KILO

KILO

INSIDE THE DEADLIEST COCAINE CARTELS— FROM THE JUNGLES TO THE STREETS

TOBY MUSE

wm

WILLIAM MORROW
An Imprint of HarperCollins*Publishers*

HarperCollins books may be purchased for educational, business, or sales promotional use. For information, please email the Special Markets Department at SPsales@harpercollins.com.

FIRST EDITION

Library of Congress Cataloging-in-Publication Data has been applied for.

ISBN 978-0-06-290529-1

20 21 22 23 24 LSC 10 9 8 7 6 5 4 3 2 1

To my mum, who pushed me to start this book.
To Monica, for helping me finish it.

CONTENTS

AUTHOR'S NOTE

Names have been changed throughout this book for the safety of some. Those of the underworld agreed to be interviewed on the condition that their names weren't used and identifying details were removed.

PROLOGUE:
SEPTEMBER 2016

PEACE! PEACE! PEACE!

You couldn't walk anywhere without tripping over the word. It was all people spoke of, all they thought of. That this wonderful word "peace" was on the lips and minds of men and women carrying AK-47s, "terrorists" in the eyes of the world . . . well, that was beautiful! Half a century's worth of fighting was about to come to a glorious end, something that many of us in Colombia never thought we would see.

And yet here we were, gathered in the middle of Colombia's nowhere, as the FARC, the Revolutionary Armed Forces of Colombia, held its Tenth Conference. More than two thousand guerrillas had marched for weeks, AK-47s slung over their shoulders, across misty mountaintops and wet jungles to get here. The comrades had come to vote on whether to accept a peace deal with the Colombian state.

The FARC was the biggest, deadliest rebel army in the Americas. Battle-tough, they'd been fighting the Colombian state, US spies, and military advisors for more than five decades, the world's longest-running insurgency. Their goal: a violent revolution to install a Marxist-Leninist dictatorship of the proletariat. The civil war had killed more than 200,000 people. And the rebels had been mainly funded by the cocaine industry.

FARC negotiators had spent four years quibbling every comma, period, and word of a 297-page document with a government team. The result? A blueprint for a new Colombia, a long-needed peace deal, investing in the countryside, education, social policies, building roads and bridges. (That the state needed pressure from violent insurgents just to provide basic services shows how abandoned parts of rural Colombia have been.) And central to this vision was a plan to end the cocaine industry, the root of so much of Colombia's devastation.

For years, the FARC had been one of the key figures in Colombia's massive cocaine industry, doing business with farmers cultivating the crops as well as with cartels and traffickers who were exporting it. They'd used the hundreds of millions to grow and expand their bloody mission of violent revolution. In return for the money, the FARC had protected the fields of coca, the bushes that are turned into cocaine. This deal would put an end to all that. With the FARC out of the cocaine business, Colombia would have a once-in-a-lifetime chance to eradicate coca from the country, ending the drug business that has haunted Colombia for the past four decades.

Now hundreds of reporters from across the world were here to watch and see what the rebels would do. If the rebels voted yes, they'd lay down their weapons. They would become civilians, ending a war their grandfathers had started. Vote no? Another generation will know war.

I was one of the journalists, here in the hopes of seeing my adopted home grasp its chance at peace. I had reported on the never-ending wars of Colombia's cocaine industry for fifteen years, making and losing friends in the bloodshed. I'd seen too many seduced and corrupted by cocaine, too many slum kids die pointless deaths, too many driven mad by the violence. This peace deal, I hoped, could begin to end the cocaine industry here. I wasn't alone.

Millions watched with the same hopes. These rebels couldn't let us down. Colombia deserved peace. And that's the history we all felt in the air. The earth told you: take a moment, breathe it in, this is history unfolding before your eyes.

THE CONFERENCE WAS TO LAST ten days and was held in the Plains of Yari. It's about 190 miles from the capital, but it's a hard twenty-four-hour drive through cloudy mountain passes and tracks so muddy they swallow motorbikes. The guerrillas had set up six camps for the thousands of guerrillas in the jungle that surrounded the open plains. They built *cambuches,* skeletal wooden huts, black plastic sheets providing the roofs. Beds were raised so the countless snakes wouldn't climb in searching for human warmth in the misty mornings. Men, women, we all bathed in the dark waters of the cool river.

An army of rebels built large tents, where after debating the peace process in the day, we drank beers, the rebels always with their automatic rifles and in their camouflage uniforms. Journalists took selfies with the top rebel commanders, as famous as pop stars in Colombia. The top guerrillas each carried $5 million bounties on their heads, offered by the State Department. Many were wanted in US courts for cocaine trafficking and kidnapping of US citizens. But here they drank beers and cracked jokes, confident in their reign of the wilderness. Above us hung huge banners of the FARC's logo: two AK-47s crossed beneath an open book (symbolizing the guerrillas' dedication to violent revolution and their self-education).

It was a time to meet old acquaintances from the battlefield. In years past, women and men of the FARC's Sixth Front rained mortars down on me and civilians. The Eighteenth Front treated me as a guest of honor in secret rebel camps as we dodged army patrols and attack helicopters. The guerrilla known as Kunta Kinte who once told me: "If you want to see weird stuff, go to war. You see strange things in war."

A guerrilla sat down next to me. Her eyes big and dark, her long black hair flowed from under a red beret with a patch of Che Guevara. Like all rebels, she was trained to start shooting at any moment. The FARC was one of the only rebel groups to let women fight on the front line. She laid her AK-47 across her lap and sipped her beer. On her nails were painted little Colombian flags, the red, blue, and yellow. She had the guerrillas' dignity, her head held high.

"Can you tell me . . . what does peace feel like? How do you live . . . in peace?"

Peace! It's obvious, isn't it? It's the absence of war. Then I thought of when people ask me: What's war like? It's more than just the absence of peace.

She looked to be twenty-five. She had only ever known war; the terror, the hatred, the frenzy of combat. All of Colombia would have to learn peace. Hundreds of thousands died in this war. Millions fled. It made Colombia the kidnap capital of the world. Worst human rights landscape in the Western Hemisphere. For what? A war that long ago lost any honor or reason.

The Plains of Yari itself had been the site of decades of war. Soldiers, rebels, death squads, cocaine cartels: they all had killed and buried their dead on these plains of jungle and empty spaces.

Each night huge salsa concerts blared out from a massive stadium-like stage constructed by the rebels. Beneath flashing red and blue lights, we danced with the rebels. Even in their camouflage uniforms and dancing in knee-high rubber boots, the guerrillas spun and twirled in grace.

Rebels looked at each other with eyes of love and sex. We

baptized the conference FARCstock. Later, there would be a bumper harvest of babies—peace babies, they'll call them. A new country was to be born. Yes, there would be problems, but anthills compared to what had been survived already. The feeling was new, something here that I'd never seen in Colombia: optimism. Planning for a beautiful future. Counting on the good.

And the peace process was already paying off—a cease-fire between the FARC and the government had seen deaths related to the civil war fall close to zero. The military hospital was almost empty; admissions had fallen by 97 percent over five years.

And South America needed good news, a continent stagnated. Next door Venezuela was imploding, a once oil-rich country sunk by mismanagement and corruption. Its people hungered and died in the absence of basic medicine. Millions would literally walk out of the country, searching for a better life here in Colombia.

The unspoken reality behind this optimism was that the problem of cocaine would finally be dealt with; everyone knows that with cocaine, Colombia will not know peace. Cocaine, the drug of glamour. The champagne of narcotics, the drug of the wealthy and those who aspire to be. After cannabis, the world's most popular drug. Exclusive and promiscuous. Cocaine follows the money. It was there for the bankers of New York and London in the 1980s, the Russian oligarchs of the 1990s. Now Colombian traffickers target China's new entrepreneurs. Nothing tells the young millionaire they've made it like a couple of extra grams of cocaine in their pocket on a Friday night.

The drug war is lost and the world knows it. President Richard Nixon declared the War on Drugs in 1971. And since the 1970s, Colombia has been trying to eradicate cocaine with American military expertise and billions in aid. The results? More cocaine than ever. Former Colombian president Juan Manuel Santos tried to discuss cocaine honestly with the world. The drug war is like riding an exercise bike. "We make a huge effort, we sweat and suddenly I look left, I look right and we are in the same place, the business continues." He was met with an awkward silence across the globe.

The FARC entered into the cocaine business, protecting plantations of coca bushes. Initially, they "taxed" drug sales in their territory. And over the years, they began exporting the drug. And as guerrilla movements across Latin America faded away in the 1990s after the fall of Soviet communism, the FARC grew more powerful than ever. The FARC became wealthy and cocaine had bought herself a bodyguard, an army that would protect her.

Now, as peace became a possibility, the amount of coca was skyrocketing. The government had suspended aerial fumigations of coca crops, capable of killing hundreds of acres of the bushes a day. Rebels had told their supporters in the countryside: "Plant more coca and when peace comes, the more coca you have, the more post-conflict aid you'll get from the government."

And as the FARC prepared for a new legal life, they were rumored to be furiously selling off their last stocks of cocaine before laying down their arms. It was their final chance at cocaine's billions. It was understandable, but they were planting the seeds of a bitter harvest.

If the FARC laid down their weapons, who would take over the territory they'd controlled for decades? In any other country, the answer would be obvious—the government, and that was the plan. In theory. But Colombia is not any other country.

Throughout its history, Colombia has always been too much for the Colombian government. Jungles too dense, mountain ranges too vast to ever be tamed by the gentlemen and ladies in the capital. In most of Colombian territory, the state exists in name alone. All that territory, filled with record amounts of coca. If the government didn't take control, the FARC's enemies would: cartels and narco-militias. And they would slaughter each other to control these lands and the riches at stake. A new round of bloodletting would occur.

That was the nightmare scenario to lose this historic moment.

This is what happened.

Instead of beginning the start of a new story, September 2016 merely turned the page on a different chapter in the old one. The treaty was signed amid great celebration by the guerrillas, the leaders, the officials, and the journalists. But this peace that arrived with the best of intentions and genuine seeds of hope was brutally damaged before it began. Peace threw the countryside into chaos.

With the deal signed, the FARC's exit from cocaine became the industry's biggest upheaval since the death of Pablo Escobar, way back in 1993. Only the Colombian government missed its moment to turn the tide in the war on cocaine. The government didn't take over the coca fields, encourage farmers to give up growing coca, or fill the void left by the FARC— the opposite occurred. Narco-militias, heavily armed men and women in uniform devoted to producing and exporting cocaine, claimed the territory once controlled by the FARC. A new round of violence was unleashed as they fought to control the coca the FARC themselves helped grow. Unarmed FARC fighters, brave men and women who laid down their weapons for a new Colombia, were murdered. Some FARC fighters abandoned the peace process and created dissident groups to keep fighting, to keep trafficking. The villages most battered by the war begged the government to fully implement the peace treaty and secure the countryside. As the cartels and narco-militias moved through the country taking over more territory, they slaughtered hundreds of human rights activists and social leaders. The billions to be made propelled these militias and cartels to more strength and power. Suddenly Colombia was back where it started, only now there were new masters of cocaine and violence, a more diffuse group of players who were more ruthless and determined to see cocaine production grow than the FARC had been. This peace will be very bloody.

The peace process delivered a record harvest of cocaine. A tsunami of cheap, pure cocaine flooded the planet. What happened in these fields of Colombia was felt in neighborhoods of Stockholm, Beijing, Lagos, Tokyo, Anchorage, Melbourne. After this peace, the United States recorded its largest-ever cocaine bust. Germany captured more than $1 billion worth of cocaine in one raid, its own record. Cocaine overdoses rocketed in the United States. Cocaine fueled violence across the United Kingdom. Cocaine set Mexico ablaze and caused a rash of violence across Brazil.

Colombia failed the world; cocaine production will flourish. And the world failed Colombia—it will fail to curb the motor of the cocaine industry: the demand for the drug from Europe and the United States. Colombia produces cocaine because the world desires it, will pay billions for it. The war on drugs and the demand for cocaine are dumping gasoline on a Colombia already aflame.

In the aftermath of this failure of peace, this failure to end cocaine, a failure to seize the future, I set out to understand the why of it—not just the failure but the drug itself. Like so many, my time in Colombia had left me cynical and cautious, and yet, also like so many others, I'd allowed myself to be carried along by the optimism of that September in 2016. The hope would slowly die as the extent of the chaos unfurled. Cocaine was killing the hope.

From years of reporting in Colombia, I knew cocaine's power. Co-caine. The name alone echoes Cain and would mark the business from the start, brother slaughtering brother. A business that corrupts countries, distorts economies, employs hundreds of thousands, and makes monsters multibillionaires. I had seen the attraction that a life in cocaine offered: thrilling, sexy, exciting, uncountable riches. And that such a life would be short was part of the deal, all those who worked in cocaine said yes.

I had seen the causes of cocaine: money, greed, power, ideology, its seductive corruption. But it was more than that. In a conflict unlike any other on earth, it was all of those and it was none of them.

Now, in the absence of the FARC, realities had been laid bare: cocaine always finds a way to survive. Today there is a new supply chain, with new players. Like evolution fast-forwarded, cocaine has evolved in this new world. To hear the men and women at each step of the chain is to understand this reality. More than a million kilos to more than satisfy the world's demand for the most glamorous of drugs. Each kilo will pass through the cocaine chain, from the fields to the cities where ecosystems of cocaine flourish and out onto the oceans of the world to reach the real cause of the drug: the consumer. And to reach that Friday night gram of fun in London, New

York, Tokyo, or Lagos, it will pass through a world of sex, riches, betrayal, and murder.

The why of cocaine isn't any single person or stage; it's all of it. And it begins with a lowly plant growing in the ground, waiting to be harvested.

CHAPTER 1

THE LAND OF LIGHTNING

IN THE ABSENCE OF EVERYTHING, YOU UNDERSTAND why cocaine. Every step forward we take, another layer of society falls by the wayside. The last hospital, the final supermarket, no more libraries. All, they flow past us as we drive ever toward the jungle. The paved roads come to their end. Now we press on beyond where the roads end. The final military checkpoint, soldiers with darting glances, worried eyes. The last glimpse of the state, the end of government. The badlands. Cocaine country. All that remains is a motorbike, the dirt track, and a jungle that embraces, that swallows. I've arrived at the end. I've reached the beginning of the cocaine trade. This is where the kilo of cocaine is born.

I roll into the Land of Lightning with a honey bear under my arm and a storm at my heels. A person of learning would call her a kinkajou, and she's the perfect companion for Colombia's jungles; agile as a monkey, playful as a puppy. I've carried my kinkajou in her tiny cage through the countryside on a bumpy bus, a boiling truck ride, and a canoe trip, wading knee-high flooded tracts and clouds of mosquitos. Now it's time to set her free.

I bought my kinkajou hours earlier from a scumbag animal trafficker in a lawless town. Behind glasses, he leered like a pimp. Sitting at the top of the fleabag hotel's staircase, he squinted at every guest walking up, asking if they wanted to a pet. He kept her in his hotel room, locked in a rusty cage. She hissed and edged away from all who approached her.

I decided to buy and free her in the jungle before he sold her to some family of brutes. He wanted thirty-three dollars. I pushed lower. He dropped to twenty-three—reluctantly. Outside came the long, jarring horn of my bus, warning departure was imminent.

After the initial four-hour bus journey, I sat at a lonely, dusty crossroads waiting for a truck to take me deeper into the jungle. The truck should have passed by forty-five minutes ago. All my kinkajou and I could do was wait.

With smooth coats of deep gold, kinkajous are mistaken for monkeys and ferrets. Here in the Colombian jungles, they're called "cuchis" or "macos." I named her Manuela.

An old woman looked sadly at the cage.

"It's a sin for her to live like that," she said. "It's like when they put you in prison."

Gently, she shared her banana with a grateful Manuela. Her paws held the banana piece as she nibbled it down. The truck arrived.

I could feel myself growing attached to the poor thing. She shivered and with each jolt of the bus she buried herself in the blanket. They're night creatures and the harsh sunlight scorched her. The midday sun was baking our truck and Manuela rolled on to her back and gasped, succumbing to the heat. I filled her water bowl, but each dwarf-sized pothole heaved the bus and spilt the water.

For all the strange looks, Manuela was a good omen. This is Marxist guerrilla country and they like to leave car bombs along these roads. Sometimes they set up checkpoints to kidnap, burn some vehicles, and kill a few drivers and split before the army arrives. They say it's for the revolution. Truth is, it's just more madness.

Still, could the guerrillas handle this scene? Imagine a guerrilla checkpoint, taking in the sight of a gringo wandering a war zone carrying a mysterious golden animal in a cage. What good is an AK-47 when you can't wrap your head around the scene in front of you?

From the truck, we transferred to a canoe, and I was nearing the end of my journey. I emerged from a canoe in a mosquito-infested river, the cage in my hand, looking like a degenerate gringo animal trafficker stealing Colombians' nature, wandering the backwaters, and selling it back to them at scandalous profits. Many Colombians expect little more from the genus gringo.

And now it is time to set her free in the jungle.

We rest at the general store next to the river, at the rain forest's edge. The jungle is ominous. I look at Manuela. Light rain tinkles on the plastic roof and thunder rumbles toward us. I ask for water. They're out. Only beer and Gatorade.

The storekeeper looks at Manuela kindly. I drink my beer.

"She must be six months old. That's too old for the jungle. The jungle will eat her alive," he says. I look at the wall of jungle at the edge of the clearing. Out there roam leopards, pumas, snakes, caimans. Slicing claws and gnashing jaws. She's out of her cage, happily eating another banana and playing with all around her. She is too trusting, too playful, too happy for this world.

"Hunters probably killed her mother and stole her when she was a baby. Then they sold her. She's too used to people now. Won't be able to survive, defend herself."

I'm surprised by the violence of my emotions for Manuela. Right now, nothing is more important to me than making sure she will have a happy, safe life. She could live for another twenty years. Cats, dogs, and parrots happily wander through the store.

I ask if the store owner wants a cuchi. He nods.

With pliers, we cut off the collar the animal trafficker had put on her. Manuela takes to the family immediately, scaling up arms, curling around necks. This family will look after her. I make a mental note to check in on her. She would have been a faithful companion. She's too young for the madness that lies before me. Ahead is the cocaine industry.

It's dusk when I set out again, a kindly gasoline smuggler driving me at breakneck speed on his motorbike along the dirt track. So far, we're outrunning the incoming barrage of lightning strikes. This is Catatumbo, northeastern Colombia, along the border with Venezuela. It's a terrain of jungles, mountains, war, a resilient people and magic. And guerrillas, cocaine, poverty, and a people abandoned by their government.

The first men and women to step through these tremendous mountains, the old indigenous, they understood this territory—hundreds of years ago they named it Catatumbo. Land of lightning, house of thunder. The land is drenched in blood. The indigenous remember—memories of horror handed down through the generations, carried in their DNA. The Spanish invasion: genocide, mass rape, slavery, bloody baptisms, entire civilizations destroyed, ancestral dreams snuffed out. Annihilations so complete entire civilizations were erased, with no survivors left even to remember them. The Spanish conquest of the Americas, history's greatest atrocity. So grotesque, so obscene it damned this continent. Five hundred years later, the curse lives on and dooms these countries to corruption, bloodshed, stagnation. The past is never dead in these lands.

The rain comes down harder. A lightning strike juicing me with a billion-volt jolt is edging from possibility to probability. We can't stop for shelter. There are appointments to keep. Each lightning bolt illuminates my surroundings, friezes of massive fields of coca bathed in white electricity. I'm where I need to be.

COCAINE'S BILLIONS BEGIN IN THE grinding poverty of Colombia's countryside. The sex and glamour of the most sophisticated of drugs, all that comes later. Right now, it's coca, the humble green bush that likes the mountains and jungles of this country.

The vast majority of Colombia is free of coca. It's a country of coffee fields, coal mines, oil fields, beaches filled with European tourists. This is the other Colombia, the one left behind. Here coca is a way of life.

Coca is a crafty bush; it hides its prize beneath a plain appearance. Standing about three feet high, its twiglike branches aim up, grasping for the sun. Gray-green branches offer up oval emerald leaves. In short, it's a bush you wouldn't look twice at . . . unless you knew of the precious alkaloid hidden in the leaves.

Twenty-five farmhands move through a field, harvesting the crops. A wall of tall, dark jungle looms at the field's edge, leaning in over the crops and the pickers. That line separates the field and the jungle, civilization and nature's chaos.

REEEK! REEEK! The sound of coca leaves ripped from their branches. Coca pickers glide, quick as whips, stripping the bushes' hundred leaves in seconds. It's a quick all-in-one movement: grab the branch at the base with two hands and rip upward. It's the sound of tearing material, the sound of a field ripped in half. Fistfuls of leaves are dropped into the large sacks tied to the picker's belt. Leaf separated from the bush, the first stage of cocaine is complete.

Cocaine is its own world, its own language. To harvest coca, the verb is "raspar," making coca pickers "raspachines."

The two seasons here in the Catatumbo are torrential rains and grueling sun. Some days you get both. Today, the raspachines wear hats and long-sleeved shirts. How do you get through the heat? Fool around all day.

"If they ever ask about Bigfoot in your country, tell them you can get one here in Colombia. He's a Bigfoot, but we civilized him."

"Watch out, he'll rape you. He'll rape you. I'm glad journalists are here to record this and denounce it. This rapist should be reported to the human rights commission, the United Nations."

"He looks like a terrorist."

"Maria, you ever fucked a gringo?"

"Shut up."

"Carlos, you are the ugliest man I've ever seen. Did they shave you to help you escape from the zoo?"

The raspachines start every day at first light, 6 A.M., and advance as much as possible in the early morning coolness. A spectral mist hangs in the dawn, memories of the night's downpour. It makes some think of ghosts.

Once, this was all jungle. Refugees from other parts of Colombia, so-called colonials, arrived about a hundred years ago and fought the indigenous and stole their land. Indigenous communal lands became individual farms of the colonials. The slashing and scorching of the jungle created fields like this one. Yet, here at the edges of Colombia, these are young lands, societies still in formation. A region where your grandfather may have killed someone for the land you live on today.

Still, the jungle remains vast and regal, sitting at the edge of our civilization watching us, ready to reign again. The rain forest bursts with life. Billions of birds, insects, reptiles, and mammals teem throughout the vegetation that stretches a hundred feet into the sky. Walking through the tangles, you feel like the first human to ever step foot here. Every leaf you pass feels like it holds a billion years of creation within. You can smell the vegetation grow. It's an endless, claustrophobic landscape of greens and browns and little else. Made up of countless creatures, the jungle feels as one. And that it wants to kill you, consume you, make you part of it.

The minute you step out of the jungle, all these sensations fade away, to be remembered like a blurry dream. The jungle spooks some. I like it.

A wilderness so dense can make you think you're more alone than you are. In southwest Colombia, there are the "Lost Cities." These are farms that are invisible by day, but the lights used to grow the marijuana crops are turned on at night, visible from miles away. In that rural whim, the farmers string the lights out in patterns, so massive hearts and huge dogs appear on the mountainside.

The deeper you get in to the rain forests, the roads disappear and travel is by river. Or air. A fleet of beautiful old

DC-3 airplanes connect these tiny jungle outposts. The silver planes were built during the Second World War but are still in use here. Every flight, the mechanic is on board. Beautiful flights on a clear day allow you to watch the sea of jungle beneath you. But when those storms clouds gather and the sky turns a thick gray, I skip the flight.

So vast are these jungles, they still house uncontacted indigenous tribes. Just a decade ago, coca farmers slashed and burned ever deeper in the rain forests, outrunning the government's antinarcotics operations, when they came upon the nomadic Nukak tribe. The hunter-gatherer Nukak, who had never touched coca, streamed out of the jungle as refugees. Many of the Nukak settled in the jungle town outpost of San Guaviare. Once the roaming hunters of the jungle, now they sit on the town's unpaved roads begging for money. Every day the Nukak lose more of their culture. They've swapped their traditional loincloths for secondhand jeans. Their jungle diet of monkey has been changed for beer and Coca-Cola. They idolize the devil-may-care raspachines who whirlwind into town every weekend to spend their paychecks on booze and hookers. Some of the Nukak women "drink beer with white man," the Nukak term for prostitution ("white man" is a term that applies to whites, mestizos, Afro-Colombians, anyone not pure indigenous).

Other Nukak saw the annihilation of their customs and returned to the rain forest. But our culture had infected them— even back in the jungle, they want our trinkets. In isolated farms deep in the jungle, the former nomadic hunters pick the crop that drove them from their homes—coca. A day's pay? A family-size bottle of Coca-Cola, the first Western product that seduced them. Another victim of the drug war.

Out here in the coca field, some of the raspachines have

small speakers tied to their belts and reggaetón—it's always reggaetón—drifts over the field. Sweat drips from their faces onto the naked coca bushes. The oldest man here is thirty-five. No job for old men.

Half the people who pick coca find their hands swell up with ugly-looking blotchy bumps. They keep picking because there's nothing else to do. The pickers bandage their hands like boxers. Still, coca cuts. After a week, every picker's hands are callused, crisscrossed with nicks and gashes. Yet there are no complaints for the only work there is. Work or starve. This is the Colombian countryside.

Seeing these twenty-five raspachines, working out in the open, is the first hint of how normal coca is in much of Colombia. And you might say it's treated like any other crop, but it's not. It's the only crop. Coca is the economy. These fields are illegal, but in these lawless lands, no one looks twice. And there's more coca than ever. More here in Colombia, more here in Catatumbo. Today the raspachines are clearing about two and a half acres of coca. Across the country, there are at least another 422,000 acres.

Colombians themselves don't consider the farmers or the pickers criminals. Everyone knows the hardship of the countryside. The land is concentrated in the hands of the country's richest. Life is close to feudal outside the cities, farmers scrabbling to survive on tiny plots of land as the wealthy acquire ever more tracts. At one point when the narco-militias were buying up land on behalf of corrupted politicians, they would offer a ridiculously low price for the land, with a deal-breaking question: "Do we have a deal or do I buy from your widow?"

When the prices of legal crops collapse, the farmers turn to coca. And that's the most obvious thing to explain cocaine—it's our legal commodities markets that drive production. It haunts Colombia every time a coffee farmer rips out his crops to plant coca. Coffee is what Colombia wants to be, how it wants to see itself, laboring to make a world-famous cup of coffee crop that delights millions every day. Coffee, the crop that helped build the nation. Coffee, the crop that could sustain a Colombia that could be.

FOR THE PAST FORTY YEARS, the raspachines have all been Colombians. It's a rite of passage for men in the coca zones, the beginning of a career in cocaine. Today, here, they're almost all Venezuelan. The border is a twenty-minute motorbike ride away. Venezuela's economy is sinking and its people are emigrating at shocking levels. Even with the world's largest reserves of oil, a socialist government riddled with corruption and mismanagement and now slapped with US sanctions has run the economy into the ground. Venezuela is unable to feed its people, who die of hunger and for lack of basic medicine. And millions are walking out to find new lives.

Maria is the only woman in the fields. She looks to be around thirty, with brown hair and white skin, and doesn't talk much. She's the butt of jokes: who did she sleep with last night, who will it be tonight. When she gets in a good comeback, a well-timed "eat shit," the raspachines point and laugh at the man vanquished, who can do nothing but shut his mouth and pick his coca.

"It's good to have this job. Pays well. It's hard but stable," Maria says. She receives $2.50 for every eleven kilos of coca she picks.

Maria remembers a life in Venezuela of going to bed hungry, of waking up to see her mother crying. As her family lost weight, she was literally starving when she walked across the border into Colombia. She kept walking and kept asking for work until a farmer nodded and sent her to the coca field.

She supports her family with the coca money. Throughout the day, the Venezuelans explain everything by "the crisis" or "the situation," as if everyone knows. And everyone in this continent does know.

I ask what was her job before this. She says she was in school—she's only eighteen. Jesus, Venezuela's collapse is prematurely aging everyone.

"It's like exercise. You get better every week. I've seen fat people arrive to the field and after two weeks, they're skinny," says Maria. "You should try it." She smiles and nods to my belly. Great, I'm getting dunked on by teenage raspachines and it's not even 9 A.M.

It's a ragtag collection: Carlos worked in a bank, Maria was a school pupil, Jonathan was a constructor, Freddy was a policeman. What unites them is that they have all given up hope of making a living in Venezuela. From the fields, all day long we see groups of skinny Venezuelans walking the dusty path looking for work.

The Colombian peasant is quiet, and humble with those he doesn't know. Soft handshakes, a stare that avoids the stranger's eyes. He wears cloth trousers, a shirt tucked in, rubber boots, and a cowboy hat. He dresses and eats as his grandfather did fifty years ago. The Venezuelans are loud and tropical, an urban culture in the coca fields: fake brand-name jeans, fake Nike caps, fake Adidas T-shirts. And all in Crocs for the puddles and streams.

The Venezuelans spend all day laughing and cracking

jokes. They're happy with the job. Earning around 50,000 pesos a day, or $17, is a good income for them compared to back home.

Carlos is so tall, I know he's Venezuelan. Sweat trickles down his face as he rips the coca leaves and drops them into his sack. It's a quiet moment across the field, little chatter from the coca pickers, only the insects chirping. He's twenty-five years old and until three months ago he worked as a bank teller. It makes sense; he has a politeness, a formality lacking in the others. I can imagine him helping old ladies with their savings accounts. Now he rips coca leaves and is the foundation for the international cocaine trade.

What did he think of the coca farmers before this job?

"I thought the pickers were criminals. Poor and without opportunities, but criminals . . ."

And now?

"This life." He laughs. "Life gives you surprises. My parents think I'm working on a pineapple farm. I'd like to, but I couldn't find any pineapples!" And he laughs. "Only coca."

How long will he stay in Colombia?

"I'll keep working here until Venezuela recovers . . ." he says, his smirk sarcastic. The joke is that there is no hope Venezuela will return to normal anytime soon.

The field has been picked to the branch. The naked bushes look like hundreds of boney fingers grasping for the sky. The coca leaves will grow back and the raspachines will return in two and a half months for the next harvest.

Today, each raspachin has picked as much coca as they can carry. Because carry it they will. The raspachines pack the leaves down into sacks the size of chubby children. A man hefts one sack as large as himself onto his shoulder.

How heavy is it? I shout.

"Ninety kilos, I guess. Yep, around ninety kilos." And he smiles—it's that common smile here that says: "All this, absurd, ain't it?" He sets off for the thirty-minute walk.

Maria sits on the ground as a friend straps the sack to her back, ropes crisscrossing her chest like a mule. Like a turtle on its back in the hot sun, Maria can't get to her feet—her friend shoves the sack from behind, pushing forward Maria, who scrambles to her feet to lurch ahead. To carry this sack only slightly smaller than herself, she's going to rely on that first push, bent ahead and hoping forward momentum will get her home.

Coca is on the move. Cocaine will eventually make it to every corner of the world and Maria is the first one pushing it forward.

There are no clouds and the sun bakes the air. The stillness of the midday heat, with only the sound of the insects and Maria's grunts. The naked fields of coca shiver in the sun.

After fifteen minutes, Maria stumbles in the dirt. She catches herself before she falls, but it's close. Her legs are jellifying. She's doubled over, her eyes focused straight ahead. Total concentration: left foot forward, right foot forward, left foot forward, right foot forward.

After twenty-five minutes, her face is covered in a sheen of sweat. She's bent over at nearly a right angle now. Finally, she reaches the edge of the jungle, and precious shade. She stands still and stares forward, breathing deeply, her eyes unfocused. From somewhere, a nest of mean mosquitos awakes. They surround us as a mist. She's motionless, too tired to bat away the mosquitos. With a grunt, she starts again along the path through the jungle.

We walk the dark path that twists and turns through the undergrowth. Finally, a clearing. It stinks of gasoline and noxious chemicals. Here stands the laboratory, and here collapses Maria.

A line of raspachines stagger in, hunchbacked with their sacks. Tossing their sacks to the floor, all sit down hard. The laboratory workers impale each sack on a meat hook that hangs from a scale. Pedro, one of the laboratory workers, shouts out the weight of the sack. The picker watches the scale as well—to know how much they're going to earn. Sometimes they smile, sometimes they're disappointed. But there's no grumbling. The raspachines treat the lab workers with respect. There's a hierarchy in cocaine and the raspachin is at the bottom.

There's a stream of weights: "Eighty-five kilos!" "Eighty-five kilos!" confirms Carlos, the bookkeeper. He's a young man, dressed in a baseball cap, rubber boots, and shorts, and that's all. He takes notes in a child's exercise book.

"Thirty-seven kilos!" "Thirty-seven!" "Ninety kilos!" "Ninety!"

Maria hands over her sack. It's hooked and Pedro shouts: "Forty!"

"Forty!" replies Carlos. Maria's eyes dart from the scale, confirming what Pedro says immediately to what Carlos is writing down. Only fools trust. At least today it's not raining: they pay 25 percent less to offset the wet leaves. Rules and regulations of cocaine.

Maria will take home 40,000 ($13) pesos today. It's minimum wage for Colombia—but a good earn for Venezuela.

She has handed off the coca to the next link in the chain of cocaine.

Everyone takes a break for lunch.

Maria walks back to the farmer's house, where tonight she'll sleep on the farmer's patio in a hammock. She'll pick coca until these fields are clean and then she'll return to Venezuela with a little cash in her pocket. She's one of the lucky ones, someone who walks away from cocaine. From now on, the noose tightens.

The coca is about to be transformed.

THIS COCA IS A PRODUCT of wild lands, long forgotten by the rest of the country. Traveling through these jungles, you pass settlements with whimsical names: Port Machete, Gringo Ridge, Happiness, The Dolls, The Shadow. It's the sense of humor of the farmers. But behind it there's a sadness—you're not expecting the pope to ever visit you if you name your town the Donkey.

From the nearest town, it's a six-hour odyssey to get here. Three hours on a beat-up highway, hoping to avoid guerrilla bombs or checkpoints. Two more hours down an unpaved road that can only take motorbikes. Reaching a river, only a ferry service crosses. "Ferry" is a grand term for planks of wood strapped onto six large barrels to keep it afloat. And "service" is generous way of saying: if the man is around. The raft holds four men and four bikes and is pulled across along a fixed rope. When it rains too much, the ferry is out.

The farmers—not the government—built this ferry to get their produce out to the world. Once across the river, it's another hour on a motorbike or a mule into the wilderness. Along the path, farmers—not the government—built small log bridges to cross streams. As I come to one of these bridges, an old woman gingerly steps on rotting logs. She looks ups at me. "And they call us drug traffickers? What drug trafficker do you know lives like this?"

Finish this exhausting six-hour trip and check the map

to see how far you've traveled: thirty kilometers (eighteen miles), as the crow flies. Imagine the cost of dragging a ton of pineapples along this route.

The center of life here is the general store. Coca farmers come from their isolated farms for a cup of coffee, a beer, to pick up supplies from the only store around. Out here, there is no plumbing. You shower and wash your clothes and dishes in an open-air shack that holds a huge barrel of water that's brought from the stream. You scoop out the water to pour over yourself with the jungle staring at your bare ass. Need a piss, step into the jungle. Need a shit, take a few more steps into the jungle.

Everyone here is self-sufficient, able to be vet, mechanic, doctor, cook, electrician or farmhand as the moment demands. A lifetime of abandon by the government has made Colombia's rural people a resilient breed.

Farmers trot by on handsome horses on their way to tend to their coca fields. A line of ten children in school uniform, sons and daughters of coca farmers, walk up the dirt track to the school. They've walked for hours to study and are excited to learn. One teacher will educate twenty students—from eight to fifteen—all at the same time. The girl at the head of the line tries to open the door. The door is locked.

"School is closed, kids. River is flooded, teacher couldn't cross!" shouts Carmen.

The children visibly deflate and start the three-hour walk back home.

Farmers set up a toll along the dirt track to fund this school at a cost of $12,000. It took years to raise the money but they finally built the school from the ground up. And where did the money for the toll fares come from? Coca sales. Why didn't the government pay for it? Good question.

"Coca farmers don't ask for anything. They just want to be left alone. If they decided to quit coca and demand their rights, for health services, education, the government wouldn't have the money to pay for it. Colombia needs the farmers to stick with coca, because if they go legal, the country couldn't afford it," says Carmen, a social leader, one day as we drink beers.

Too many men in the countryside have the reputation for drinking away what they earn. It's the women like Carmen who organize, who get results. She's a bundle of energy, moving like one life isn't enough to get everything done. She is asking local authorities for funds to build bridges so the farmers can transport legal crops out of these backwaters to market. She dreams of a true crop substitution program, bringing coca farmers and the government together to hammer out a real deal that would see the farmers leave coca and leave it forever.

Like everyone, Colombia's violence has bled over her. Her husband was murdered by soldiers who lied and reported him as a guerrilla killed in combat—all to receive bonuses. Known as the "false positives," the scandal broke in 2008. The Colombian army—backed with US aid—was slaughtering thousands of civilians and dressing them up as rebels in return for bonuses, promotions, holiday days. It was the logic of a civil war that was judged solely on body counts. Not how many schools or hospitals were built, how many jobs created in the countryside. No, the number of dead. And the number of those left to kill.

It's when Carmen thinks you're not looking at her that you see the sadness in her black eyes.

Like much of the country, Catatumbo allowed itself to dream of a new future with the peace process. FARC rebels had controlled parts of Catatumbo for decades, imposing their own order through the barrel of a gun. Then they surrendered their weapons and the territory. And for a couple of years, there was a sense of optimism as Colombians embraced the peace process.

Then politicians who had thrived in the war politicized the peace, accusing the government of too soft a hand. And the government lost interest. Farmers had hoped the government would arrive with health clinics, infrastructure projects, new schools. Instead, new narco-militias arrived for the coca. And the countryside slid back to war.

Since peace was signed, dozens of narco-militias have sprung up; they're rebel groups with military hierarchies, with men and women in uniform and heavy weaponry. They claim some political ideology, from Marxism to far-right politics. The narco-militias control the cocaine industry in the countryside, the cultivation of coca leaves and the production of pure cocaine, cocaine that they sell to the drug cartels based in the cities, made up of the urban narcos.

They rule in their territories, dictating what crops farmers can grow, even settling disputes between quarrelling neighbors. In some zones, they forbid the farmers from planting anything but coca. They eye as hostile anyone who wants to get rid of coca. Social leaders like Carmen have been killed by the hundreds since the beginning of the peace process.

The list of narco-militias fighting for the coca can get confusing. The National Liberation Army, or ELN, are Marxist rebels, inspired by the Cuban revolution. They're big on kidnapping and blowing up oil pipelines. Then we have the so-called dissidents of the FARC, guerrillas who broke away from the FARC when it made peace with the government. They're off to a strong start, bombing and killing soldiers and police.

Then there is the Popular Liberation Army, or EPL, a Maoist communist insurgency that went full narco decades ago. And there is the AGC, the largest cartel in South America, whose politics are far right. It's also known as the Gulf Clan Cartel. ELN, FARC, EPL, the AGC—a war of the alphabet. The United States lists some of these groups as terrorist organizations but calls them all narco-traffickers.

Bombings are regular. Children are recruited to fight for the militias. Political candidates campaigning are gunned down. Starving Venezuelans are press-ganged into the militias. Tens of thousands flee their homes, trying to outrun the fighting. Throughout this territory, the groups fight each other and the army and enter into temporary truces, before reverting to war. The only constant is the pursuit of coca and the kilos of cocaine. Catatumbo is just one corner of Colombia. It's a picture repeated across the country.

Many out here fear the army. A general was quoted as suggesting the army should ally itself with one group of traffickers in order to combat another. "If we have to murder, we will murder," he said. Out here in Catatumbo, a civilian was shot dead by a soldier who then tried to bury his body. The crime only came to light when thirty of his friends and neighbors marched in to look for him and found his cadaver.

And the war burns. The air force bombed a FARC dissident camp, killing at least seventeen. The president called the operation "impeccable." Two months later, a senator revealed that at least eight of the dead were child combatants, one as young as twelve. The children had been forcibly recruited by the dissidents and were now killed by their own government. The senator had to flee Colombia with his children ahead of all the death threats he received.

A very violent peace.

THIS COCA LABORATORY OPERATES ONLY because it has the permission from the FARC dissidents who rule from the jungles. And right now, the coca is about to change. To evolve.

"Laboratory" is a grand term for wooden poles buried in to the earth holding up a roof made up of large sheets of black plastic. Even with no walls, it's gloomy inside as the five men prepare for the day's work of turning coca into coca paste. Huge barrels stink of gasoline and ammonia. This is their office. They start at 6 A.M. and work until 4 P.M. Like office workers, they eat lunch here, listen to the radio, chat, and joke around. Here they will turn the coca leaves into coca paste, a brick of dried powder that is just one stop short of pure cocaine.

Small amounts of coca are legal for the indigenous who consider it a sacred plant. Wandering the countryside, a policeman is not expected to rip out every coca bush he sees. If a policeman sees a coca laboratory, he's expected to take it down and make arrests. In the fields, it's coca. Here in the laboratory, it's the beginning of the cocaine conspiracy. And people act like it.

Still, a couple of months ago, soldiers walked into this coca lab and sheepishly asked for some gasoline for their motorbikes. The lab workers gladly filled a canister with gasoline while everyone pretended not to notice the mattress of coca leaves.

At first, the lab workers are not interested in talking. "What's the recording for? You better not be with the police. What part of the United States are you from?"

"Not a gringo. I'm from England."

"Ahhhhh, a gringo from England. You saw the match? What did you think?" says Pedro.

This fucking question. I'm half-American, half-English. For

all my time in Colombia, I've always said I'm English. Americans aren't too popular in the cocaine countryside, given the billions the United States spends on fighting the cartels, guerrillas, and cocaine. So, I'm British. With these words, people relax. And I can work.

And then came that fucking football match. Colombia and England faced off in the World Cup. After an ugly game, England won. Colombians felt they were robbed (they weren't). Now every Colombian wants to hear the English man say Colombia should have won.

"It was an ugly match."

Pedro is pacified and allows me to stay in the laboratory. Right now, there's work to do. Pedro and Carlos empty the sacks of coca leaves on to the floor. A one-ton mattress of green coca leaves. It's irresistible—some raspachines dive on top of it, like kids into a mound of snow.

"Stop it!" Pedro yells and the raspachines stop messing around and file out. He cranks up the wood chipper and it whirs away. Pedro thrusts armfuls of coca leaves in and out sprays shredded coca. It takes about two hours to pass a ton of coca through the wood chipper.

The farmer's wife arrives with lunch. Today it's chicken, rice, yuca, and a bottle of apple soda. Colombians are serious gourmands and lunch is the countryside's most important hour. Now is the time to talk.

"This helps keep people alive. But no one is getting rich off this," Pedro says pointing to the lab. Carlos runs through the farmer's costs to process a ton of coca leaves: $250 for the coca pickers, $80 to the laboratory workers, $150 for the gasoline, other materials another $50.

"He's left with $200 . . . That's not much," Carlos concludes. That's $200 every ninety days and it comes expensive—

the farmer now lives outside the law. Someone steals from him, threatens him, slaps him like a dog? Well, live with it, because with a field full of coca, he's not phoning the police anymore.

Farmers used to grow seven, eight hectares of coca and could make decent money. But the fields became too easy for the police to spot and swoop in and destroy them. Now almost all farmers grow a hectare or so.

"Across Colombia, a lot of people look to the coca because it produces a lot of jobs. Not riches, but a lot of jobs," says Pedro.

For the men here in the laboratory, coca exists because of the poverty of the countryside. It's that simple: give the farmers an alternative and they'll ditch coca now. Pedro used to grow coca until the government arrived, promising to help transition him to legal crops.

"The government told us they would help us if we grew cacao. The kilo was three dollars. And that's an okay price. It promised to help us export the cacao. But the government made some deals and flooded the country with cheap imports . . . It's now a dollar a kilo. You can't cover costs at that price. So, what did the people do?" He sweeps his arm around the laboratory.

Pedro interrupts himself: "Do you believe in God?"

I communicate with a nod, a shrug, and a firmer nod.

"Good. Can't speak to anyone who doesn't believe in God. So, as I was saying . . ."

Where else in the world can you be thrown out of a coca laboratory for being an atheist? Nowhere, that's where. Only Co-Lom-Bi-A.

Pedro picks up his story again—he was out of the laboratories for sixteen years. When the price of cacao dived, he asked his cousin for work. So, it's back to the labs.

"I've got four hectares of cacao, but here I am working in the laboratory. It's not paying. I had to come here, leaving my wife and kids back home."

He earns $16 a day and he'll be gone from his home for three months.

"Here in the countryside, ninety percent of people just survive. What does that mean? You work to eat, not to have. Not to make money. Be it coca, cacao."

Lunch is finished and now is the obligatory postconsumption chat to ease the digestion. And all want to keep talking because the endless dysfunction of Colombia is a source of fascination for every Colombian. Colombia, the enigma that befuddles its own citizens. Rebels, prostitutes, soldiers, taxi drivers, priests all try to understand why Colombia is the way it is: violent, charismatic, corrupt, happy, swimming in cocaine, a tragic beauty.

The main culprit is always corruption. This is a country where the top anti-corruption official is arrested on charges of corruption, where the anti-kidnapping cops are found running their own abduction rings, where drug cops are found on the cartel's payroll. Daily stories emerge of politicians, police officers, military officials, public servants on the take. And still the corruption rolls on. Corruption keeps the country ignorant; it distorts. Corruption kills.

"Where you're from, the politicians don't steal everything?" asks Pedro.

"No! There are corrupt people . . ."

"But less than here? Here they steal everything . . . We should have the best highways in the world, but look at them . . . We need schools, highways, we need business. What are we going to do with yuca and coffee if people don't have the money to buy them?"

This is frustrating. I've heard it all before. I ask: How will it ever change if Colombians don't change it and throw out the corrupt politicians?

"But if you're poor here, what can you do?"

A history of political violence that murdered would-be reformers has taught Colombia to be cynical. It's a widespread cynicism that often assumes the worst, that treats every accident as one more piece of treachery. The cynicism has become the bane of too many. If the game is rigged beyond hope, what's the point of trying to change things, too many ask. They've convinced themselves nothing will change. I've never met a people so proud of their ability to live through anything, but so pessimistic about the chance of changing it.

I ask about the FARC's peace process.

"War and cocaine. Everyone gets rich off of both. That's why it won't end," says Pedro. "This industry isn't what it used to be," says Pedro. "Before, the coca farmers made good money. They sold their coca, spent the weekend with two, three prostitutes, brought their whiskey, and returned home with still enough money to make the wife happy. Now . . ." His voice trails off.

The reason is that the price of coca has remained the same for the past twenty years. All other prices have gone up—the prostitutes, the booze, food—but the coca paste still sells at around $400. Yet it's all they've got. This part of the country has been growing coca for the past three decades, but no one's seen as much coca as there is now.

The chat is winding down. It feels like there's not much more to say. The mulch of coca is spread across the floor. Carlos tosses an ammoniac solution over it. He dusts that with a mix of cement, lime powder, and ammonia. The ammonia fills my lungs, like a chemical weapons attack. I rush outside and gasp the air. The workers in the laboratory laugh.

Two of the workers march up and down over the mulch, mixing it all together with their rubber boots. They look like old Italian grandmothers crushing grapes for wine. They smirk, aware of how ridiculous it looks. For all the billions made, the production is still rustic.

The mulch is shoveled into huge metallic barrels and the gasoline is added. Around seven of these barrels are needed to hold the ton of coca leaves. There it's left to sit for three days. The gasoline extracts the coca base.

They roll out drums packed three days earlier. The drums are drained. The gasoline now holds the cocaine alkaloid. A filthy mulch is left behind in the drum and that's tipped out into mounds next to the lab, out in the open in the clearing.

At one corner of the clearing is a muddy chute that leads to a stream. It carries all the chemicals and dredge straight to the pristine streams. This happens thousands of times a day across this country, acids and gasoline dumped in the streams. Add the thousands of acres of rain forest chain-sawed down to make way for new fields of coca, and cocaine ain't exactly environmentally friendly.

Pedro's pouring out the final solution into a barrel, passing it through cloth, ensuring any solids are left behind.

"Dip your finger in and lick it."

I lick my finger gingerly. It tastes like gasoline but it immediately puts my tongue to sleep. That was cocaine's breakthrough: as an anesthetic back in the 1880s.

This solution will dry and solidify and become coca paste—one step short of pure cocaine. A ton of coca leaves has been turned into a kilo and a half of coca paste.

Pedro grabs one that dried out today, a dirty whitish and yellow solid blob.

"A kilo and a half!" he says, putting it in a tatty plastic bag. He steps out of the lab and gets on his motorbike and revs the engine. He'll drop the coca off with the farmer who owns the coca field, passing the coca paste up the next link of the chain. The motorbike's gas tank has a sticker: If God is with me, then who would be against me?

THE SUN SETS ON ANOTHER day of coca harvesting. In Catatumbo, the sun rises at 6 A.M. and sets at 6 P.M. Twelve hours of light. And you feel every second of the darkness. Night is a life of torches and candles, with little to do. A few nights a week, the family of the general store will crank up the generator—the only one for miles around—and power up the television— the only one for miles around. The family watch their soap operas in the shack. Quietly, respectfully, out of the darkness come the coca pickers from nearby farms. They pull up plastic chairs in the dirt outside and watch the soaps through the open doorway, twenty-five feet from the screen. Pigs and chickens wander through the rows of plastic chairs as the farmhands watch a soap about cocaine cartels. On the screen, impossibly beautiful white women and men move through luxurious penthouses dressed in the latest fashions, all financed by cocaine. I look at the viewers—the dark-skinned men and women sitting in plastic chairs in the dirt, swatting away mosquitos, relaxing after a long day picking coca.

Then it's sleep. Nights are so hot, you drift off in sweat. Here we sleep in thunder, always thunder in Catatumbo. There are more lightning strikes in Catatumbo than any other spot on earth. The storms feel like barrages of artillery. The rain ham-

mers on the metal roof. For three hours, the lightning illuminates every hole, every space between the wooden slats of my
hut. The roars of thunder cascade to crescendos lasting minutes. The storm crawls closer and closer. Now, roaring above,
reverberating in my chest, kicking my organs around.

And, finally, the storm crawls on to torment the neighbors.

The next morning, a woman stops by the general store.
It's another sunny day; still there is thunder to the north of
us. She's around thirty with that distinctive guerrilla physique: healthy and large thighs—the heavy carb diet and long
marches of a life in the rebels. She possesses the confidence
absent in a typical farmer; her back is straight and her eyes
meet my own. Small farmers live on the margins. The guerrillas teach them they are the future of the revolution. I know
she is a guerrilla; she knows I know. These are things that are
not said openly.

"Laws in Colombia are for assholes," she says, sitting in
the shade. She and her husband grow coca. "The government talks about the coca farmers as if they're to blame for
everything. Every day the cocaine is leaving through the
airports, the ports; why isn't that declared a national emergency? They don't because that's where the billions of dollars
are being made, not the thousands of dollars here."

She wears black leggings and a black Donna Karan T-shirt.
Guerrilla style is always black—tougher to spot at night.
Shadow fashion.

"It's sad and inevitable. The government will come and rip
out the coca crops. That will make the zone even poorer—if
you can imagine that—and the violence will get even worse."

She shakes her head as if saying, None of this needs to
happen.

One night, the gasoline smuggler motors over to Venezuela

to buy crates of beer. Coca growers from miles around come to the general store to drink. It's been a long week of harvesting coca and making coca paste. The kilos of coca paste are tucked away in the huts, ready to be taken to market.

In the distance, a full-on electrical storm is under way, huge clouds illuminated from within, a light show of the heavens.

Carmen's mother is celebrating her birthday. Salsa plays through a small speaker. Couples dance. All the young men give the birthday woman a twirl for a song. A couple of ten-year-old girls ask their grandfather to dance with them. They spin and glide to the tropical rhythm.

"How do you like our lives in the countryside?" a farmer asks. "I bet it's too quiet for you. We like it like this. Quiet and slow. After two days in town, it's too much for me."

I ask about the violence.

"Now, no one really knows what's happening. Under Megateo it was all different . . ."

And that opens the floodgates for everyone to talk about their favorite rebel leader: Victor Ramon Navarro Serrano, known by everyone as Megateo. A legend, a man who could only be born out of the jungles and mountains of Colombia. Drug lord, warlord, and a bandit beloved of the people. Pablo Escobar, Che Guevara, and Robin Hood, all rolled into one.

Growing up in the mountains of Catatumbo, Navarro Serrano was bright and ambitious. Colombia's rigid feudal hierarchy wasn't going to work for him—he wasn't going to work himself to death in a field. Born poor and die poor was no deal. The quickest way to be someone in the Catatumbo was to join the guerrillas. The guerrillas in his town were the Maoist Popular Liberation Army (EPL). Over the course of the 1990s, the EPL shrank from a national guerrilla movement to only ruling Catatumbo. The EPL raised money for its fight by "taxing" coca sales, turning Catatumbo in to a sanctuary for cocaine, a regulated zone where cartels could come. And in 2000, Megateo took control of the EPL and became the warlord of Catatumbo. The EPL pursued cocaine to keep fighting against the government. Slowly but surely, the group started fighting the government to pursue cocaine. Cocaine had seduced another.

"He was a revolutionary, but you know what cocaine does to you . . ." says a farmer.

Megateo turned the EPL into a uniformed cocaine trafficking militia that spouted revolutionary slogans. He never stopped wearing the military uniform befitting a guerrilla insurgency, but as cocaine took over, the narco within came out. Gold chains, expensive watches, flashy SUVs, costly escorts flown in, gold pistol-shaped medallions. Narco style.

One farmer tells how Megateo famously asked his lovers to tattoo his name next to their vaginas. It was a golden ticket ensuring that Megateo would take care of the woman.

"He always helped people out if they needed it. If a mother couldn't feed her children, he would pay for her shopping every month."

What you hear in the farmers' voices is a nostalgia for stability. When there is one warlord, everyone knows the rules and there is peace. When there are two warlords, there is war. And the farmers always die first.

"If something happened, you could speak to him. If someone stole your motorbike, or a man touched your daughter, you could send a message to him and he would take care of it," says another.

When the state won't do its job, a line of villains wait for their chance to step in instead.

The EPL slowly turned from a revolutionary organization to a well-run narco-militia. With a multimillion-dollar bounty on his head, Megateo invested heavily in snipers. His men couldn't stand and face the army and the police, but they could score big in hit-and-run operations. These mountains became shooting galleries, knocking off police and soldiers.

Megateo's story ended as it must, as Megateo knew it would. Megateo bought a mobile antiaircraft missile launcher to take down the helicopters that plagued him. Except the arms dealer was an undercover army agent and the rochet launcher was booby-trapped. Megateo was eager to try out his new toy. And the army agent politely excused himself to a safe distance. Megateo pressed "Fire." All they ever found was one leg.

With Megateo gone, Catatumbo became an open war zone as all the other militias came in.

"We never should have killed him," someone in the army will tell me later. "He put order in Catatumbo. Now it's a disaster."

THE NEXT MORNING, I LEAVE. The rain has flooded out the river. Nothing to do but wait for the boat. And among those waiting for the boat is a farmer with a backpack.

The kilo of coca paste and I are leaving the Land of Lightning.

This kilo will travel thousands of miles, throughout Colombia, across the Pacific Ocean. It will pass through the hands of criminals; it will witness greed, betrayal, and despair.

On the horizon another storm gathers.

CHAPTER 2

LA GABARRA, LA GOMORRAH

IT'S FRIDAY AFTERNOON AND LA GABARRA is cranking up for an un-forgettable weekend. Now that cocaine is funding the party, every weekend is unforgettable. La Gabarra is firmly under the sway of cocaine, the white madness.

La Gabarra is the next link in the chain of cocaine. It's the hub for the cocaine industry for this part of Catatumbo, and similar towns are spread across Colombia's coca zones, marketplaces where farmers come to sell their coca paste. Thousands of kilos arrive here, brought by farmers out of the jungles ready to unload their coca paste to the illegal militias who will then refine it into kilos of pure cocaine that they can sell to the cartels. Today buzzes because it's market day.

It was a priest who recommended I visit this town.

"I don't mess with the mafia," the man of God had told me when I met him, as he made the sign of a gun, pulling the trigger repeatedly. "This is the only part of Colombia with three guerrilla groups: FARC dissidents, ELN, EPL. And the mafias . . . all the mafias are here with us."

This priest was gruff, uninterested in courtesies. His manner was: here is the truth, so listen to it or fuck off. We met in his office, as two fans whirled against the heat. He wanted to explain cocaine's stranglehold over his flock. He jotted calculations on a piece of paper, mumbling as he wrote: "Seventeen thousand hectares times by eight hundred dollars . . ." He multiplied the number. His eyebrow rose as he looked at the total. "More than thirteen million dollars every two months. That's just coca paste."

That's nearly $80 million a year—for the lowest rung on the cocaine ladder, in one corner of Colombia.

"These are the people that run this, operate here. I'm not getting involved in what they're doing so they can come and kill my family, kill everyone down to my dog."

He read the disappointment on my face.

"I'm not going to tell you anything—all I can do is just give you tips and you go investigate. It's much worse than what you see. The people tell me. The dissidences are growing much quicker than anyone realizes. Big warlords are coming in to take charge. The killings, the war is going to get much worse." He stopped talking abruptly, hearing someone outside his door, and after sending the man on his way, the priest waited until he knew we were alone.

"Strange people everywhere . . ." And he continued. "It's the law of silence here. We see all of these killings, but no one knows why," he says. "Before, during the war, someone was killed and the killers would say: 'We killed this person for this reason, that reason.' Now people are killed and no one claims them. Just silence. This peace . . . it's killing us."

He paused for a moment.

"You want to see all the militia members, the coca farmers, the traffickers, all drinking together? The disorder, the drunks, the social decay, the prostitutes? Go to La Gabarra. You'll see it all there."

And so, with the blessing of this man of God, that's where I find myself, in a modern-day Gomorrah. Battered old trucks roll into town, men and women hanging off the doors, sitting on roofs. At the village entrance, the trucks dump the young raspachines and coca farmers. At La Gabarra's river dock, long motorized canoes carrying twenty people pull in, so weighed down by passengers, it seems everyone might sink before docking.

The sunset hits the dust as it hangs in the air. Streets are packed, a fun-fair atmosphere. Families walk through the middle of the unpaved streets. Hundreds of raspachines are in town to blow through the money they earned sweating in the fields. They're in their finest threads and fresh haircuts. Raspachines deserve their own collective noun: a riot of raspachines.

The streets smell of roasted chicken, meats on sticks sold by food carts. Raspachines pass bottles of rum back and forth as they crack jokes or stop to lose money at the makeshift roulette wheels. Indigenous women with beautiful colorful necklaces sit by the roadside, selling their trinkets. Everything here is designed to separate the men from their money, like a Las Vegas for coca farmers. They'll spend it on booze and women. And the rest . . . well, they'll just waste.

Just because this village doesn't respect the rule of law, that doesn't make it lawless. It's the law of the narco-militias and they rule with an easy trigger. Their snitches are on every street, watching. They pretend not to look at you as you pass, but turn around sharply and you'll catch them looking straight at you, phone in hand communicating to their bosses.

The militias knew I was coming before I got off the bus. And they'll keep watching me until I leave. Like everywhere in the coca zone, the narco-militias had approved my visit. If they hadn't approved it, they would have stopped me along the route to ask what I was doing. And if they didn't like my answer, they would have taken me into the mountains.

Everyone smiles and through the air passes that electrical feel of money changing hands at a fast pace. Stores are open late tonight, to sell clothing to the raspachines, stereos to the farmers, motorbikes to the drug traffickers. Two men walk through the streets carrying a large plasma TV, offering to sell it to every drunk who stumbles past. Prostitutes wander the streets in pairs, taking a break before the heavy work begins later tonight.

These lands have the feel of the Wild West. Territory is stolen from the indigenous. A man can't count on the law to protect him. Today's gold rush is coca. Some sell the coca; some sell the herbicides to grow the coca; some sell their bodies to the men who sell coca. It's a frontier spirit here. A town by the side of the jungle, a people at the edge of civilization.

Like any boomtown, money stenches the air. Children screech with glee doing wheelies on shiny new bicycles. Young men rev Japanese-style motorbikes up and down the main strip, winking at the girls. Flashing stores, owned by loud gregarious salesman, sell huge television sets and the latest fridges. Many of the stall owners have come from outside of Catatumbo, lured by the money. Cocaine causes huge waves of migration across Colombia, as salesmen and prostitutes travel miles, attracted by the unmistakable smell of coca farmers with cash.

An energy buzzes that promises riches, sex, and death. It's not that anything is possible, it's that someone *is* going to do the unthinkable. Want five hookers, ten kilos of cocaine, and an AK-47? La Gabarra is the place for you. A Casablanca of mud, beer, and cocaine. Tonight is for drinking, buying, and fucking. And anyone who leaves town sober, unfucked, and without a plasma TV never should have come in the first place.

THE DEALS ARE DONE IN hotel rooms, in people's homes, out of sight. Once the cash is in the farmers' hands, they head out in to the night to spend. Coca farmers and raspachines start the evening in the pool halls, and so do I. There are eight pool tables and a large bar where large bottles of beer are drunk quickly. For some reason there's a framed poster on the wall of W. C. Fields holding an eight-ball. On the pool tables are photos of blond women on all fours looking over their shoulder with a sultry look. The photos are fading from too much staring. Above us is one of the town's brothels, so a man need only stumble up one staircase once he's good and drunk.

Pool halls are the workingman's weekend hangout, a cacophony of roaring laughter, drunken stumbles, and blaring music. A woman jokes with friends loud enough for me to hear: "Leave him with me and I'll make him a daddy by morning!" These lands have spent decades learning to laugh even in the shadows of the militias, cocaine, and violence.

And they are ever present. A month earlier, just twenty miles from here, men walked into a pool hall. It was 3 P.M.: the balls were pocketing, the beer flowing, and the songs blaring. The men pumped the pool hall full of bullets. There were nine dead, among them a social leader.

Tonight the pool hall blares out the *corridos prohibidos,* jaunty songs about the narcotics trade and Colombia's endless violence. The sound track to Colombia's conflict, oral histories put to music. Now plays Uriel Henao's "The Child of Coca," the story of a young boy who travels to a coca zone in search of parents who abandoned him. Instead, he finds a job.

> *Now, I'm in the mountains of Colombia*
> *Picking coca, because there's nothing else to do . . .*

The boy discovers that his parents were murdered in the drug trade. By the end of the song, the boy has become a man, a drug lord. He promises vengeance on the "cowardly dogs" who slaughtered his parents.

Next to me at the bar, a business deal is going down. Two men are dressed as cowboys, all in white. They're the best-dressed men in town and decked with beautiful cowboy hats, *sombreros vueltiaos,* distinctive to the Caribbean coast. And I'm certain they're drug traffickers in town to buy merchandise that they'll take back to the coast. Men like this are negotiating multi-ton deals of cocaine. One is showing his drinking partner his beautiful hat's impermeability by pouring beer over the top. The cowboys look amused by their surroundings, the coca farmers, and the raspachines. They give off the air of finely controlled, methodical violence. Crazy and tough can be faked. The aura of being intimate with violence can't.

As one of few foreigners to visit Catatumbo, I'm attracting curiosity. A drunk old man comes over, his white T-shirt dotted with fresh bloodstains. A machete swings from his belt in the beautiful scabbards of the countryside. I imagine he's another coca farmer. I figure it best not to ask about the bloodstains.

"They call me 'Highway Machete.'"

Why's that?

"Lots of fighting. On the highway. With my machete. Took a man's arm off."

I drink my beer.

"Never started a fight myself. But I always ended them."

He drifts off into the crowd of the bar, his machete swinging and a bottle of beer in his hand.

A young man approaches. He's thin, with a black mustache and a *corte paisa,* a mullet. Drunk already, he begins to talk. People here feel comfortable talking, confident that everyone else in the room is into much uglier things.

"There's going to be a big meeting of the FARC dissidents tomorrow. . . . Come, come and see. It will be great. I don't think they'll kill you if you get there."

I guess he's twenty-seven years old. He's dressed in a black T-shirt and black quick-dry trousers. There's the confidence in his bearing, the steel of a guerrilla. He says he has been a rebel with the FARC's rivals, ELN, for five years. But he's contemplating a change.

"I want to join them, but you have to be careful with the FARC. They'll kill you for anything. You piss them off once, they say, 'Go do this job.' You go there and wake up dead."

I ask what type of revolution he'd like to see: Cuba, Venezuela?

Suddenly his voice is 100 percent sober, measured.

"I should be treated the same as everyone else. That's the revolution I will die for."

Out in the town, a river of young raspachines moves through the mud streets, laughing and drinking. Across Colombia, everyone is always taking photos on their phones, selfies, photos with friends. Here I don't see a single person taking a photo. Why? Because you don't know who else is going to be in the background of your selfie, and a photo like that will get you killed.

BOOM! Everyone seizes up. Shoulders hunch. Heads duck. An old woman cackles. It's her firecracker. Some laugh. Someone angrily shouts: "Don't do that!" She cackles harder.

Packs of young men move through the streets. Like all country boys, they're polite, stepping aside to make way for people, holding open doors. And in a town run by militias, it's good to be polite to strangers when you don't know who they are.

The town has the feel of repressed violence, of a snake coiled. And sometimes it breaks through.

The fists hammer in a flurry. Immediately the two men toss their shirts to the dirt. Good defenses—both young men take up the boxer's stance. In seconds, sixty men and women surround the two fighters. Men climb on trucks for a better view. Children worm their way through the crowd to a front-row view. Stray dogs join the throng, wagging their tails, happy to be included. The fighters lunge, thrust forward, and tumble backward and the crowd flows around them like a shoal of fish.

This fight is brutal and the crowd grateful. Both men work with their hands for a living, and now these hands connect solidly. The leaner man's punches land as wet thuds on his rival's face. Blood sprays in the streetlight. Ultraviolence. The leaner man unleashes a tornado of blows, connecting again and again to the torso and then the head. Under the onslaught, the man steps back and stumbles. He falls backward, hitting the dirt hard. It's lost.

The lean man leaps astride him, pinning his arms with his legs. The lean man deliberately, slowly raises his arms. Down they come.

On the man's face.

Like fucking pistons.

More blood squirts into the air.

Under the barrage to his face, the man goes limp. Only his head jerks from side to side with each blow.

The flurry of punches ends. That was adrenaline-spiked fight-or-flight. Now come slower, harder blows. This is darker; this is killer. The man on the ground is no longer a fighter, he's a victim. A man is being murdered. The crowd stops cheering. Silence save for wet, hard thuds.

After ten seconds, his friends pull him off. Amid hugs and backslaps, they lope off into the night. The loser lies motionless. A mask of blood stares up at the stars. Half the crowd fades away. The body moves and there is audible relief. Now the crowd can enjoy it again. Girls with their dates giggle and laugh. Two ten-year-old boys mock fight, imitating the kicks and punches they just witnessed.

BOOM! Everyone ducks again. And then the cackle again. "Goddamn it! Don't do that!" someone shouts again. Another cackle.

After a long three minutes, the man clambers to his feet.

"Where did that faggot go? Where is he?" He wobbles.

A dwarf with a hunchback steps up to the man and speaks softly. And then he walks the man off. I look down and see I'm standing in the blood splatter. Time for another beer.

THE NEXT DAY, I WALK around town. It looks like any of the hundreds of other market towns in rural Colombia that sell coffee, vegetables, and fruit. There is a church. A large school, meant to educate hundreds of children from the surrounding mountains. Families eat at restaurants and window-shop. Still, La Gabarra has a feeling.

I walk to the medical outpost. Behind closed doors, doctors see the teenage pregnancies, the bullet holes, the STDs, the machete gashes. Doctors know the truth of a town.

On the locked metal door hang two sheets of paper: "There is no treatment for malaria" and "There is no doctor." The clinic is closed, all the medical staff relocated after constant death threats from the militias. Locals have marched and protested. But the doctors have yet to return.

The only justice here is of the rough frontier kind. No one believes in the police. A month earlier, a Venezuelan immigrant stabbed a well-loved hairdresser to death. The crowd fought off soldiers and police to burn him alive in the middle of the street, a shrieking body aflame. A witness made sure to tell the journalist who wrote up the story that "it smelt like roast chicken."

The humor of the violence takes some getting used to.

Gun battles break out regularly as the different militias vie for control of La Gabarra's neighborhoods. The shoot-outs don't resolve anything but add to the death toll.

"The Grim Reaper continues to stroll undisturbed through here" writes a local newspaper to explain the homicides. This region, the municipality of Tibú, will end the year with a homicide rate of 240 per 100,000. Put that in context—the most violent city in 2018 was Mexico's Tijuana and that had a rate of 138 per 100,000. Most of Tibú's killings will remain unsolved. But hold on, someone estimates the homicide rate might be double as militias disappear their victims, burying them in shallow graves. Catatumbo has more mass graves—running into the hundreds—than authorities can investigate. This is no longer violence. This is an epidemic.

As bad as La Gabarra is, it has improved.

The modern history begins with floods of farmers arriving,

displaced by a Colombian civil war so tremendous it's simply called "the Violence." The man and women who make their way to Colombia's most isolated stretches are called *colonos*, colonials. The colonials arrive and fights immediately begin with the Bari indigenous. From the beginning, there was something in these lands that brought out the evil. The first settlers grabbed as much land as they could defend and began to work the land.

"At the beginning, many people worked on the large farms. And strangers would come from outside the region and work two, three, six months. . . . Then the worker would say: 'Right, I need my money because I need to return home.' The landowner would say: 'Okay, let's take a look at the work you've been doing.' And then: Bam! Bam! Bam! . . . to avoid paying them, the farmers would kill them and bury them in the farm . . ." says Antonio, a pleasant, thoughtful man who teaches at the local school here in La Gabarra. "Catatumbo was founded with so much bloodshed. And that's why it's remained so violent ever since."

If you want to understand small-town Colombia, find the old-timer teachers. They're the town intellectuals, the possessors of the gossip that will become town history. You'll find them in white plastic chairs outside their home, in the shade, passing around a family-sized bottle of Coca-Cola and chatting. They reminisce and are grateful that someone listens. To listen is to tell them their memories matter.

In a town so small, they can pinpoint the man who brought coca to La Gabarra, way back in the 1990s. Don Julio brought coca from the south of Colombia, where coca grows naturally. He brought 150 cuttings of coca, buried in earth, hidden in a large plastic container. He disguised it by putting an ornamental plant on top. It was an immediate hit.

"Many people who had previously said coca was bad now started working in coca once they saw how much money it moved," says Juan, an old man now in his seventies.

"All the other crops were abandoned, because it took three hours to get them to town and if the highway was damaged by rains or a bombing, you could wait days for them to fix it. So it cost you money to sell the produce. But make coca and you can put five kilos of coca paste in your backpack and get on a bus," says Antonio.

It's the same story all over Colombia. Once a few farmers start planting coca, the price of food goes up as it has to be brought from outside. That pushes more farmers into growing coca. Soon, all the farmers in town are growing coca. Coca's takeover is complete. This is every coca town's golden age—when they revel in the money. And the killings have yet to begin.

"When it first came, it spread so quickly across the region and people thought it was amazing. 'Look, he's bought a car because of coca.' The stores were packed, the brothels were packed. Everyone wanted to be a cocalero!" says Antonio.

"The money flowed! It was so much money, it was incredible. You would see people laying out stacks of cash on tables, building little castles on the tables with the wads of cash."

Suddenly the tiny town now had ten brothels, filled with prostitutes from around the country. Groups of women rented entire buses to get here. Towns deeper in the jungles saw stables of prostitutes charter airplanes to arrive to the distant boomtowns.

"We realized that the town was losing its mind."

Coca became currency. Short on money? No problem, pay with grams. When the town was good and under the control of coca and everyone was happy, that's when the killings started. The honeymoon was over. It had become one more battleground to be fought over. The coca, the money, had attracted Colombia's rebels.

"A friend of mine got drunk and started saying stupid things, things he didn't need to say. They came for him and left his body on a riverbank."

As violent as the guerrillas were, the true horror was coming.

"You have to understand—there are two histories. There's before and after the paramilitaries came. . . ." says Juan.

The paramilitaries were a far-right militia, supported by rich farmers, parts of the military, politicians, and drug traffickers that battled the Marxist rebels. Throughout the 1990s, they carried out a dirty war against the FARC, slaughtering any civilian suspected of links to the guerrillas. In truth, the paramilitaries were fighting to seize the coca fields from the rebels. And the paramilitaries had noticed the millions to be made controlling La Gabarra.

In August 1999, the people of La Gabarra knew the paramilitaries were rolling through the region. The tension was rising in the town. The paramilitaries were known for their ferocious massacres. Chain saws, torture, rape, machetes— this is what makes up a paramilitary massacre. But the army still had a checkpoint at the entrance to the town.

"Such a coincidence," Juan says, the bitterness still there twenty years later. "Friday morning the army took away the checkpoint. And Saturday night, the massacre happened. . . . The checkpoint was there all the time. So why take it away Friday? What a coincidence," says Juan.

He heard the gunfire all night and wisely took cover.

"In the morning, I woke up at six thirty and I asked my neighbor, 'What was all the shooting last night?' He said:

'Teach, go and see.' I said: 'Go and see what?' 'No, just go.' And when I went . . . I was stunned to see all of those dead, all the bodies. So many."

The massacre left at least thirty-nine bodies dumped around the town. Villagers say the true figure was higher—more were shot and tossed into the river and others were taken away and never seen again. Even now, Colombia doesn't know how many were killed.

The paramilitaries took control of La Gabarra and terror reigned. The paramilitaries murdered all those with links to the rebels. A darkness took hold of the town—it turned blood simple. Old scores were settled, property coveted and taken—all you needed to get someone killed was to whisper to the right person that they were a guerrilla. The people of La Gabarra had been handed a toy of death. And they played with it like any one of us would—badly.

"Civilians were murdered because people were inform-ing on them, pointing out to the paramilitaries anyone they wanted and saying they needed to die. Many times it was to take away a business, a farm. They even killed a man to take his girlfriend."

What were the police doing? What did the army do to stop the madness? Local politicians? In La Gabarra much of the local authorities were bought off by the paramilitaries.

"They were more into looking after the paramilitaries. It was a rabbit hunt, honestly."

As in much of the country, the paramilitaries were car-rying out a dirty war striking at left-wing civilians, human rights activists. And they worked with parts of the army.

"The military couldn't grab just anyone, so they told the paramilitaries: 'Hey, there's a guerrilla, he's dressed in this T-shirt.' And the paramilitaries would travel all throughout the neighborhoods on motorbikes and cars looking for their targets. They'd find him and: Pow!," says Antonio.

The coca had turned the town mad. The bloodshed deepened the insanity.

"We've been desensitized here—because in that time, if you saw a dead body, you would say: 'Oh another dead body.' You'd walk around it and that was it."

One green truck inspired terror by its appearance alone. La Ultima Lagrima, the Last Tear, was driven by a particularly sadistic paramilitary commander.

"Anyone who got into that truck, never returned"—he gives a dark chuckle at the madness of war—"they were taken and"—he whistles—"shot."

The paramilitaries changed the way coca paste was sold. Previously farmers had sold to cartel emissaries, selling to the highest bidder. The paramilitaries made the farmers sell directly to them at a price—roughly four hundred dollars—decided by the paramilitaries. The paramilitaries, with high-ranking traffickers in their central command, exported the cocaine abroad themselves.

The paramilitaries demobilized in the early 2000s in one of Colombia's countless peace processes. As the paramilitaries left La Gabarra, the FARC returned. As long as coca is here, La Gabarra is a patch of ground doomed to be forever fought over. Now three militias are in the town: the ELN, the FARC dissidents, and EPL. They've kept the system—demanding farmers sell straight to the rebels. And they've kept the same price established two decades ago.

The teachers watched the children they taught grow into underage assassins. One killed more than twenty for the ELN. Another hunted for the FARC, killing more than forty. "Including a young boy. The boy didn't have any family so would ask for food from the army, the police. For that, they killed him."

Antonio guesses that 80 percent of the economy is based on coca. And if it is to be taken away, the town will fall into catastrophe. Children starving, everyone out of work, the gasoline of the economy gone. It's happened to other coca towns across Colombia.

But that's for the future—the grim reality is that coca is the only option for now.

"We tell our children in our classes: coca is bad. We try to show the children other paths," says Juan. "A student will tell me: 'Teacher, I won't be in class next week, I'll be picking coca.' And they'll tell us: 'Look, teacher, what you earn in a month, I earn in a week.'"

"What has us fucked up is the stigma we have. Outside of here, if you say you're from La Gabarra, you're marked. You're a bad one. We want to get rid of this image," says Juan. "There are good, honest, hardworking people here."

I ask him what identity he would like to see associated with La Gabarra. He shrugs. A Gabarra free of coca is almost too difficult to imagine.

SATURDAY NIGHT. NOW THAT THE kilos have been sold, drunken coca farmers will splurge on booze, women and the latest electrical appliances—flat-screen TVs they'll carry home by motorized canoe, strapped to the back of a mule to climb a mountain and finally reach a wooden hut where it will be powered by a diesel generator. Cocaine doesn't make for good savers. It's an orgy of beer, sex, and consumerism. Drink, fuck, and buy!

The tradition is to sell the kilo of coca paste and burn some of the money in the brothels. It's still early and the women sit at the tables chatting, lazily eyeing each man who comes in. A weird scene of bared behinds, lingerie, and bored faces. A pole stands in the middle of the dance floor. Blue bulbs give everything a feel of under the sea.

The administrator comes over and has a beer. She's around thirty-five years old and funny. She has a tough job, keeping the prostitutes and drunken raspachines in order.

"It's hard controlling the women. Making sure they're working and not fucking off, not fighting each other," she says.

"The men usually are respectful. But sometimes . . . Last night, a girl didn't want to drink. A man said drink it. She said no. He poured it over her head. She took that same bottle and cracked it over his head. And then all the other women joined in. Start with one, they all join in. They fight all day but if a man fucks with them, an instinct kicks in."

Almost all the women working inside are Venezuelan. And most of the raspachines are, too.

"The Venezuelans work harder than the Colombians," she says. I shudder at the word "harder." "I've only been doing this job for a month. It's been a shock. I'm learning a lot," she says, forcing a smile and downing her beer before returning to behind the bar. The bar has a huge metallic grille they can pull down if it gets too rowdy.

Prostitution is a hierarchy. At the top of the pyramid are women who charge tens of thousands of dollars a night, switching between drug lords and politicians. Near the bottom is sleeping with drunken coca farmers and coca pickers in a war zone. And dangerous: Become a girlfriend to a militiaman, you're no longer a civilian. You're in the war now.

One prostitute was hung from a tree in Catatumbo. Her one-year-old baby was left crying and shivering beneath her corpse as it swung in the wind. Something so macabre was a punishment, a message meant to be seen, so none dared cut her down. She swung and the baby cried until her family arrived to cut her down and save the baby two days later.

Here, in the brothel, the classic *corrido prohibido* by Uriel Henao "I Prefer a Tomb in Colombia" comes on and everyone's head bobs. The song is based on the words of Pablo Escobar.

I'm conscious of what I'm doing
I know too that it's a big crime
Poverty brought me to this life
Although too late, I regret it

An obviously pregnant woman sits on a raspachin's knee and as the chorus comes on, "I prefer a tomb in Colombia," they belt out the words, the beer slurring their words.

Poverty brought me to this life
But it's too late for me
To leave drug trafficking
It's very tough
Because a lot of people depend on me. . . .

On the wall, a poster outlines the rules for the prostitutes.

Fights = $33
Missing work = $15
Messy room = $15
Stealing or drug use = Suspension
Using cell phone during work = $15
Leaving work without permission = $15

Beneath, is a reminder that each client gets twenty minutes in the room. And finally, the opening hours:

Monday to Friday 7 P.M.–1 A.M.
Saturday: 2 P.M.–3 A.M.
Sunday: 9 A.M.–1 A.M.

Brothels run as factories.

The brothel seduction is well established. A man will call a woman over to his table. If she wants to, she'll go over. She decides who she has sex with, but the administrator is watching and this business only works with a high turnover. The two will drink what's on the table. The two will dance for a number of songs. And then hand in hand, they'll go to the doors at the edge of the room. She'll charge twelve dollars for the twenty minutes. His night in the brothel is usually finished, although sometimes he'll come out and take his seat at the table and get back to drinking. And she'll have a quick wash and then back out to earn some more money.

A beautiful woman grinds on a young man's lap. She's in perfect fitting white shorts, and a tight bra top. She grinds, rounding over the man's crotch. She has him hypnotized. She catches me staring and she smiles and winks. It's a wink that says: Baby, it's all a game. Don't take anything seriously. Nothing lasts. Nothing is what it seems. Nothing means anything. The nihilism of the brothel.

A salsa song comes on and this scene is transformed to elegance as the prostitutes dance with the coca pickers. The moves so fine, such rhythm, I enjoy the show.

A YOUNG MAN SITS DOWN hard next to me. He's drunk. He says to call him Cristian. He starts talking, spitting constantly. He's Venezuelan, and like all of them, he picks coca to send money back home to his one-year-old daughter and wife. He makes around $170 a week. "I save my money. That makes me different from all the other raspachines.

"It's embarrassing that our women are here as prostitutes. Five years ago, it was all Colombian women in Venezuela who were the prostitutes. When we wanted to come to a place like this, we would say: 'Let's go visit the Colombians.'" Another chuckle.

He looks at me, studying me. He turns back to the woman stripping around the pole.

"It wasn't just the crisis that brought me here . . . I was a policeman. And a killer. And a policeman."

He was a policeman in a small town in Venezuela. As the economy sank, crime exploded, enveloping his town. He and two other cops became a unit of dirty cops—killing all the criminals in his hometown.

"We were paid to clean up the town. Me and my friends, we cleaned up the whole town. We killed all the criminals. All the thieves, the drug dealers, the killers for hire. A man who robbed old ladies, we would go to his house and shoot him dead. We killed them all."

Crime went down in his town, he says. "The criminals feared us. We made a difference."

It's called "social cleansing"—local businesses pay money to the police to murder junkies, prostitutes, small-time drug dealers. Some of the killings Cristian did for free.

"But we weren't criminals. You see the difference between us, don't you? The sicarios (paid assassins) killed to kill. We killed to save our town. We never enjoyed it."

He spits.

"There was one drug dealer and we went to his house. We shot him up. No one had paid us for this job. We did it just for the town. To help. The faggot didn't die. . . ."

The man survived and talked to authorities. The police started investigating all the other dead crooks. Investigators swooped, arresting Cristian's partner. Cristian managed to escape across the border to Colombia.

"I'll never go back. This is it for the moment. . . ." He sweeps his arm around the brothel, the stripping hookers and the passed-out raspachines. And he smiles at what his life has become. Is the story true, or a way to say: "Hey, I'm different from these loser coca-pickers. I was somebody once!" who knows?

"Enough of this," he says firmly. "Let's go to the next brothel. The women are more beautiful. I'll pay for you."

I politely decline, but he's getting boisterous. He's been sipping some Venezuelan rotgut. I tell him firm and strong to stop being annoying. He takes it once. But he's big and he's getting drunker and meaner. He won't take it a second time.

Outside ten motorbikes roar to a halt in front of the brothel. These are not the raspachines or farmers inside. These are drug traffickers. Their bikes are imported Japanese hyperbikes. The men have the look that says violence is part of their daily job. All are in their twenties except the obvious boss. He's a cracked face in his fifties, a large gold chain around his neck. He has that aura of repressed violence. And the fat man next to him is the one who carries it out, the type to fight the wind. Fatso stares me up and down. They enter but walk out shortly after. They take their menace somewhere else tonight. They'll ask after me tomorrow morning.

Back inside, Cristian is well on drunk and obnoxious. I sit at another table.

A crash, a scream, a smash. Cristian is by the bar up front, waving a metal stool. The women behind the bar slam down the protective grille, just as Cristian smashes the stool against it. A second's hesitation and the steel stool would have smashed into their faces.

Cristian shouts, threatening one and all with the stool. His face is contorted in rage. There's the killer inside he's been carrying around since he fled Venezuela. His friends try to calm him and he violently pushes them away. Another coca picker puts his hand on his shoulder. Cristian tosses the stool and stumbles to a seat by the wall.

A squad of police arrive dressed for a war zone. Worried about drug traffickers, militia members, they come in with fingers on the trigger of their machine guns. Cristian is shouting; a prostitute is bouncing up and down on the lap of a raspachin. The police smirk to themselves at the state of it all. Cristian is hustled out. The police check every man's ID in the brothel.

The policeman looks at my ID.

"It's your birthday."

Yes, it is.

I SPOT ROSARIO GLIDING THROUGH the brothel. She's graceful as a cat, a smile fixed on her face. Long black hair falls down her back. Tonight she's on that ancient mission of separating a sucker from his money. I ask for an interview and I'll pay her rate—twelve dollars for twenty minutes (half goes to the brothel owner). Her time is money and it's the right thing to do. She says to come back the next day. I do.

She guides me to her room and leaves me for a moment. She

lives here with another young woman. And this is where she has sex with the clients. There are two single beds. At one end of the room is a large barrel of water. In it floats an empty plastic tub and next to it, a stained porcelain toilet. There's no running water in La Gabarra—washing is by dunking plastic bowls and drenching yourself. The toilet flushes by filling it up from the barrel.

Ten pairs of shoes sit on a shelf: trainers, sandals, and a pair of gold high heels. High heels in a town without paved roads. A Che Guevara baseball cap hangs off a hook on the door. It's the kind of thing young rebels give as gifts. Two fans whir in the stifling heat. Vast, colorful, and unidentifiable stains mark the room's ceiling. One tiny window. It's grim, like a cell.

She returns. As she closes the metal door, three prostitutes outside eye me meanly, mouths itching to gossip. I grab my phone to start taking notes. Rosario doesn't move—she's pressed up against that metal door, staring at me.

"They tell me you're one of the bad ones. Are you a bad one?"

Tears well in her eyes. Her eyes implore me: "Tell me I haven't put myself in danger by talking to you. . . ." I tell her that I'm writing a book, that I promise her family will not find out what she's doing (Rosario is not her real name); no one in the town needs to know that we spoke. I tell her that in my years working in Colombia I've never got anyone killed for my reporting. I silently curse the bored prostitutes outside.

"Please don't tell anyone that I spoke with you. Please."

There is a look of childish innocence on her face. Her eyes say: "Please don't get me killed."

I tell her: Trust me. You won't die.

Rosario is from the Venezuelan town of San Cristobal,

about six hours away. She has a two-year-old son, who lives with her mother. Rosario says her mother thinks she works in a restaurant. I wonder if the mother really does believe that.

"The situation in Venezuela forced me to do this. It's the only way I can make something for my son."

As a teenager, Rosario wanted to be a forensic investigator, those who scour crime scenes for clues. As she talks, I see the traces across her face of the young girl she once was and her dreams of a life. Before becoming the woman who has sex with drunken coca farmers for money.

She got pregnant and started working in restaurants in San Cristobal.

"Study doesn't pay. Work doesn't pay in Venezuela. You're on your own."

She and five friends got together and planned a trip to Colombia. Living on the border, they had heard of La Gabarra. They knew it was synonymous with cocaine. There had to be money there. They just never thought of the violence.

She arrived four months ago. She drank to get through her first experiences having sex for money. She cried whenever she was alone. Life in the brothel doesn't give much time off and she hasn't seen her son since arriving. Her friends couldn't handle the job, the violence of La Gabarra. The weirdness of it all. They left. She needed the money. She stayed.

If Rosario can sleep with five men a day, good. Eight men a night is better. If she does that—she makes forty-eight dollars. Most days, she doesn't make that. But the weekend is when she's going to make the money.

As a prostitute, she's come to know everyone in La Gabarra. "It's a strange little village. You can see the money here. This country is so . . . different than Venezuela. I didn't realize what Colombia was like. It's a country where even the smallest town has had its own massacre."

She still doesn't understand the violence that swirls around, only learning to keep her head down. The killings terrify her. When gun battles occur, she hides under her bed.

"It's tough living here. You're always dealing with men from one militia or another. And you have to be neutral, right in the middle. If you don't . . . you're a target," she says looking at the floor. Even the bodies of prostitutes can be battlegrounds.

"It's difficult sleeping with these men when you know what they do. . . . Toby, the men here do terrible, terrible things. They kill for any reason."

She has a thin face, with long black hair that falls to her hips.

I ask what the worst thing is working here. She looks at me in disbelief.

"This!" She points to the bed. Tears well up again in her eyes. And I realize that she thinks—she knows—I don't understand how this job torments her. "Toby, I have to do this!"

"Saturday and Sunday are the worst." That's when the most money is made—and she sleeps with the most raspachines or coca farmers. I try to console her, but it's futile. Nothing I say will change the fact she needs to have sex with many men tonight and tomorrow and the next day.

"I'll keep doing it until I can't any longer. But I can't much longer."

Her youthful face is offset by a deep cynicism in her eyes. Whatever twists and turns her life takes, La Gabarra will mark her for life. Hopefully it will become a dark memory that only occasionally makes her shudder. But it will always be there.

"This life is gross, it's disgusting."

As we speak, she takes the decision.

"I'm leaving this week. I can't take it anymore."

Where to?

"Bogota. Anything is better than this. One day La Gabarra will change but I won't be here. It will get better, I'm sure."

"Toby, why do you do this" Here she points to my phone, where I take notes.

Journalism?

"Yes."

I do this because I hope what I report will change the world. If the world knows the truth, things can change.

She smiles at me sadly, a look of infinite pity.

"You can't change this world. When I'm finished for the night, I always read the Bible." She points to hers on a bedside table. "We are in the apocalypse. There's so much evil in the world. The innocent are cheated, murdered, raped. Countries are at war. More war. Strange things happen that we can't explain. This is our world. This is what we deserve. . . . But I don't deserve this life."

Such life has passed across this face, through this body. This woman has seen more of humanity in this ghastly cell than I'll see in several lifetimes.

"How old are you?"

"Nineteen."

BY SUNDAY AFTERNOON, THE EXODUS from La Gabarra has begun. The kilo of coca paste has been sold by the farmer for around $400 to the militias. It will be taken to a nearby laboratory, where it will be turned in a kilo of pure cocaine. The militias will then sell it to the cartels for around $1,600 a kilo.

Drunken farmers rise from the tables they drunk at and slept under. Coca pickers, beers in their hands, fall into the canoes at the village's port. Laughing and merry, they climb aboard the trucks that are preparing for the long journey back to the mountains. Bottles of rum pass back and forth. The coca pickers look forward to another week of sweating in those fields. The farmers have bought their rum and paid for their women and now return home with a few dollars in their pocket and a sad story for their wives.

I jump on my bus out of town. As the bus curves out along the mountain high roads, I think on those I've met. There's something I've never seen before—these men and women really do want to give this up. They've lived with cocaine now for a full generation. The good times, the bonanza is gone, and it's not coming back. All it is now is a drag. Cocaine is nothing but bloodshed without even the good money anymore. These farmers don't want this life anymore. All they want is a government to step up and help them move away from the coca. A visionary government with a real plan to eradicate coca, working with farmers, would find willing allies in the countryside. Build the roads and bridges that allow them to transport legal crops to market.

Unfortunately, there is little visionary in the drug war. The United States, Europe, the Colombian government all continue to treat cocaine as a war. Coca is to be destroyed, cocaine seized.

That's my next stop.

CHAPTER 3

SISYPHUS IN THE COCA FIELDS

TUMACO IS A PORT IN THE MIDDLE of thick jungles that line the Pacific Ocean. Here there are mountains, perpetual rain, neck-deep poverty, and more coca than any other region on the planet. It's cocaine heaven—dense jungles providing cover for the coca and the laboratories, and a coastline to ship the cocaine out to the world's biggest consumer of cocaine: the United States. Naturally, it's the center of the government's attempts to eradicate coca—destroy enough coca, goes the thought, and you can't make those kilos in the first place.

Traveling to Tumaco feels like a journey to another planet. The propeller plane hums happily through the blue skies of southwestern Colombia. A beautiful flight attendant dressed in her blood-red uniform collects my empty coffee cup with a smile. Out the window, mountain ridges and peaks alone pierce the mattress of clouds below. The captain announces our imminent arrival and we gently sink into the clouds. The sun disappears and dense Pacific rain clouds batter the plane, heaving us to and fro. Out the window, the gray is so thick it swallows the end of the plane's wing. Ten minutes of this and we're out, two thousand feet above the earth and with the endless Pacific Ocean ahead of us.

The port relies on fishing, cocaine, and not much else. Entire neighborhoods are built on top of the ocean. Wooden huts balance on stilts, lattices of rotting timber in the Pacific. Paths of wooden planks supported by stilts connect the houses. There is no plumbing in these huts; the human waste cascades down to the ocean below—where people bathe.

The Pacific Coast is one of Colombia's tragedies. It's been abandoned by the central government to ravenous corrupt politicians. The Pacific Coast is largely Afro-Colombian. The region has given the country some of its most important artists, making Colombia a world power in salsa music. Yet, amid the jungles and the near constant rain, the region simply does not progress. The people of Tumaco are warm and generous, but trapped in tragedy.

For most of its existence, Tumaco lived off fishing. Then two decades ago, the government attacked coca crops in southern Colombia. The coca farmers and the narcos came to Tumaco. And they never left.

Traffickers are rife throughout the port and the surrounding mountains and jungles. Now what was once a quiet fishing town, has so-called casas de pique, chopping houses where traffickers' enemies are dismembered alive, body parts tossed into the ocean. The police bust them when they can, but few residents inform on the chopping houses no matter how loud or prolonged the screams. It's the quickest damn way to end up in one yourself.

And the peace process that upended Catatumbo has wrought chaos here, too. Under the FARC, there was a grim stability. Now there are too many new militias to count, all out for the coca.

Once Tumaco became the world capital of coca, it also became ground zero for eradication. For the past two decades, Colombia has been fumigating coca crops using small planes. It started out with American contractors flying these two-seater planes through the mountain valleys, fumigating the coca fields beneath with herbicides. Flanked by heavily armed Black Hawk attack helicopters, these planes could dump gallons of the glyphosate-based herbicide Roundup deep in rebel territory, fumigating hundreds of hectares of coca in a day. The rebels would shoot the planes up and back at base the pilots could count the new bullet holes.

Meanwhile, the contractors, who worked for companies like Dyncorp, were easily identifiable in Bogotá's handful of pubs. The pubs had the feel of a Graham Greene novel— Russian spies, Drug Enforcement Administration agents, drug traffickers, actors all rubbed shoulders in these pubs. Even the FARC tossing a grenade into one didn't stop the drinking. And like so often, the grenade didn't kill the foreign targets but innocent Colombians.

Colombia was the test run for the United States' latest experiment: to hire private mercenaries to carry out actions in war zones. This policy would be greatly expanded in Afghanistan and Iraq. But it started here, fumigating poor farmers' fields.

This was all part of a US-funded Plan Colombia back in 2000 under President Bill Clinton, which gave billions to Colombia to fight the rebels and aimed to slash cocaine production by half. Now that we have the world largest cocaine crop ever, the Colombian government's new goal is to cut coca production in 2023 by half. The drug war doesn't move backward or forward; it simply turns in circles.

Out in the countryside, complaints started appearing: legal crops were getting wasted as well in the drizzle of Roundup, impoverishing innocent farmers. Some questioned whether there might be health issues in spraying men, women, and children with industrial herbicide. One Ecuadorian community said the herbicide caused birth deformities. In the United States, a groundskeeper won a court case for $289 million for his terminal cancer because, the jury ruled, of his exposure to Roundup. Lawyers are now soliciting claimants for class-action lawsuits against Roundup in TV commercials running in the United States. The World Health Organization said in 2015 that glyphosate, the main ingredient in Roundup, is "probably carcinogenic to humans."

This is what the government had been using to drench one of the most biologically diverse environments in the world. The government suspended the fumigations in 2015. Washington and a new administration are keen to start fumigations again. One governor who opposes the fumigations saw his visa to the United States canceled as he tried to travel to attend a United Nations climate summit in New York.

Without aerial fumigation, it left the government with only manual eradication to destroy the coca crops: units of small farmers ripping out the coca crops, under heavy police guard. And there's more eradication here in Tumaco than anywhere else.

The antinarcotics base here in Tumaco is the center of the drug war on Colombia's Pacific Coast. It's heavily fortified, ready for any attack. Attack choppers fly in and out of the base all day long. Colombia's antinarcotics police combat daily the deadliest, most heavily armed cartels and guerrillas in the world—they're trained for that, equipped for it. Units of antinarcotics police are on full alert, sitting on their backpacks, rifles on their laps, ready for the order to hit the jungle. This base has three missions: capture/kill the biggest drug lords, seize cocaine, and destroy the coca. This isn't law and order. This is war.

Still, it looks like an invading army—inside the base, the police are indigenous, mestizo. Outside the population is almost all Afro-Colombian.

As I walk into the base, a bulky forty-year-old man with a short haircut walks past, handcuffed and with a poncho slung across his shoulder. I nod to him and he nods back— two men passing each other. Two men doing their job. Me, here reporting on the cocaine trade. William, getting busted for shipping tons of cocaine through the Pacific Coast on its way to the United States.

Seven hours earlier, William's night was going real bad. He was with his family, feeling safe, as he had paid local taxi drivers to warn him if the police were coming. Twenty elite cops eluded the taxis and busted into his home. Now William and his family were on the floor, hands behind their heads, rifles pointed at their skulls. They'd been hunting him for months after finding two tons of cocaine in the Pacific Ocean in a vessel. Get that to New York City and it's worth $90 million. Now William is here at the base, being formally charged. He'll be extradited to Texas. He's facing decades in an American prison, but he seems calm. For these traffickers, this is their moment in the ring, facing the bull. Feel the fear, but only a coward shows it. And I doubt he's scared. These men lead lives of violence and mayhem. William knew the knock was inevitable: a police raid or an enemy's bullet.

I sit with the Junglas commandos, the police's elite troops. They've picked up the swagger of the US advisors who trained them: millimeter haircuts, wraparound sunglasses, gymed-out bodies. I ask one: If you could take down any villain in all of Colombia, who would it be?

The guy licks his lips, like he can taste it. With a malicious smile, he says: "Guacho. I want Guacho."

THE IMAGE HORRIFIED SOUTH AMERICA: a video of two Ecuadorian journalists and their driver pleading for their lives, padlocked chains wrapped around their necks. The three stood next to each other, their arms wrapped around each other's shoulders. Tired, dirty, they were worn down. It's April 2018 and it's the first "proof of life video." Javier Ortega spoke directly to Ecuador's president: "Our lives are in your hands. . . . All they want is to swap their three men detained in Ecuador for our lives, for our three lives, to let us go to Ecuador safe and sound."

Ecuador breathed a sigh of relief—the men were alive. But who in the twenty-first century puts chains and padlocks around the necks of free men? The savagery. The cruelty.

Ortega, Paul Rivas, and Efrain Segarra were reporting on the spike in cocaine bloodshed along the border of Ecuador and Colombia. In a small town, they were kidnapped by "Guacho." Now he was telling Ecuador what he wanted for their lives.

"Guacho" is the type of madman who is thriving in the new Colombia. A tall, skinny kid, Walter Arizala Vernaza grew up in the rural misery of the Colombian-Ecuador border. A region abandoned by both governments, drug lords and Marxist rebels ran the zone. In regions like this, the first man in uniform that children see is a guerrilla passing through. Like millions of others, Walter had few options in life so he joined "those from the mountains," the Marxist rebels of the Revolutionary

Armed Forces of Colombia, the FARC. Still in his teens, he took the war name "Guacho." Smart and brave, he was put in a mobile combat column. These were the rebels' shock troops, a life of constant marching and fighting, fighting and marching. The rebels' job was to fight the army and protect the coca crops that were spreading rapidly throughout the zone.

Guacho rose through the ranks of the FARC to become that most dangerous of men in Colombia: a midrange commander. These are the men who convert the boss's orders into reality—packing the cocaine onto speedboats on moonlit beaches, planning and executing ambushes on enemies. Men of action and violence. And after they've mastered the finances and the bloodshed, midrange commanders are perfectly suited to grab the crown themselves.

It would take peace for Guacho to make his move. After the peace agreement was signed, the guerrillas moved into government-approved camps and began to disarm. Guacho complained that only the rebel leadership was reaping the rewards in the peace process, leaving the midrange commanders behind. In rallying against the peace process, his best ally was the government itself. The accord was signed with much fanfare, dignitaries from around the world watched the president and the FARC's leader put pen to paper. The civil war that had held Colombia back for so long was gone. The country's potential could be unleashed.

And yet the government lost interest. Jobs, training, stipends—the government bungled it all. The process's optimism was snuffed out. Violence spiked and rebels saw that Colombian society was apathetic in welcoming them to their new lives as civilians. The peace process became politicized. Politicians who had thrived in a Colombia at war seemed out of place in a Colombia of hope. Their speeches nipped at the ankles of the peace process. And the government did little to respond. By incompetence or corruption, Colombia let its once-in-a-generation opportunity slip through its hands. Hundreds of highly trained, dangerous guerrillas grew frustrated with the peace process—and returned to the jungle.

"We didn't see any need to continue with a process that the government wasn't living up to, not with us nor with those who live in the countryside," said Guacho in an interview with television channel RCN. He has a small mustache and that way of speaking on the Pacific Coast: higher-pitched, slow, as if weighing each word all with the lightest lisp. Over his shoulder is slung his automatic rifle. His bodyguards circle him, their guns at the ready.

Tumaco was one of the towns hardest hit by peace. Displacements and forced disappearances are up. Sexual violence is common. Women are abducted off dirt streets and raped for days on end. Heavy combat lasts for hours. Men like Guacho looked out over the zone of Tumaco and saw that the government was not coming. Instead, other criminal groups were taking over the coca crops and the cocaine trade. Many were old enemies of the FARC and were relishing the opportunity to settle some scores now that the guerrillas were unarmed. Guacho was right to worry—more than 160 ex-guerrillas have been murdered since the peace process began.

And like so many times in Colombian history, a group of men and women walked off to the jungle and formed a new rebel group, dissidents of the FARC. Former Marxist rebels trained in tactics, ideology, now focused on trafficking cocaine.

The world was about to learn how lawless this new war is. And Guacho was about to become world famous.

Tumaco's violent peace bled across into Ecuador. Car

bombs, heavy drug violence, this was all new to Ecuador, a small country trying to progress. Ecuador's top reporters wrote on the deteriorating security along the border. At the beginning of 2018, a team from Ecuador's leading newspaper, *El Comercio,* returned to the border to show how Ecuador was suffering Colombia's chaos. And they disappeared.

Latin America was transfixed by the case. Marches and protests were held across the continent to demand their liberation. Ecuador was united.

A march was held in Quito to support the three. As thousands filled the country's main plazas, Ecuador's president addressed the nation.

"Ecuador is in mourning," he said, his voice choking. He told the country that the three were dead. The demonstration descended into howls and tears.

This was the new violence. The FARC didn't kill journalists—they had the institutional knowledge to understand it was counterproductive, that it would only bring blowback. Guacho and the new generation of warlords were not operating by the old rules. The murders put Guacho at the top of the wanted list for both Ecuador and Colombia. Colombia announced three thousand extra troops to take down Guacho.

"This peace has been very deadly to us," a farmer in Tumaco tells me. "Before, we knew the rules of war. When something happened, we knew who to go to. There was someone who knew the FARC and you could send a message. Now? No one knows what's going on. There are no rules left."

As we speak, she tells me that a fifteen-minute drive from where we speak, corpses still litter the highway, from a clash between Guacho's men and troops. The authorities hadn't got enough security together to collect the bodies.

Let's go.

The old woman starts to cry.

"Please don't. They'll kill you."

She's probably right.

And it's Guacho's territory that I'm flying to to see the eradication efforts.

"THE BLAST WAVE EXPLODED HIS eyeballs," Major Jaime Aguirre says.

Some soldiers tell you these details because they dig your reaction. This major seems bummed out by the ordeal. A small IED hangs off a coca bush, a meter off the ground. A civilian coca eradicator walks through the bushes. By remote control, someone detonates the explosive. The blast wave blows out his eyeballs. A live, screaming skull with holes for eyes. No one will forget that day. A Black Hawk evacuates the eradicator from the coca field and flies him to the closest hospital, forty-five minutes away. For five hours, doctors try to stabilize him. A massive, final heart attack kills him. He was thirty-three. That was Friday. Today is Sunday.

Colombia is covered with IEDs, land mines, and unexploded ordnance just waiting to go off with a bang. Only Afghanistan and Cambodia see more injuries from mines. Small land mines aim to blow off just a foot. Huge explosives are hidden with the malice to massacre dozens in a single blast. Tens of thousands are scattered to protect coca.

Dropped off into the middle of enemy territory, the eradicators spend months slowly moving through the zone, ripping out the coca crops. Even with two heavily armed police troops for each eradicator, they're easy targets. Occasionally, the narco-militias launch full-on attacks. More common are land mines. They slow down the eradication and make it as painful as possible. Take my coca, I'll make you bleed.

These civilian eradicators, dressed in their blue shirts, have some of Colombia's most dangerous jobs. Explosions kill two, three, six. A donkey wandered into a coca field. Reaching the eradicators, it detonated—the rebels had loaded it with explosives. Two died that day.

Here with antinarcotics police, you feel the pressure they're under. The suspension of aerial fumigation helped push Colombia to a record cocaine crop. The United States is angrily demanding that Colombia reduce cocaine production. The government is promising that it will.

The antinarcotics police are responsible for the manual eradication. Whenever you speak to the antinarcotics police, the deaths in the coca fields weigh heavy on them. There's a bitterness that aerial fumigation was halted, sending the police and the civilian eradicators back into these literal minefields. This human toll is the backdrop to every conversation.

"When we see the huge number of deaths we've had, when we see the number of police and civilians mutilated, we need to ask how good is manual eradication compared to aerial fumigation," says Major Cristian Moreno, who oversees Tumaco's manual eradication program.

He doesn't hide his bitterness. Like many, he doesn't believe that aerial fumigation harms. He thinks coca growers shamed the government out of its best weapon against coca.

"It's very tough to see people who are working alongside you today, and tomorrow, you're walking along and just because of an IED, it finishes your life, it finishes all your hopes and dreams. We've had very athletic people mutilated, crippled. And as much as it keeps happening and as much as you witness it, it will keep hitting you hard."

The police know the truth of Colombia and the misery that births cocaine and the global demand that sustains the business. The antinarcotics police understand their job is a global one, they are the first line of attack in an earth-wide drug war that reaches every corner of the planet. That each kilo is one less not just for Colombia but the world. The antinarcotics headquarters has a statue of an agent holding the planet aloft. But the solution to cocaine will involve us all across the world. Yet the police are sent to the darkest corners and ordered to bring down cocaine by themselves.

"There's been a huge lack of development here; the state has been absent. And not just the security services, but all parts of the state. And the state should arrive to all parts, build roads, and create opportunities and show people that drug trafficking isn't their only option."

The police organized a mini-marathon in the town of Tumaco and were amazed by how many young men and women turned up—exactly the youngsters most likely to be written off as gang members and traffickers.

"We realized how many people in Tumaco like these things, but they're never available."

Moreno understands the why of coca, but wonders how these families think it will end.

"You've got couples out there, with four or five children, and you ask them: What future are you offering to the kids? The only dreams these kids will have is to join the illegal groups or keep growing coca."

Will you ever see a Colombia free of coca?

Pause . . .

"It's a difficult question . . . because really . . . in the near future, I can't see it. While this whole industry continues and while it keeps being so profitable, it will keep on."

The conversation winds down. He looks out the window. "It's impressive how much damage we Colombians do to each other."

IT'S THE ANTINARCOTICS MORNING MEETING. Each department head looks exactly as you'd expect: the head of intelligence sits in the corner with that ability to fade into the background. The pilot is in his flyboy jumpsuit. The head of the Junglas commandos swaggers in his sunglasses. Two missions today: 1) fly out to the jungle to check in on the manual eradicators, and 2) send a small group of police who will fumigate manually. Fewer officers, less protection, but more agile. Fly to the heart of enemy territory, destroy the crops, and get out before the militias can attack.

They discuss the day with all possible contingencies: attacks by Guacho's fighters, explosions, heavy combat, helicopter accidents. All the different ways to die.

Someone hands me a form to sign. "To execute this dangerous professional mission and to board these mobile vehicles, I am totally conscious of the risk that this represents to my life. . . . I assume exclusively all the responsibility for the risks this represents." Sounds about right. This is a red-hot zone. I'll have to wear a helmet and bulletproof vest.

The mission was suspended yesterday because of the weather. Colombia's Pacific is one of the wettest places on earth, daily downpours that drop nearly forty feet of rain a year.

Those who fly the Black Hawks say that Tumaco ticks every pilot's nightmare checklist. Regions so mountainous you can't find one piece of flat land to land a helicopter? Check.

Thick, low-hanging clouds making helicopter flight impossible? Check. Tropical storms that appear out of nowhere to ground your chopper? Check. Mountain ridges so high, even flying at altitude a well-placed sniper might be hiding at your eye level, locking the target, squeezing the trigger (the pilots won't fly at less than 1,500 feet). Check.

One of the pilots takes me to one side: "The helicopters land at an angle out there." He points to the jungle beyond. "Remember that when you're getting out of the helicopter. We had one guy run out and the helicopter decapitated him. Be careful, please."

The Black Hawks whir on the helipad. Nothing like that sound—motors pounding and air-gliding. I run to the chopper doubled over.

Within seconds of takeoff, the Black Hawk glides over the Pacific Ocean, Tumaco behind us. And in a minute, the city is gone. The landscape is breathtaking—virgin rain forests carpeting all the land and mountains rising out of the green. There's an old joke that only soldiers and guerrillas know truly how beautiful this country is; they turned some of the most gorgeous stretches into war zones no one else can visit.

The antinarcotics officers are decked out in sunglasses and machine guns. In the chopper is that undefinable atmosphere of men with guns ready to kill. One rests his head on his rifle's butt, mumbles, and crosses himself. War prayers.

Gocho the bomb dog is next to me. He's a Labrador, happy to be along for the ride. He tries to get comfortable on the floor, moving his body between a forest of heavy boots and upright rifles. Labradors and heavy machine guns, a strange mix. On both sides of the chopper, gunners scour the landscape for enemies. One gunner's helmet has the punisher skull on it.

Their fingers are on the huge 7.62 mm cannons. These cannons explode men and do it thousands of times a minute. Firing, they sound like grinding metallic death.

Out the window, it's uninterrupted jungle, greens and browns of rain forest and not a sign that a human being has ever passed through.

The pilot announces we're landing and an energy jolts through the men—like a muscle flexed. I think on the land mines below. My checklist: avoid stepping on fresh earth, dodge piles of leaves or twigs, don't touch shiny trinkets, step exactly in the same spot where the person in front of me stepped. I tell myself this will save me. The illusion of control, the delusion of safety.

The chopper lands hard, smack in the middle of a coca field. We're all out the doors, running doubled forward. The pilot's not turning that engine off—first sign of shooting, he's airborne instantly. We scramble to the undergrowth at the field's edge. I have no idea if the militia is nearby, watching us, ready to fire on us. Running for my life, I stomp on fresh earth, plunge through a pile of leaves, kick an empty Coke can.

The police take up their position, rifles ready. The helicopter takes off. The thundering machine of war leaves us to the sounds of the countryside: the chirrup of the insect, the call of the bird. We're alone. With rows and rows of ripe coca.

The police set up a security perimeter around the field the size of four football fields. Gocho the bomb dog runs through the coca, sniffing out any IEDs. An officer follows with a metal detector. The fumigation team hurriedly strap canisters to their backs. The countdown has begun: we're in Guacho's territory and there are not enough men to defend against an attack. This is a lightning strike: fly in, destroy the coca, and get out.

"Here there are enemies all around us, so we're heavily armed. We check everything, check it with our intelligence units, and then we come in, hitting hard," says Captain Max Perez. He's in his late thirties, hair starting to recede. He's spent years busting up laboratories and taking down traffickers. Now he's in the manual eradication program. I like him.

We're so far from civilization, it feels prehistoric. Huge insects seem unused to humans: finger-sized bugs smack against your chest, falling to the ground. If it weren't for the coca, I would think the Black Hawk was a time machine that dropped us off 50 million years ago.

A policeman takes a chain saw to the tree in the middle of the field to make a bigger landing patch for the helicopter when it returns. He doesn't seem too interested in where the tree will fall. Two officers and I jump to avoid being crushed by the falling tree.

"Today we're here, tomorrow we'll be somewhere else, and then we might be back here. The population doesn't know where we'll arrive," says Captain Max.

The policeman with a gas mask and plastic overalls has the canister on his back. He sprays all the coca with the herbicide. The bushes start to wilt—they'll start to die three days from now. The police estimate that within two weeks farmers could replant the coca.

Heavily armed men risking their lives to destroy this meek-looking bush—it is an absurd sight.

Perez calls for the helicopter to pick us up. In the field, the policemen light a bonfire, a column of black smoke for the chopper to see. Landing, the Black Hawk throws up a world of dirt and twigs. And we're off to see the manual eradicators.

Flying over the jungled hills, Captain Max points out the window. Beneath us stretch long fields of coca.

"It's in indigenous territory, so we can't enter and rip it out," he says. These are thick, mama bushes of coca, fat with leaves. I spot the telltale black plastic roof of a coca lab. He stares at all the coca, slowly shaking his head. Across Colombia, reserves have been allocated to the dozens of indigenous communities that live here. The police avoid enforcing the law in these zones save for the most serious of crimes.

The Black Hawk comes in low to a clearing next to the tiny hamlet of Marranera. We jump out, again making for the jungle's edge. The helicopter flies off, the sound of its engines slowly dying in the hills. Brushing away branches and leaves of the jungle, the police and civilian eradicators emerge. A young, pale-skinned police captain orders them into formation: the eradicators get in line along with rifle-armed police and twenty anti-riot police. The eradicators are dressed in their regulation blue shirts, their rubber boots already caked in mud. The anti-riot police are decked out in their black "robocop" armor, thick shields that cover legs, chests, and arms. Sweat dribbles off their faces, standing in the 95-degree jungle misery. I'm drenched in my bulletproof vest and helmet. I toss them into the undergrowth to pick up later.

"Good morning," says Captain Carlos Andres Cadena, and all reply: "Good morning."

"Today is another day of manual eradication, gentlemen. The word of the day is security. Security above everything else. Your security and where you step. Discipline and control."

The anti-explosives team—a bomb-sniffing Labrador and a metal-detector-waving agent—take the lead and we all file out for the kilometer march to the coca field. Now life moves fast: the dog barks twice, an officer asks: "Why's the dog barking?" and two gunshots boom out.

We scramble to the undergrowth. At the jungle's edge, police take up defensive formations: on one knee, rifles aimed. I scurry for my body armor. No one knows where these shots are coming from. Or where they're going. In the jungle, the captain crouches next to me.

"Sometimes it's fireworks," he says, unconvincingly. "But we're always ready."

More shooting and everyone flinches. These aren't fireworks.

"Probably better if we move here," the captain says, and we scramble a few yards deeper into the jungle. Five anti-narcotics police run to the middle of the clearing; in a line they drop to one knee, guns forward, aimed. From the undergrowth, more men cover them. Is this serious fighting? Or some drunk peeling off shots into the jungle?

The shots aren't getting closer and they're clearly from a handgun, not a rifle. So after a couple of minutes, we move out to the coca fields.

We arrive to the field and the anti-explosive dogs run to check. Once they make camp, the eradicators will rip out all the coca within a four-kilometers radius. The militias know which fields will be worked and they have the time to plant the IEDs. These IEDs can cost a dollar to make, so the only limit is the supply of malice. God knows when Colombia will be free of these IEDs. So much risk and pain for such a plain-looking bush.

As the police pass through the fields, they have the experts' appreciation of the coca bushes, the farmer's work. "These look beautiful," says one. "These crops are more organized. They're being cared for. They don't let them fade away like the other farm," says the captain.

I look up at the wall of jungle around us. The fields are in these pinpricks in the jungle; a hole, slashed and burned out of the rain forest. Through a drone, we see a column of black smoke a kilometer away, a farmer likely burning more jungle to plant coca.

The eradicators form a line. Two together working: one digs the hoe into the dirt, the other grabs the bush, yanking it out of the ground. The sound of the crunch, the rip of a plant out of the earth, reminds me of the raspachines who move through the fields, collecting the leaves.

This coca bush is ripped from the earth. These, though, are fertile lands; throw some seeds on the ground and within three months you can be harvesting coca again. I wonder how many times coca has been planted here, ripped out, re-planted. An eternal, pointless circle. It feels like a cruel, divine punishment. Like Sisyphus, condemned in the dreams of the ancient Greeks to push a boulder up a hill. And in this divine punishment, the rock would roll back down before he ever reached the summit. And this will go for eternity. Sisyphus is the patron saint of the war on drugs.

From the surrounding jungles comes a constant chatter of insects. But good God, it sounds like they're laughing at us.

Most of these eradicators are former coca farmers. The police won't let them work near home: too easy to identify, too easy to murder. Here, they all live in a camp. Each living space is a hammock under a mosquito net and a plastic sheet for a roof held up by wooden stakes. Muddy paths connect each living spot. They've only been here for five days and in another five days they'll pack up camp and move on.

Each day begins at 5:30 A.M., in the morning darkness. They wash in the cold stream, an invigorating start to the day. Invigorating is an English synonym for "testicle-shrinking cold."

At dawn they march out to destroy the coca. And maybe, to some it feels like putting their shoulder against a boulder. They rip out coca crops for eight hours and trudge back to the camp. They have an hour to play cards, read, and listen to music. And then lights off.

"At sunset, six P.M., everyone must be in their beds or hammocks and in total silence. The illegal militias could attack us at night. So we need silence to hear if anyone is coming in the darkness," says the captain. Police stand guard all night.

Julio is twenty-six and from Caqueta, another coca zone.

"Where I'm from, you don't tell anyone anything. And all this talking to others, well, you don't do it there because you can't trust anyone."

When he goes home, Julio tells friends and family that he's been picking coffee. He tired of a life in coca, always looking over his shoulder.

"When I was planting coca all I thought about was planting more and more and more and cutting down and burning the environment so I could plant more and more."

He likes being in touch with nature, the birds, the reptiles, the frogs.

There's no booze, women, or social contact except with their colleagues, all deep in the jungle. It's like a crusade of warrior monks out fighting evil, deprived of life's pleasures. And they do this for three months.

"Some people get here and they love it and they stay. The type of men who don't like society, and here they can be by themselves," says Captain Cadena. "How you survive the jungle depends on your values, your principles."

Here in the camp, the joke is how much will kill you. Bullets, land mines waiting for your soft step are just the beginning. Malaria-fat mosquitos torment you in the fields. Want your diseases more exotic? A dose of flesh-eating Leishman-iasis? (Forty eradicators in Tumaco have succumbed to these diseases.) After a day's work, climb into your hammock and get bit by the poisonous snakes. Wake up in the morning, get your cup of cold stream water, and get poisoned.

"At our last base, just eight kilometers from here, someone poisoned the water. How did we know? My order is every time you're getting water, check the fishes. If there are fishes, that tells us the water is clean and we can use it. At that river, one of the boys saw fish floating, dead. We looked a little more upriver and all the fish were floating," says the captain. Fruit on the branch was also banned after they discovered poison had been injected into some apples.

Does it frustrate him that they may replant the crops you risked your lives to rip out?

"It's probable that when we go, a month later the people will go back and plant the coca."

And with that he turns away. It seems maddeningly frustrating—risk your life in this harsh job and then see that it was all for nothing.

"It's frustrating because the job was supposed to be done," he says. "I always say the coca bush isn't bad. . . . It's what they do to the bush that is bad."

A YEAR ON THE RUN as South America's most wanted man finally caught up with Guacho. He was killed in an army operation. His death has made no difference to Tumaco. He has already been replaced. Everyone is expendable. And all the while, the coca keeps growing. The boulder still won't reach the summit.

CHAPTER 4

COCA STEALS THE SOULS OF TOWNS

THE WAY TO END COCA IS TO offer the coca farmers a new life and get them to rip out their crops. The government's own figures show this: when coca is eradicated, a third is replanted. When the farmer is paid to remove it, just 1 percent return. It takes money, patience, and time.

The bus shudders along, hugging the mountainside and so far avoiding the fall into the abyss. These Andean valleys are filled with cool morning mists so thick you can swim them. Rising higher, jungles are replaced by forests on a slant. Life on a mountainside is lived at an angle. Towns perch on the incline waiting for any good avalanche to sweep them deep down into the valley. This bus is heading to one-such town, Briceño.

"I had sixteen children," says a wizened old indigenous man. He's proud—and he should be. "We didn't have television like you young ones," and he cackles. It's an old joke, but he's got to be near ninety. He wears a white cowboy hat. His smile shows what a woman in Virginia once called "summer teeth"—summa there, summa here.

"Three of them I lost to this town Briceño. One was killed in a motorbike accident. The other two were killed by the violence," he says. The violence. Live here long enough, specifics become irrelevant. What does it matter when, why, or how they were killed? It doesn't. "The violence" explains it all.

"Now Briceño is much calmer. The fierce are all in the cemetery. And the rest all ran away scared."

The bus keeps working its way up the mountainside, one curve at a time. Fifty feet a curve, fifty feet another curve, fifty feet a curve. A young child vomits.

"Yes, the town is different now. Still, I don't leave my house when I'm here. I'm too old not to be scared. What's the point of getting this old and being murdered?" Can't argue with that.

There's nothing more to be said, so he cracks open the bottle of aguardiente and pours me a shot. I neck it—with a grimace—and hand the plastic cup back. He fills the cup again.

"Drink two if you're a man," and he hands me the cup.

It's 7:30 A.M.

Briceño is a sad, poor town. A beautiful church looks over the central plaza. But even at 9 A.M., half the stores aren't open. The town was built on the backs of cattle and coffee, industries that allowed the farmers to live in dignity. No one got wealthy, but they raised families with their heads held high. They collectively built the town up, kept it clean, bought from each other. They took pride in their town and its good name. Then came cocaine.

Briceño is a strange choice to carry the hopes of a country. As the FARC and government negotiated peace, they jointly announced a commitment to eradicating coca. The government would work closely with the town's coca farmers, overseeing a comprehensive crop substitution plan. One and all understood the importance: everyone knows there will never be peace while there is coca. And no one was as surprised as the good people of Briceño, Antioquia. The future of Colombia. A Colombia in peace, free of coca.

And honestly, the farmers were delighted that anyone had even remembered them.

That was the dream. And it worked. The farmers ripped out all their coca. Until it stopped.

He goes by the nickname Pollito, little chicken. He's come down from his mountain farm six hours away to meet me here in the village restaurant. He is thirty-one years old, a former coca farmer. Pollito is that type you meet in Colombia's countryside who could have gone far in life with access to education. But no, the countryside punishes its sons and daughters.

For his entire life, the FARC controlled these lands. On these mountainside fields, farmers grew coffee and raised cattle, with small plots of foods to feed their families. Aside from the occasional clash between the FARC rebels and the army, life was calm and predictable.

At around the turn of the millennium, a poor family returned from a trip. With coca seeds.

"He had been very poor. Suddenly he was buying bags and bags of food. He starts buying cattle. I remember he bought a car. It was an old Toyota, but here it was, wow! His family started buying better shoes, better clothing. Then came gold chains and bracelets. And he built up his house. A drastic change. . . . So, the people said: 'Let's all get involved!'"

And the cycle begins: Coca lifts the town out of poverty.

It's a boomtown. Prostitutes roll in; salesmen arrive with their appliances to sell. And the money keeps streaming in.

"This is what we need, to plant more coca. More, more, more . . . We never realized what this would bring. In that moment, it was healthy, calm."

What did the people of Briceño think of the people consuming this thousands of miles away?

"The people here used to say: Great, now we're planting coca, forget the gringos. They're the ones who bring the money to our country. . . . Let's produce it here. And send it there. What do we care? Forget them. With their money, we'll live much better here."

The cycle kept grinding forward: the town started to count the cost of cocaine. Other militias arrived for the cocaine. The dead started to appear. Families broke up as farmers ran away with prostitutes. There were mass displacements as the militias fought. A culture of fear and distrust arose. Crime soared. A society broke down. Still, cocaine had her claws in the town. No one would return to poverty. Briceño couldn't give up the coca. What was once a town of upright coffee farmers and cowboys was now a debauched town of drunken coca farmers.

"If we look at everything coca does, it's a cancer. This destroys your life. It physically destroys your life. It destroys your family. It destroys everything. Little by little it destroys everything to such a point that everyone, all of us regret we ever planted a single seed of coca."

The government proposed to the people of Briceño that they be the pilot in the peace plan's experiment to replace coca. Many wanted to accept the government's offer, fed up with coca, the income not offsetting the murder and mayhem of the crop. But others were wary, the old wisdom of the countryside that says not to trust the government.

Pollito found himself in Bogota. He visited the infamous open-air drug neighborhood called the Bronx.

"What did I feel when I saw all the people walking in circles? I felt that the people were the blood of my blood, my Colombian brothers who were deep in drugs because of Colombian society. . . . All of us are to blame. It's not just presidents, politicians. We're all guilty. I believe that every Colombian who grows coca, we're hurting our own country," he says. "I thought we're destroying our country. At the next meeting of farmers, I told them of the Bronx."

The farmers listened to Pollito and voted to rip out their coca bushes. The government announced the plan and ministers arrived for their photo ops and speeches.

"These people wanted a change, more than just getting away from this precarious life of the coca. . . . They said: 'We're going to change. We're going to have a better life. We'll have a school. A park for the children. We'll have education.'"

The plan went this way: The small farmer ripped out his coca. Officials from the United Nations would verify that the coca crops were gone. Now verified, the government payments would begin: $700 every two months for a year, money to survive on. At some point during the first year, the families would receive $600 to plant legal crops to feed the family. As the project went on, the families would receive a one-off payment of $3,000 to begin an agricultural project: pigs, chickens, pineapples, anything that wasn't coca. And in the second year, another $3,300 to finalize the project that would get the farmers off the coca.

Hundreds of families went home and ripped out their coca.

And Briceño became entirely free of coca, a huge victory in the war on drugs.

"We were optimistic. We were proud—the country was watching us. We had dignity again. We did our work as we promised we would. And the peace process meant everyone was thinking about the future."

It had been a full generation since Briceño left cattle and coffee behind. And many had forgotten how to manage legal farms. They had become coca farmers and coca farmers alone.

"It's very difficult after twenty years to say you're going to change an economy that gives you money, that gives what you need . . . to now grow something else."

As the first year came to an end, the government payouts never appeared. The government seemed to lose interest. Farmers faced ever-larger bureaucratic hurdles. No government money, no coca money. Briceño had nothing.

"The people switched from coca and now they don't have anything. Why? Because they've been waiting for the government to honor what was agreed . . . When we took out the coca, we were left with absolutely nothing."

An indifferent government, an impoverished population—the old problems reappeared.

"Briceno lives in a precarious situation. Many people have had to leave. Some now rob for food. Others take day jobs on other people's farms."

Illegal militias are recruiting the disillusioned young men. It's not a difficult sell: come join us, carry a gun, see the respect in your neighbor's eye. Or sit a rot on a mountainside like a country bum. The old cycles grind forward.

"I see the poverty much worse than it was twenty years ago. Because they had coffee, they had cattle. Coca took all that away."

If something doesn't change, he believes Briceño will return to coca.

"It's not that the people want to go back to the illegal crops, no. The people of Briceño don't want to return to the illegal crops, because of all the problems they brought us. Why do we have to do it? Because of the inequality. Because of the lies. Because of the delays to all that was promised. Because of these programs and promises that never left an official's desk."

And what the government was doing to the people of Briceño it turns out it was doing to tens of thousands of farmers across the country, as well. They eradicated 35,000 hectares. But only one in ten families received all the money.

As the government let the security situation spiral out of control, it was impossible to travel to parts of the country to verify the coca had been ripped out.

And a new government announced that it preferred to forcibly remove the coca. It's almost as if the point is not to win, but just to keep the war on drugs going.

"If I had finished schooling, if I had studied, if there were good access to roads, good education, if I could sell my products easily, yucca, plantain, coffee, I would be happy and I wouldn't be thinking of planting illegal crops, because I'd have opportunities," Pollito tells me.

The chat is over and he needs to get his mule ready and return the six hours to his farm.

CHAPTER 5

A HISTORY OF COCAINE IN FIVE NARCOS

IN THE MOUNTAINS SURROUNDING LA GABARRA, THE narco-militias turn the kilo of coca paste into cocaine. Clandestine laboratories work as factories, employing twenty men and churning out tons of cocaine a month. The coca paste is dissolved, brought to heat, and mixed with acetone and hydrochloric acid to produce cocaine hydrochloride. Stacks and stacks of microwaves dry out the cocaine. Each kilo is weighed to the gram and wrapped as a brick. And on each kilo is slapped the laboratory's logo. Versace, Gucci, Apple, Corona. Cocaine loves capitalism.

Weekly, the police launch operations to dismantle these labs, seizing cocaine and blowing up the structures. All it takes is another $50,000 and seven days of construction and you've got another lab ready to produce the cocaine. The demand isn't going anywhere, so neither are the labs.

The narco-militias sell these bricks to traffickers for around $1,600 apiece. The new owners decide where it's going. If it's to feed a Europe greedy for cocaine, the brick heads east, crossing into Venezuela. In an impoverished Venezuela, it's not difficult to find officials to bribe. From Venezuela, sometimes the bricks go straight to Europe, like the Air France flight—Caracas to Paris—that was found with 1.3 tons of cocaine aboard. Sometimes the kilo's route to Europe passes through Africa, forging a trail of murder and corruption. Colombian narcos have settled in very comfortably in Guinea-Bissau where they oversee the trade.

If the trafficker wants to send it to the biggest market in the world, the United States, then he sends it west. Kilos are packed in a truck for half a day's drive. It's heading for Medellin.

ROLLING ALONG THE MOUNTAIN PASSES, the kilo leaves the jungles and the narco-militias behind. Ahead is the world of the urban narcos, those experts in getting the cocaine out of the country and the dollars in. The kilos enter into a vast ecosystem of cocaine. Drug lords, accountants, cartel soldiers, killers for hire, lawyers, witches, lovers, and pimps all work together, feeding off each other in a world funded by cocaine.

The backdrop to this is the city of Medellin, an embodiment of Colombia's struggle with cocaine. Medellin is the afternoon sipping rum listening to tango music. It's the typical heavy lunch of rice, sausages, plantain, beef, and beans. It's the beautiful massive bronze statues of men, women, cats, and horses by the artist Fernando Botero in the city center. It's the taxi driver's joke. It's the beautiful weather that feels like the "forever spring." It's the narco with his arm around his lover in the expensive restaurant. It's the corrupted politician; it's the human rights defender defying the death threats to keep working. It's sitting with the families on a Sunday as they picnic at the airport fence as planes come in to land just fifty feet above your head. It's looking up and seeing mountains in the background wherever you look. It's the American retirees in the Juan Valdez coffee shop still bitching about Hillary Clinton. It's the New York gay couple clutching their copy of *48 Hours in Medellin* and eating lunch. It's the thumping nightclub that will keep going until midday Monday. It's a squalid slum with no dirt roads. It's the shiny new shopping center. It's riches. It's poverty. A city with voltage. Medellin defies words.

Medellin is the city that most resembles Colombia, a people made up of mestizos, Afro-Colombians, and the indigenous. Its inhabitants love their city more than anything else and are mystified that the city is not the Colombian capital. Cold, wet Bogota is the seat of government, but for much of Colombia's history, Medellin has been the industrial heartland. Buoyed by bonanzas of gold, coffee, and other industries, the city thrived. The booms birthed in its people a natural inclination to be entrepreneurs. And as the economy prospered, waves of art would be created. Film directors, artists, authors, musicians have all been produced by these streets.

The people of the city and surrounding region are called Paisas. The women pride themselves on being Colombia's prettiest, important in a country that tunes in to watch Miss World every year (how important? One newsmagazine ran a front page of a photo of the new Miss Colombia being crowned.

At the bottom of the cover in smaller type read: "The Massacre in Segovia"—that bloodletting, which occurred on the same night as the pageant, killed forty-six people). The Paisa is an enigma to the rest of Colombia, embodying the best and worst of the country. The rest of Colombia knows the Paisas as smart, hardworking, devoid of sentimentality, conservative. And perhaps a little fast and easy with their business ethics. When Colombians tell jokes about the fast-talking used car salesman, it's always a Paisa. Paisas even look different from the rest of the country—the fairest skins in the country belong to the Paisas.

They're understandably proud of their city. Toss some trash on the street and someone will rightly call you a pig. Store owners and housewives sweep the sidewalk in front of their stores and home as part of their daily chores. When a tiny piece of graffiti was found on a wagon on Medellin's metro, it outraged the city and made national news. And that's Medellin's ambition—it's still the only Colombian city with a metro.

This civic pride has a dark side. Paisas are not supposed to speak of the city's ills in front of strangers. Journalists report angry phone calls from officials in city hall complaining about stories that reveal the city's problems, especially in the international press. "Why do you speak so badly of your hometown in front of the world?" These people really hate international stories about the city's history of drug trafficking.

In Medellin, with a booming economy in the first half of the twentieth century, the working classes and middle classes were able to build neighborhoods up, with distinctive architecture. Then in the middle of the last century, a civil war exploded in the countryside, pitting Conservatives against Liberals, called the Violence. Waves of displaced arrived to the city fleeing bloodshed and poverty.

Empty-handed, they took over land at the city's periphery. Land invasions they called them. Families built wooden shacks and started looking for any work. Misery belts surrounded the city. Every new wave of arrivals built ever higher on the mountainside. Peasants brought the trauma and violence of the countryside. And those who couldn't make it in Medellin spread out across the country. Paisas are Colombia's wandering merchants—travel through the country, deep in the jungle, and the village store is likely run by a Paisa.

A recession struck in the 1970s, just as cocaine was taking off. If the economy had been stronger, could the city have fended off the drug's expansion? Who knows. As people lost their jobs, cocaine snuck in and never left.

It was the mix of the misery of the slums with the ingenuity and hard work that would make Medellin the center of the cocaine industry under Pablo Escobar. Throughout the 1980s, the city was awash with money as the city went cocaine crazy. Cocaine dollars flowed through the economy. Rich families, boys from the slum, all worked together to meet the American demand.

Escobar and other traffickers formed the Medellin Cartel and dominated the cocaine trade in the 1980s. Escobar created his own private army of killers, which he called the Office of Envigado. They were responsible for collecting debts owed in cocaine. Their motto: Debts get paid with money or with your life.

It was in the days of Escobar that narcos became a fixture of the city. To this day, you'll spot them. It's like living in New York and seeing the Wall Street brokers. They're not on every corner, but if you know what to look for, you'll spot them. A style, an attitude. Every Colombian can spot a narco and most swerve to avoid them.

Escobar remains a divisive figure. Polite society, those with a microphone, those who have power, say Escobar was a monster, a stain on Colombia's history. It's the message every tourist hears. In this telling, Escobar is the Colombian version of Adolf Hitler.

Like everything in the drug war, the conversation in Spanish is different. So, slow down, grab that shot of coffee you see everyone else drinking, and stroll through a working-class neighborhood in Medellin. Speak Spanish and you'll hear something different. Sure, many hate Escobar, but many adore him. The old-timers reminisce over the booming economy under Pablo.

"Only those who didn't want to work, didn't work in the time of Pablo," says one old man.

Pablo remains El Patrón, a word that means so much more than simply "The Boss." El Patrón is not your office manager; a patron employs you, ensures you have food to eat, holds the power of life and death over you. It's an old-style term for a society that can feel feudal.

Every Sunday, flowers are left at Escobar's grave just outside Medellin. He's the Robin Hood Paisa, the barrio boy who made it in a system rigged by the same families who have owned this country for hundreds of years. And when he made his billions, he never forgot the poor, goes the legend. As the politicians robbed, he built up a neighborhood—Barrio Pablo Escobar—for the homeless that still stands today. Here old ladies grow angry when asked about Escobar's victims. "Pablito," they'll tell you, was innocent, the victim of government lies. When people know the game is rigged, they adore the outlaw. John Dillinger, Bonnie and Clyde all knew this.

Did he care about the poor or was he like the politicians who came before and have infested this country since, simply buying the people's love for his own ends? It's impossible to know.

On Escobar's orders, thousands died as he battled the government and rival traffickers. His war was so disruptive to cocaine trafficking, the drug industry united to bring him down. To save the cocaine business, the godfather of cocaine needed to be eliminated. The alliance worked with Colombia's police, army, the CIA, the DEA, and a far-right militia. And once Escobar was shot down in 1993, the governments of Colombia and the United States announced the end of the cocaine kingpins, that a corner had been turned in the war on drugs. It would be the same message every time they killed the next kingpin for the next three decades.

Escobar's death allowed the cocaine industry to return to business as usual. Any hope that his death would dent the trade was quickly snuffed out when his successor emerged. Not all Colombians know the name Diego Murillo, but everyone knows the nickname "Don Berna."

Don Berna's life exemplifies how cocaine and far-right politics mixed to ally itself with large parts of the Colombian state to attack Colombia's left-wing politicians and civilians. Berna was rising through the Medellin Cartel when Escobar killed his bosses. He helped bring Escobar down, later grabbing what was left of the Medellin Cartel. For the next fifteen years, he ran Medellin's underworld with a firmer grasp than any before him, eclipsing even Escobar. Every trafficker had to pay him a percentage on each kilo moved. His was a power so strong, that in public, people would whisper his name, knowing his spies could be anywhere.

He promoted the Office of Envigado into something special—an arbiter in cocaine. Feuding traffickers would go to the Office and state their case, and the Office would make a ruling. The men of cocaine were trying to impose order on the chaos of cocaine.

And if someone had been ripped off, the Office would recover the money—for a cut.

During the late 1990s, the civil war intensified in the countryside and some feared the Marxist rebels of the FARC could topple the government as the army suffered defeat after defeat. In the countryside, off-duty soldiers, politicians, and wealthy landowners came together to create an illegal far-right militia, the AUC. Known as "paramilitaries," they carried out a dirty war on the rebels and civilians. The AUC would fight the FARC for control of the countryside.

Drug traffickers like Don Berna had become huge landowners themselves, so they allied with Colombia's rural elites to attack the FARC. They joined the AUC, turning the organization into a massive drug-trafficking army. Don Berna and other traffickers saw a chance to grab the land and the coca the rebels of the FARC were protecting. The urban narcos went to the rural countryside in order to control every aspect of cocaine—from the coca leaf to the kilo sent abroad. Don Berna and other traffickers put themselves in uniforms and told the country they were saving Colombia from the communist menace. Drug traffickers had become patriots.

The AUC would unleash Colombia's worst violence. Whenever the AUC fought the rebels head-on, they tended to lose, lacking the conviction and training of the die-hard revolutionaries. Where they triumphed was in a vicious dirty war on civilians they accused of supporting the rebels. The AUC slashed and chain-sawed their way through the country, murdering anyone even suspected of links to the rebels. They killed thousands of innocent civilians along the way.

The AUC's hit list grew to anyone who opposed their land

grab and drug trafficking. They slaughtered journalists, human rights activists, environmentalists, teachers, trade union organizers, politicians. They employed tools of mass sexual violence, and torture, and made massacres so commonplace, a slaughter of a dozen civilians would barely register in the news. All of this occurred with help from parts of Colombia's army, business leaders, and politicians. The AUC claimed to control a third of Colombia's congress and later dozens and dozens would be imprisoned for links to the group, which was officially listed by the United States as a terrorist organization. The secret police was so infiltrated by the AUC and weighed down in scandal, the government simply disbanded it.

The FARC were rooted out of much of Colombia in part thanks to this ferocious slaughter. The government entered into a peace process with the far-right death squads in the early 2000s. This was another reason why Don Berna had entered into the political AUC—the position of the government is not to negotiate with drug traffickers. But it will negotiate with armed political actors. Still, the commanders had expected an easy way out, thanks from the political class for pushing the rebels out of large stretches of the government. Impatient, they started to hint that they might know things that could implicate high-profile Colombians. It backfired.

The government alleged the commanders were continuing to carry out crimes and extradited Berna and the others to the United States in 2008 to face charges of drug trafficking. Berna was sentenced to thirty-one years. Medellin's criminals were stunned. A single king meant order. Disorder erupted as drug traffickers warred to be Berna's heir. Two traffickers fought for control of Berna's cartel, the Office of Envigado. The war lasted three years and probably killed more than four thousand people, only ending when the police arrested one of the traffickers. His rival took control of the city. That he had to fight so long and hard for the crown meant he would always temporarily hold on to it. Other drug traffickers rose in the shadows. It was no longer the rule of one king. No, now it was a democracy of drug lords. A corruption of drug lords.

THE TRAFFICKERS OF YESTERYEAR WERE easily distinguishable. Many had roots in the countryside. The traffickers put their money into fine horses, their girlfriends' bodies, and massive, luxurious haciendas. One friend of mine told me she was invited to a drug lord's party. The driver picked her up from Bogota and drove her out to the eastern plains. Arriving at the gates of the hacienda, the driver pointed to the small single-propeller plane waiting for her. The flight took twenty minutes to reach the main house of the hacienda.

These traffickers brought the rural fashions to Colombia's most expensive restaurants in the biggest cities. These drug lords enjoyed the attention their cowboy hats, ponchos over their shoulders, and potbellies commanded. These were not men of high culture. Their humor was always dull-witted and medieval. Common at narco parties were fashion parades and stripteases of dwarves, which they found hilarious—as humorless as it was cruel. These traffickers' very existence was a middle finger to the refined elites who had plundered Colombia for centuries.

These were larger-than-life figures. One trafficker explained his fortune as coming from winning three different lotteries one December. Others bought football teams and tried to bribe their way to international trophies. They rigged beauty pageants to crown their girlfriends. Escobar built a zoo and opened his own theme park, Hacienda Napoles. Here he showcased artifacts from other outlaws like Al Capone's guns and the car in which Bonnie and Clyde were killed (or at least that was what was promised—narcos are famous for being ripped off).

They went by strange nicknames, such as "Mueble Fino" ("Fine Furniture"), "Desalmado" ("Soulless"), "Gatubelas" ("Catwoman"), and "The Chess Player," who founded the Cali Cartel. One of Pablo's killers called himself "Earring" because he said he was so close to everyone's ears, hearing everything that was going on. A good nickname disguises and intimidates.

And cocaine has a habit of driving the top drug lords mad. A potent mix of countless money and the power of life and death over all around them drives them as insane as any Roman emperor. The money indulges every whim. Every desire has been sated, every fantasy purchased, every perversion serviced.

Over the years, cocaine became more of the establishment. A new type of trafficker emerged, what the InSight Crime think tank called the "Invisibles." These were men who could blend in as prosperous businessmen and with lower profiles keep trafficking that much longer. Cocaine became corporate. It infiltrated through the cracks and grooves of Colombian society and the international economy. Multinational banks launder the money. Their money flows through the legal economy, building shopping malls and funding start-ups. Now the money is laundered in plain sight in the middle of the legal economy.

And the narcos ascend to the highest circles of society. One dangerous narco was arrested living in the same apartment complex as Medellin's mayor. Cocaine is now the establishment.

Benefiting cocaine's rise to the establishment, it needed less violence. Medellin's homicide rate collapsed even as cocaine was more prevalent than ever. What had once been one of the world's most dangerous cities now doesn't even make the top fifty. Cocaine traffickers had learned that more violence brought more trouble, interrupting the only important thing—the flow of cocaine. Truces between cartels and the city's gangs have delivered peace for its inhabitants. "Pax Mafiosa."

The falling homicide rate has allowed the city to reimagine itself. Medellin has fashioned itself a tourism destination: a city of restaurants, nightclubs, and museums. Talk of cocaine is seen as impeding this renaissance of the city. To the annoyance of many, there are now "narco tours" where tourists are taken around the sites of the drug war: the famous bombing of the Monaco building, the house where Escobar was shot dead and his grave. Some end with meeting Escobar's brother Roberto, who tells the backpackers to stay in school and don't do drugs. The hint is that this is all in the past. That's the conversation in English—Medellin has overcome all its problems. The tours don't offer trips to the nightclubs where the narcos still party.

The cartels are still very much alive, though. In the absence of Don Berna, Medellin is now straddled with two main cartels and possibly hundreds of independent drug traffickers working for themselves. The Office of Envigado and the Gulf Clan cartel hold sway over different parts of the city. They live in an uneasy truce, neither strong enough to grab control of the city—for now.

Still, all have seen massive growth in scale, in part because of simple, yet crucial, shifts in how they run their businesses. When cocaine took off in the late 1970s and '80s, Colombian traffickers sent the drug directly to the United States. There Colombian networks distributed the cocaine. And the Colombians reaped the billions. The United States wised up and increased patrols of its borders to stop the cocaine deliveries. The Colombians felt the sting as their shipments were seized. Time for cocaine to evolve.

And who knew the 3,145-kilometer US southern border better than Mexican smugglers? In the 1990s, Colombian cartels began selling directly to the Mexicans, largely abandoning its export routes straight to the United States. The Colombians were renouncing retail and embracing wholesale. At first, observers couldn't understand why the Colombians were forgoing the big profits in direct sales to the United States. Get a kilo of coke directly to Miami and it will get you about $25,000. Mexico nets you about $10,000.

"You get less money but you don't have the hassle of trying to get the cocaine into the US. Let the Mexicans deal with that. They get it across the border or not, it doesn't bother me. The cocaine has already been sold," says one trafficker.

Lower profits, but more guaranteed supply. It's the type of business decision that a CEO would make.

This flood of Colombian cocaine made the Mexican cartels fantastically rich, propelling men like Joaquin "El Chapo" Guzman to unimaginable wealth. As always, after the money came the slaughter as Mexican drug lords warred over the billions to be made.

Dodging navies and coast guards throughout the Pacific Ocean, Colombian traffickers started to use El Salvador, Honduras, and Guatemala as transit points to Mexico. Already precarious, cocaine tipped these countries over the edge. Politicians, presidents, and generals were corrupted by the easy cash to be had.

Juan Antonio "Tony" Hernandez was arrested in Miami. "Hernandez was involved in all stages of the trafficking through Honduras of multi-ton loads of cocaine that were destined for the US," said the Manhattan US attorney Geoffrey S. Berman, where Hernandez was sent to be tried. Hernandez is the brother of Juan Orlando Hernandez, president of Honduras.

In 2017, Fabio Lobo was sentenced to twenty-four years for exporting "huge quantities of cocaine into the US" using "his father's position and his own connections to bring drug traffickers together with corrupt police and government officials." Fabio's father, Porfirio Lobo, was Honduras's president from 2010 to 2014.

Mario Amilcar Estrada Orellana was running for the presidency of Guatemala when he was charged by a US court with "conspiring to import cocaine." With his accomplice, he offered to appoint people who would turn a blind eye to traffickers' activities if they funded his campaign. He also asked for help recruiting sicarios to kill political rivals. Thoughtfully, he and his accomplice offered to provide the AK-47s.

Corrupt cops, customs officers, politicians—cocaine pays for them all.

Gangs earned fortunes transporting the drugs through their countries. The easy millions fortified the gangs, such as Mara Salvatrucha and Barrio 18. They in turn made their countries the world's most violent. The bloodshed provoked a mass exodus of Central Americans fleeing the reign of the gangs, with hundreds of thousands marching through Central America, heading to the United States.

The cocaine corrupts the authorities, creates the impunity, and fuels violence in the region.

From Colombia, the traffickers watched these countries break down into savage violence. But it wasn't their problem—they assume violence is the normal state of life.

Cocaine alone wasn't responsible. But it plays its part.

STILL, THE TENUOUS PEACE IN Medellin has its threats. And the ascendant Gulf Clan cartel is one of them.

In 2012, when Daniel "Loco" Barrera was captured, the Colombian president addressed the nation and said the "last of the big capos" had been captured. "He's spent twenty years dedicated to doing evil to Colombia and the world."

Loco had been South America's most wanted drug lord at that time. The Americans were desperate for him, offering rewards of $5 million for information leading to his capture. Loco was an old-style trafficker, with a belly full of beef and beer and a poncho slung over his shoulder. He had the look of a man who would burp in your mother's face.

Authorities said his organization exported thousands of tons of cocaine, 720 tons to the United States alone. Loco was now Public Enemy No. 1. The hunt was on. The mythology of the underworld was that Loco burned his fingerprints off with acid to go undetected.

Loco had risen from the coca region of San Jose de Guaviare. In the legends of the underworld, Loco earned his name killing the six sicarios who had murdered his brother. A *patrón. Un hombre.* He snatched control of much of the industry throughout eastern Colombia. He became wealthy beyond imagination buying cocaine from the Marxist rebels and selling it to the far-right death squads, the AUC. Both groups were in a fight to the death but they somehow ended up in business together—the paramilitaries knew their money would strengthen the rebels. The rebels knew that the paramilitaries would make fantastic profits that would be spent buying ever-better weapons to kill the rebels. The usual madness of cocaine.

An intense multinational operation had caught Loco in neighboring Venezuela, just ten miles from the border with Colombia. He's flown back to Bogota. Loco begins to chat with the policeman next to him.

"It's more difficult to go shopping for food than move a thousand kilos," he tells the police.

But what this cocaine mastermind really wants the police to know is that there's a monster growing in the underworld.

Unprovoked, he issues the warning: "If you don't watch out for Urabá . . . If you don't watch out for Urabá, easily four hundred more people could be killed."

Urabá is the northwestern jungle region that borders Panama. Barrera is sharing the mafia's deepest secret—a new monster is coming.

"This Otoniel that's there, he's an animal. He's an animal."

Dario Antonio Úsuga, known as Otoniel, is a rising drug trafficker. Barrera is gesturing, in a pleading tone, trying to convince the policeman.

"You can't let these people be killed."

There's a sadness in his eyes—he's not getting through to the police.

"Does this person deserve a chance to live? Boss, he doesn't deserve it."

Loco is warning them: I am not the last great capo. Out there, in the jungle, something evil and powerful grows. It's the Gulf Clan cartel.

The Colombian state did not listen.

Otoniel leads the world's largest cocaine cartel, the Gulf Clan cartel. Even in the depraved world of drug trafficking, Otoniel is a degenerate. With the power of life and death over thousands, and more money than can be counted, Otoniel's fetish is underage girls. Families are threatened into giving up their daughters. Some search Otoniel out to offer their daughters—for a price. And their underlings imitate their bosses. The Gulf Clan trafficker "Gavilan" notoriously suffered from a host of serious sexually transmitted diseases but continued raping underage girls.

They've created this empire in northwestern Colombia, in the province of poverty and violence known as Urabá.

The Gulf Clan rose out of the ashes of peace. Around 2006, when Colombia carried out a peace process with the AUC, only the top bosses were interrogated and many of them simply refused to hand over assets or reveal the truth of the conflict. The midrange commanders, those who carried out the killings, who loaded the cocaine onto the boats at midnight, the government made promise to behave and go home.

And that's what the Úsuga brothers did, Dario Antonio and Juan de Dios (Juan of God). They came home with all that knowledge of cocaine routes, killing, and contacts in the military. They joined with another paramilitary leader and began trafficking cocaine.

They cornered northwestern Colombia, the dense jungles of Urabá, which connect Colombia and Panama. The rain forest there is so dense it's the one gap in the Pan-American Highway, a 18,000-mile highway that runs all through North, Central, and South America. From here they expanded. They moved east along the Caribbean coast and south down the Pacific Coast. And then to Medellin.

They came in from the countryside, taking over neighborhoods at the city's edges. The Office of Envigado put up a fight. And the violent fight rolled over the city. The most senior traffickers stepped in and demanded peace. The Gulf Clan was allowed to keep their neighborhoods. The truce remains to this day—but is so very, very fragile.

The Gulf Clan was a rising monster in the underworld—but they weren't known nationally. The country would learn of the cartel in death. Antinarcotics police were tracking the brothers for months. They had managed to turn one of the underage girls Juan de Dios had raped into an informant. She led them to a New Year's Eve party, deep in the jungle.

The police surrounded a house. One policeman told journalist Germán Castro Caycedo that the police saw someone moving and shouted out to surrender.

"I am a man of war. I don't fucking surrender!" And he shot at the police. The police mowed him down. It was Juan de Dios. Juan of God. Dario escaped and became the sole leader of the largest cartel of cocaine on the planet.

The clan would make the country sorry for the death of Juan de Dios. It announced a two-day "armed strike"—in provinces throughout northern Colombia, everyone was ordered to stay home; businesses remain closed and transportation ceased. Anyone breaking the curfew was to be killed. And a bounty would be paid for every cop killed.

I was with the police in the town of Zaragoza, Antioquia, when one of these armed strikes was called. This was a large one, spanning eight provinces, a quarter of Colombia. Over the two days, there were killings, shoot-outs, and vehicles burned. I was in the police base, in their control room, as the details streamed in. All bad. A bus burning. Police officers killed in a neighboring province. A police outpost fired upon, two officers injured. A shopkeeper shot down. Grenades tossed at a business. WhatsApp messages offered three hundred dollars for every police officer killed. The Gulf Clan had surprised the police, leaving them impotent.

The armed strike had achieved its aim—a total show of power. It was front-page news and led all the newscasts. The Colombian state looked powerless.

"Just like the time of Pablo Escobar," said one police officer to himself.

The government launched Operation Agamemnon in 2015 to destroy the Gulf Clan, backed by CIA support. The aim was to overwhelm the Gulf Clan and take down its leader in three months. Five years later—nearly three thousand arrests, more than one hundred dead cartel members, eighty dead policeman, hundreds of tons of cocaine destroyed, and more than seven hundred properties seized—the clan still breathes. It grows in the lands that the FARC abandoned with their peace deal.

Undoubtedly, the clan has taken heavy blows. Otoniel is one of the wealthiest men on the continent, but police say he lives as the most miserable of peasants. He moves from jungle hut to hut on the back of a donkey every night as he outruns the antinarcotics forces. Hundreds of millions of dollars, if not billions, and nothing to spend it on. Cocaine does enjoy her jokes.

The Gulf Clan is the focus of Colombia's antinarcotics operations. Weekly, another arrest is made, another boat is captured laid down with cocaine, a trafficker is captured, a laboratory is burned down. Yet none of it makes any difference. And when Otoniel is killed, it won't slow cocaine's flow by a second.

THE KILO HAS ARRIVED TO a safe house where it will sit while its owners decided where it goes. Will it go abroad and get the gringos high? Or send it to the gangs of Medellin to sell to the home market?

While the kilo waits, an entire ecosystem of cocaine swirls around the brick.

CHAPTER 6

THE COMBOS

BRYAN HAS A BUSY FRIDAY. HE NEEDS to run his gang, solve a murder, oversee street drug sales, keep control of his barrio, wait for the mechanic to pass by and change the serial number on his new stolen motorbike, avoid the police, and take his husky Juana for a long walk. And he's starting the day with a hangover. The one that will kick his ass? Juana.

He rubs his eyes.

"We went long last night," he mutters. It's midday.

He wanders through his sparse home built of wooden planks, cinder blocks, and cement. No glass in the windows, only bars. Like a cell. Out the back, the view looks down on the whole of Medellin, two and half million souls. A million-dollar view in a thousand-dollar shack. He bathes, tipping tubs of cold water over his head, and brushes his teeth. There's no running water in the barrio.

His teenage girlfriend prepares him some breakfast as she yawns, wearing panties and a small T-shirt. She looks to be fifteen.

On the wall is a painting of a horse in the countryside. Opposite it hangs a meter-high painting of Jesus on the cross, beneath him: "I trust in you." In front of Jesus sits the stolen motorbike, the incriminating serial number still there.

His mother arrives. She's in her late thirties; slim, made-up, dressed in sweatpants and high heels. She's brought Juana, who strains at her leash, a skinny husky with arctic blue eyes. Juana jumps up, paws thumping on Bryan's chest, squawking that husky talk.

"She needs a good walk."

"Yes, Mom."

In a few minutes, he's dressed. He drops a chain with a crucifix over his head, sticks his gun in his waistband, and grabs Juana's leash. As he speaks, his braces catch the light and, I think: Christ, he's running this neighborhood and he's barely out of his teens.

THE COCAINE TO BE TRAFFICKED abroad is stashed in a safe house. The cocaine to be sold here in Medellin is delivered to the slums and sold to the gangs, combos, like Bryan's. The combos break the kilos apart, tossing them into a blender, the blades slicing the cocaine into powder. Aspirin or borax is poured in to cut the cocaine, making the kilo go that much further. The young men work late into the night, packaging each gram of cocaine into little paper envelopes.

Medellin is plagued by hundreds of combos, who have carved the city into fiefdoms. The combos are strongest, more open in the slums that encircle the city, where they have created parallel societies. With a mostly absent state, rules, taxes, justice, even borders are decided and administered by the combos. In the slums, people don't pay income tax; they pay extortion to the combos. What occurs in the slums happens with the combos' say-so or it doesn't happen at all.

Each combo answers to a drug lord or a cartel; the traffickers provide the combos with the drugs, the combos kick back some of the profits. And when the next drug war sweeps the city, the combos will serve as soldiers for the front line.

Combos who try to break free from the cartels are taught a lesson, quickly. La Terraza worked for Don Berna, killing his enemies: human rights activists, rivals, and Colombia's most famous comedian, Jamie Garzon. La Terraza demanded a route to traffic cocaine abroad. Don Berna told them no and war was declared. La Terraza got some quick, harsh blows in, murdering Don Berna's brother and confidant. Don Berna responded with a methodical slaughter of the combo. After months of murder, a decimated La Terraza was invited to sign a truce. On their way to sign, the combo's leadership was ambushed and nine of them were murdered by the side of the road.

The combos are so well known, newspapers report their wars, their triumphs and defeats. The Agony, the Banana-boys, the Edge, the Combo of the Cow, the Cross, the Christ, the Bald Ones, the Faith.

The slums are the meat grinder for a never-ending supply of young men ready to die in the country's different wars. There's no great mystery why. Little work, less future. The misery of the countryside explains the coca. An urban misery provides the young men and women for the combos. Unemployment is over 10 percent and half of those with a job work cash in hand with no contract. The legal minimum salary is around $250 a month. Millions don't even earn that. The economy limps forward, overly dependent on extractive and finite industries like coal and oil. Colombia is one of the world's most unequal countries, a tiny oligarchy that lives as royalty while the vast majority toil for little.

Most young men and women in the slums don't join the combos. They try to live legally, trying to get by. But they face discrimination in the classist Colombian society. Over dinner parties in the wealthy oases of the city, among people who see each other on the newspaper's social pages, words like "disposable" are used to describe those in the slums (there's a joke in the slums that the crime section of the tabloids where they show photos of the latest murder victims is called "the social pages of the poor").

But crime—now there's a life with a future, admittedly a possibly very short future. They know that to enter into this life is one long act of suicide. But . . . the money and the respect make it worth it. The young men know the combos are training ground for future gangsters. Shine on these streets and you'll be invited to work for the cartel. For the kids who have chosen this path, a life in cocaine is like a life in Hollywood.

DANGEROUS PLACES SHOULD BE DIFFICULT to get to. Bryan's barrio sits high up the mountainside and has a nasty reputation. The first taxi driver says, "There, I don't go," as he drives off.

I get smart and flag the next taxi down. When he stops, I slide into the backseat and then tell him where we're going. He doesn't like it but he starts driving—up.

Medellin sits in the Valley of Aburra. Look at the mountainsides that rise above the city and read the social geology of the cliff face. Each layer is another social class; the higher you rise, the lower you sink. At the bottom starts Colombia's small middle class. Edge slowly up the mountainside and it's solidly working class. Creep higher, the houses get smaller, the incline sharper, a mix of working class and the underclass. Near the mountain peaks, it's wooden shacks and unpaved roads. Here live the recent arrivals from the countryside, displaced by slaughter and poverty. In Colombia, the social classes are immovable as the rock strata. Born poor, die poor.

We drive up the steep roads on our way to Bryan's barrio. Kids on their bikes bomb past us down the road. This is "gravity biking," where the kids reach speeds of 70 miles per hour racing down the mountainside. It's exactly as dangerous as it sounds. Once at the bottom of the mountainside, the kids turn their bike around, grab on to the back of a truck heading up, and return to the summit.

As we drive, the radio reports the latest narco scandal. A woman invites dozens of people for a free holiday in Chile: the four-day bus journey, the food, accommodation, all free. The bus crashes; twenty-three corpses are strewn across the highway. Then the drug dogs bark. Amid twisted metal and the dead, police find 80 kilos of cocaine and 600 kilos of marijuana. The police had never seen this way of shipping cocaine. Constant evolution.

The story cheers the taxi driver up no end.

"You get a free trip! Free hotel! Free food! And now you're all dead! Hahahahaha," he says slapping the steering wheel, looking over at me, making sure I get the joke.

We're dropped off at the main road. The taxi driver spins the car around and is gone. The final stretch must be walked: the roads are too narrow, steep, and unpaved for cars.

A young man sits on a corner, watching everyone who enters.

The entire neighborhood lies on an incline. Children kick balls on the street, carefully because if they roll down the hill, they'll never stop. Grandmothers stand and chat. Small stores dot every block. Narrow alleys ready for mischief run between the houses. Out of open windows wafts music: old tango melts to salsa, which turns to reggaetón. Old women sweep the dirt road in front of their homes. It's that Paisa pride.

Through these roads, a bouncing Juana yanks Bryan. Everyone gives him a "Good afternoon," "Hello," or "How are you?" Bryan replies to all of them.

"This is a good neighborhood. People are humble. They're all poor. We have all sorts of people here: tough, good, hardworking," he says.

He has a good grip on his barrio. Juana . . . not so much.

Bryan's first stop is the *plaza,* the drug spot. The dealer sits in a shelter that looks like a bus stop. He's wearing long denim shorts, a mullet, smoking a joint. The look of a kid skipping school. A cloud of sweet-smelling *cripy* smoke hangs around him. Under a rock, in a black plastic bag, are packed thirty envelopes, each a gram of cocaine.

This kilo has come to its end, here at this plaza—from the leaf to consumption. This is what propels the whole business—that moment the consumer hands over the cash to the dealer. The grams are sold and then the cycle begins again.

He pats Juana.

"Nothing better than a dog. I had a pit bull. The nicest girl. Always playing. I had her for six years. Then some *malparido* shot her two months ago. What sort of animal shoots a dog? We took care of him."

For years, stung by the international stigma of being painted as drug traffickers, Colombians would reply with "Colombia may produce cocaine but Colombia doesn't consume it." And it was true. Until the traffickers realized the large home market they had ignored. So they set some tons aside for their own people. The profits were smaller, but so too were the risks: there was no threat of extradition.

At three dollars a gram, cocaine took off. Artists snort it at parties, executives use it to sober up after one whiskey too many, and taxi drivers take hits off their keys to stay awake on the lonely night shift.

Still, others detest the business, never forgetting nor forgiving how many Colombians cocaine has killed. For millions, the very idea of drug use is reason enough for anger. These Colombians are outraged to see how casually drugs are consumed in cities like London and New York. Outrage turns to fury when an unwitting English or American makes a joke about drug trafficking. Every Colombian has that story of the idiot foreigner who jokingly called them a drug smuggler.

In the slums, it's through weed and cocaine that the combos earn.

Bryan takes a seat next to him and we sit and hang out, looking out over the barrio. The dealer offers me a toke of his joint—I take one. But that's it—there's work to do.

A man dressed in a black shirt and black trousers walks past us quickly, like he's late for work. He puts on his white priest's collar as he trots by.

At the whine of every motorbike, everyone looks up—instinctively. Here, bad news arrives on the back of motorbikes: cops or rival combos. Bryan asks how sales are.

"You know, it's good. We sold joints, some *perico*, boss," says the dealer, using the slang for cocaine. A spot like this should be shifting fifty grams of cocaine a day, each gram wrapped in a little paper envelope.

"See anything strange?"

"No. Everything calm."

Bryan looks at him, as if taking in his answer.

"Hear anything new about the kid?" Bryan asks.

"No, boss."

We leave the plaza and Bryan explains. Two days earlier, a young man was found dead in a dark alley. Head shots. Murdered like a villain, the young man was a civilian, on the straight and narrow. Bryan asked his boys and they swear it wasn't them. Bryan lets Juana off the leash and she bounds down the block.

"We have to clear this up, find out what happened. Because if it wasn't us, then who was it?"

Who does he think it could be?

"It could be our enemies, making a move to come into our territory," he says. "We need to know."

It doesn't even occur to us that the police would seriously investigate the crime and find the killer. The combo will find out who did it.

Juana chases a peep of chickens as they feed on a patch of grass. Bryan calls her back and she returns, eyes filled with regret of all the chickens missed.

BRYAN IS TWENTY-THREE YEARS OLD. He's friendly and welcoming to me, but it's easy to imagine him bullying kids for the short amount of time he spent in school. He's big and surprisingly fast.

As we walk back from the plaza, a loud whistle pierces the air. Five seconds later, a police motorbike turns on to the road, two cops riding. It's coming toward us. I pull my cap down. In this barrio, a foreigner is immediately suspicious and I don't have a good reason for being here.

I turn to Bryan—who's gone. Juana sniffing the dirt is the only evidence he ever existed. Juana realizes she's free and bolts for the chickens, who flap their wings and squawk.

An old woman laughs.

"Juana is going to end up paying for those chickens."

The police take a turn higher up the mountainside.

Another whistle slices the air and Bryan rambles around the corner, grinning at his vanishing act. I don't know if he's wanted for arrest or if it's just the gun. Juana trots back. And the chickens are unharmed.

Bryan took over the neighborhood when the last chief was gunned down. And someone younger will replace Bryan the day he's killed. If Bryan can manage his neighborhood successfully, boosting drug sales, and show enough cunning and violence, he might get noticed and get hired by the traffickers. He would start out as a cartel dogs-body, called here "dog washers" because often their job is . . . washing the traffickers' dogs. But it's a foot on the ladder. And if you're smart and vicious enough, you can rise through the ranks.

One dog washer became a successful trafficker. At his wedding to a beauty queen, he was given expensive cars, envelopes of cash, and one drug lord gave him a chess set, each piece made of solid gold. Why the chess set?

"It's where you can see a pawn fuck a queen."

Bryan runs his barrio with the instincts of a slum Machiavelli.

"You have to control your turf. If someone gets out of control, you have to fuck them up. . . . Out of control is when people say things they shouldn't. Telling us what they will or won't do. You get three or four rebels, they can start a revolution."

As the barrios' rulers, the gangsters act as police—investigating murders and enforcing rules.

"If the young ones misbehave, we'll always give them a beatdown. . . . A few weeks ago, a boy brought someone into the neighborhood to *stick* [kill] someone. We found out and beat him up. That's the warning. But if they keep doing it, we have to *justice* them."

That crime lingo, the poetry of the slums. Colombians are natural poets, loving to roll words around their mouths before inventing a new term. Murder can be expressed as "make them see the devil," "putting dirt on someone's chest," "to fall in love with someone," and "sucking gladiolas." To be in danger is "to carry a tombstone around your neck" or "to stink of formaldehyde."

Jobs are scarce and bad here. Women work as domestic help in the wealthier homes below. There's a joke in Latin America: you employ a maid or you are the maid. Others sell cigarettes, candy, books on the street.

I want to speak to the people about life under the combo. It is impossible. The combo would know exactly who spoke to me. And the people would have things to say. The combo earns good money extorting all the people under its rule. Everyone pays: businesses, civilians. Extortion is paid just to live in your house, perhaps thirty cents a week. Here it's called "vaccination."

The combos themselves were an answer to the police's inability to enforce the law. Many of the combos started out as vigilante groups to protect neighborhoods from preying criminals. In turn, they became the predators. When the government is absent, monsters take over.

"The government does nothing for us. This road we're

walking on? We built this," says Bryan. And it reminds me of the FARC rebels I once watched build a road because the government never would.

"You built this?"

"Well, people in the community did."

Politicians remember these barrios every election season. They come by with sweet speeches and cash ready to buy votes. Votes can run as high as thirty dollars each, so politicians go into debt to win the elections. Doesn't matter because if they win they make it back and more awarding contracts and receiving hefty bribes. Corrupted voters selling off their votes, predatory politicians paying for the ballots, you weep for the honest caught in the middle.

The corruption convinces the young that crime can be a way of life. If lawmakers steal, why be the sucker who lives correctly? Rightly, the combos consider themselves amateurs compared to the crooked politicians.

"These politicians have our country fucked," says Bryan. "They steal everything. That's the biggest problem we have—stealing politicians."

In these slums, there's a nihilism about anyone's chances in this life. Bryan's hope is to run the barrio and move on to the cartel. But there's a realistic appreciation of Bryan's chances in life. I ask him about his future.

"I've got my bags packed, I'm ready," he says. It takes a second to realize—he's saying he's ready to die. Other phrases include "We're living in extra time" and "we're born to die."

He tells me that he's got his funeral all planned out—loud music and an all-night party.

It's nihilism but it doesn't feel grim. It doesn't depress; it is simply accepted. Even in the shadow of death, the social law in Colombia is to enjoy yourself and don't be a downer.

WE WALK A LITTLE WAY along the road. A teenager sits on a corner. He's dressed in shorts, trainers, a basketball shirt, and a baseball cap. He plays with a branch. The boy is a lookout.

"Buddy, everything good?"

"Yes, boss," the teenager replies.

This is the limit of the combo's territory. Medellin is sliced and diced with "invisible borders," lines that separate combo territory. People are regularly gunned down for crossing them. At this border the order is: kill any unknown young man who crosses over—on sight.

I ask what would happen if I crossed.

"Buddy, I wouldn't. . . . But if you're really stupid, and you ignore the advice of a friend, then it depends if you've been seen with us or not. Let's be optimistic—you haven't been seen. Then the sons of a bitch over there will grab you, take you, and interrogate you: Where you from? What are you up to? Then the bullet. That would be if you're a regular Colombian like us. But as a gringo, they'll kidnap you and hold you for ransom until your family hasn't a penny left. Now, if they have seen you with us, and I'm sure they have . . . well, brother, you get the bullet, too."

Tension is high with the neighboring combo, but no one calls it a war. Yet.

The last major round of gang violence was a decade ago. The wars can be filled with sickening violence—gang rapes of family members, relatives tortured, drive-by shooting massacres. Kill a gang member and to go to the funeral and kill some more. Acts of hate birth new killers hungry for vengeance.

"We've had peace for some years now. The big guys came in and told us we needed to make peace," says Bryan, looking over at the world beyond this invisible border.

Not the government or the mayor's office. It was the cartels that enforced peace, ordering the combos play football matches and hold block parties to celebrate the peace.

"These conflicts are normal," he says. "We have to be prepared. And if you're not ready, they'll dead you."

Recently flareups have occurred across the city. Combos battle intensely for weeks and then things go calm. Bloodshed spikes in one part of the city, dips in another, and so it goes. No one can explain what's happening. It's an underworld without order.

IT'S ANOTHER DAY, ANOTHER BARRIO, another combo. In the darkness, looking for enemies to kill, Jesus thinks on a life that brought him to this. He sits in an abandoned, decrepit shack. It's at the far edge of the territory his combo controls. With another gang member, Jesus keeps watch over this invisible border.

The gang worries "the other side" will launch a night attack. With a small squad of hard men, ready to kick in doors and shoot men dead as they sleep, you can seize a barrio. Territories belong to those who take them. So Jesus is on lookout. As the hours go by, he thinks on a different life.

"I think on the men I see every day, I see them walking home at seven P.M. They've finished their day of work. Time to be with their family. I see them out with their wives, their children on a Sunday all eating ice cream." These are the men he thinks of as he waits with a gun in the dark.

"It's a better life than sitting there waiting to get killed."

And when he thinks of leaving the combo, reality asks the question: "But how am I going to fill my fridge?"

We're sitting outside a little store and we're on our second beer. His shift starts later tonight. He limps—two months ago, a bullet struck him in his ankle during a shootout.

"The other side did it. A man they call the Rat. The other side. They want our barrio," he says. "We won't get just him. . . . There were others with him. We were standing at the border. We wouldn't let them in. We were all armed. All armed. We almost all killed each other."

Cocaine has made him her soldier. He is one of the men who will kill, who will die in a gang war. The constant wars have conditioned these men to think that reaching thirty is a miracle.

"It's adrenaline. Your heart races a thousand beats a minute. But obviously you get tired. This life tires you. You don't know if you'll get home alive. Whether your family will get word you're dead, that your corpse is being picked up off the street by the police."

The store owner comes over and sets down two more beers.

"You never think in the future or the present. You don't think about tomorrow, if you'll be alive or dead."

Jesus has a small frame, large glasses. He has been in the combo for the past thirteen years.

"Since I was ten, I've known the wars."

It's a common tale: His father was murdered when he was a baby. His grandmother raised him, but couldn't control him. Wild, he idolized his uncle and his godfather, both in the combos.

"I saw them with drugs, armed to the teeth. I said: this is great!"

He started with little errands for the gang: hiding a gun, carrying bags of drugs. He got wilder, smoking weed, snorting cocaine, and dropped out of school. Now he's in the combo—full-time. Generations follow generations into crime.

"I need to make every week one hundred and seventy dollars. I need that money for my family, that money in my pocket," he says. When times are good, he'll pull in two hundred dollars a week.

"When times are bad, and there isn't money around for all of us, we can get thirty-three dollars. And then I have to go out and make the money anyway I can. How do I get it outside my barrio? The bad way," he says.

This combo is famous for nabbing motorbikes.

"We had a gang member and we did a robbery. Thank God, I didn't get identified," he says. The police identified his partner. They bombarded the barrio—police checkpoints at every entrance, helicopters buzzing above. All looking for this one man who was moving from house to house at night. The police understood there's no loyalty in the underworld—so they kept the pressure on. All those helicopters and police patrol, and drug sales fell to zero.

"They fucked up the plazas," he says. "We made him turn himself in. 'Turn yourself in or we kill you. We kill your family. With all this going on, we can't eat. You're not eating, I'm not eating. The plazas are hit, they're seizing the merchandise.' . . . He got five years."

The police eased up. But their rivals keep up the pressure.

"Two months ago, two homeless men came into the barrio. We found out they weren't homeless, just in disguise. They were taking photos of us, the barrio, where we were hanging out. A week later, we caught them. We saw the photos on their cell phones. And we had to . . ."

Jesus is smart, self-aware. Anywhere else, he'd have a path to a different life. Here he falls into grooves of violence, long carved out by men that came before him. He knows it's too late for him, but not for the younger kids in his neighborhood.

"A thirteen-year-old comes to me. I tell them to go back to school. Now we beat gang members who take drugs in front of kids. 'Hey, here comes a kid, hide the joint.' It's a bad example."

But the kids keep trying to join, to be somebody.

"They watch documentaries about Pablo and they want to be like him. But they don't think about what it means . . . he died on a rooftop. These are the kids who always wanted to be bad since they were born. They've grown up with bad role models. Like uncles."

But this life of crime is a con, a barrio tale told to seduce young men who don't know any better.

"I'm worth nothing. My life is always a struggle but all for nothing," he says. "People who are worth something? People who studied, struggled, got a job, got a career, and a house for their family and can provide for them. A man like that is worth something."

He wants out before he becomes like the rest of the combo.

"This is a life for sons of bitches," he says. "I want to change. I see the older men, they've got no regret left. I look at them and think they've got no futures . . . everyone dies."

He dreams of owning a legal motorbike.

"With a good bike I could be a messenger. We could leave this behind."

The dreams of Colombia's poor are always so humble, so unambitious, yet impossible.

"That's our fate: we think nice thoughts, but must live badly. But as they say: dreaming costs nothing."

We finish our beers and pay. He looks to the border, and the house where he will keep watch tonight. He knows what there is in that house. He also knows that there is no longer any place to go except to that house.

THE FIRST TIME I MET Jesus, we had completed an interview about the peace process and how it would affect Medellin's underworld. We finished and I flagged a taxi on the street.

"Toby, can I ask a favor?"

What do you need?

"Can you take me to the hospital? I want to see my son. He was born last night."

Jesus had been in the shack, watching the border when his son was born, and when his shift ended, his boss ordered him to meet me for an interview.

We arrived at the hospital. His girlfriend was in bed, beaming at her twelve-hour-old boy. She smiled at Jesus as he walked into her room, which she shared with six other patients.

He kissed her but coolly: the old macho thing—not too much affection in front of other men. She handed him their baby.

"You're going to be a champion. A tough guy," he said looking at the baby's face.

As he talked, her smile faded. A look of fear slowly crept over her face as she saw the two together. Generations follow generations.

THE MECHANIC HAS PASSED BY and changed the numbers on Bryan's new bike. We walk up the mountainside. As we move past shacks, small dogs yap at Juana, but she's too dignified to reply to the mutts. We reach the lookout. Below, Medellin rolls out before us. The tall buildings concentrate in the city center. Planes land and take off in the middle of the city. Countless barrios rise up the mountainside on the other side of the valley. The lush greenery of the mountaintops encircles us.

It's a long-running irony that Latin America's poorest have views the rich would kill for. But right now this view feels taunting—a reminder of all that Bryan can't have and never will.

"I can go to a few neighborhoods, those of our allies. But most of the city"—here he waves at Medellin below us—"I'm not welcome."

If he enters most combos' territories, he'll be shot on sight.

I ask what he thinks of the city.

"This is the best city in the world. The people. There's nothing like Medellin. I wouldn't change it for anything."

Looking at Bryan, I try to understand why Medellin churns out armies of these young men. Poverty is part of it. Large families are often crammed into small shacks. They struggle for enough to eat and basic services of electricity and water are spotty. Most of the households are headed by single mothers, deadbeat dads are common. The culture of the city venerates these hardworking mothers making it on their own. There's a saying: "Mother? There's only one! Dad? Any old son of a bitch!"

But poverty alone doesn't explain it. Nearby, Bolivia, Nicaragua, and Ecuador are all poorer than Colombia. But they don't have their own armies of young men turning to crime.

The old-timers sitting on Medellin's street corners have their own theories. "It's the culture of 'easy money.' These kids don't want to work, don't want a regular job. Just the money right now. And whatever they have to do for the money, they're going to do it," says an old man sipping his beer.

"Easy money" is the culture that mocks the person who goes out to work every day, when the bandit can earn twice as much robbing someone. The culture of cocaine created a whole mentality that infected parts of the country: "The smart live off the dumb." The cocaine culture also left a deep cynicism of Colombians about their compatriots. Every foreigner is warned in earnest terms to be careful not to be ripped off when out and about. Colombians feel overly protective of their foreign friends, going to great lengths to safeguard them from the "bad Colombians." For many, the foreigner is an innocent sucker.

The sun sets and Bryan and I grab a table outside. I buy some beers. It has the feel of a small village. All these boys were born in the city, but their DNA is country—their parents, grandparents fled the rural violence and tried to re-create that small village feeling in the concrete. We're drinking at a small store, and as the *Corridos Prohibidos* flows out, Bryan tells the man behind the counter to put on techno. Bryan hasn't found out who killed the man in the neighborhood—he'll keep looking tomorrow. His combo still controls the neighborhood. Tomorrow, another kilo of cocaine will be dropped off, cut up, and sold off. So, a successful day.

A young man rides up to our table on a motorbike.

"Que chimba your motorbike," Bryan says—"Chimba" is a catch-all term in Colombia that stretches from pussy to the best.

"Yes, brother. It was left all alone on the street. Obviously, the owner didn't want it." He laughs. "But I did!"

"This kid is crazy," says Bryan laughing.

"How you doing?" he asks Bryan.

"Relaxed, brother," answers Bryan, patting the outline of his gun under the T-shirt. A number of girls have emerged from their houses. They're made up, their hair done; they pull up chairs to sit next to Bryan. He looks at the girls to either side of him and smiles.

And they start laughing. And I laugh. I pour another beer and Bryan snorts cocaine off a key. Not one of these men around this table will reach thirty. And we keep laughing.

CHAPTER 7

OUR HOLY VIRGIN OF THE ASSASSINS

PRAYERS FOR MURDER IN A GODLESS WORLD.

In front of the Virgin Mary, the killer kneels. The Virgin looks down on him with a mother's unquestioning love. A bow of the head, eyes squeeze tight, he mutters the Assassin's Prayer:

"If there are eyes, don't let them see me
If there are hands, don't let them grab me
If there are feet, don't let them catch up to me
Don't let me be surprised from behind
Don't let my death be violent,
Don't let my blood spill,
You who see all,
Know well my sins,
But also, you know my faith
Don't abandon me. . . . Amen."

He crosses himself. A chaste kiss, lips brush the bullets hidden in his hand. Now the bullets are blessed. He struts down the steps and sits back on the pew.

"We ask for protection for ourselves and . . . death for the others, those we're going to murder," says Cachote. "It's a ritual of death we perform here."

A gun and the favor of the Virgin of the Assassins. That's all he's got. Cachote is a killer for hire, an assassin. A sicario.

Cachote's job is to protect his drug lord boss and protect the kilos of cocaine as they are stashed in safe houses—and to die if need be. The combos deal on street corners. Cachote works directly for the drug traffickers who export the cocaine. Now Cachote has young men sit outside the cocaine safe house. He checks in with them throughout the day to make sure nothing is out of the ordinary, no thieves casing the warehouse. There's a whole class of criminals crazy enough to steal from the drug lords. If there's a police raid, a theft, a bolt of lightning that loses this kilo—his boss will ask questions. Coincidences are unacceptable.

"If anything happens to it, it's me finished. There's no trust in this world, and that's the way it should be. If there was trust, people would steal everything. No. I can't expect anyone to trust me because I not going to trust anyone," he says.

Prolonged exposure to murder corrodes the soul, unhinges the mind. Killers for hire, police investigators, drug lords all know this. It's the price of the job. The only men who don't regret a life of death are the psychos.

In the drug war, the corpses come surging as a tsunami. Territory, a street corner, a kilo—there's a million different reasons to kill. Those who survive this war are grateful, because they know the bullets didn't catch them because of dumb luck. Of course, "survive" is relative—no one gets out of this life alive. It's just that death comes around a lot sooner in the drug war. One man nicknamed Iguano confessed to killing two thousand people. What do you do with that information? Jack the Ripper had his fill at five. The knowledge alone that a man like Iguano exists is enough to change you. The spectrum of evil is broader than you thought. The dark knowledge expands the mind, stains the soul.

In Europe and the United States, the middle class are sheltered from reckoning these truths. Our murders come in novels, and are solved in forty-two minutes by attractive cops on the small screen. Murder is committed by Hannibal Lecter and solved by Sherlock Holmes. And when caught, our fictional murderers are overwhelmed with remorse for the innocent lives they've snuffed out. In the drug war, men and women murder for a wage.

A third of all people murdered today will die somewhere between Mexico and Chile. Day in, day out. Drugs, drug lords, and drug-dealing gangs have made Latin America and the Caribbean the deadliest region. As the deaths mount up, minds come undone. To keep our sanity, our minds turn numb to the dead. If one were to look head-on at the wave of death of the drug war, to truly understand and feel each killing, it would fry the brain. The numbness cools and soothes, an air bag for the mind. Now dulled, we can take in the battlefield and all its cadavers. In the morgue, at the crime scene, by the mass grave, we learn they lied when they told us children that each life was precious. No life is precious. Innocent. Bystander. Civilian. None are to be mourned. Because if you break down and cry for one, good God, how will you ever stop?

In this carnage, death becomes a profession, and men become artists of murder.

The rule in cocaine is that no one gets away with anything. When a big cocaine bust occurs, the police know there will be a trail of bodies. The drug lords and their sicarios work their way along the chain of those who knew about the shipment, killing all suspects. Ninety-nine dead innocent men to catch one guilty man is the deal in cocaine.

If someone screws up, Cachote may deliver the verdict. If Cachote slips and the block of cocaine is stolen, he should make peace with the world before the other sicarios arrive. This is a life on the front lines of the drug war, one of thousands of hired guns for the white queen.

The sicarios are the cartels' military wing, the enforcers. In this ecosystem they are order, equilibrium, an answer to the problem. From outside, the killings look like chaos. That's the thing no one understands: In a world of chaos, the sicarios are order. The killings are their version of a justice system. In the legal world, screw me over in a land dispute, I'll see you in court. Burgle my house? I call the police. But when I'm in cocaine, I go to the men with the guns to restore justice—my version of justice.

"In the underworld, no one can file a criminal complaint, so they hire the sicarios. They hire us."

IT'S A FAT, MEAN SUN. Its rays fall straight down, burning shadows off this open-air religious shrine, the Virgin of the Mystic Rose in the south of Medellin. Half a dozen pilgrims sit on the benches in front of the Virgin Mary. She's dressed in white and blue, crowned in gold. The devout pray. A rare moment of serenity in the insanity.

Hundreds of pilgrims come each day to pray for divine help. Small plaques clutter the shrine—every surface covered in the notes of granite gratitude to the Virgin for prayers answered. Jobs, health, and love divinely given, humanly received. The people of Medellin are born traders, their religion gloriously transactional: deliver my prayers and I'll buy you a plaque. They know the truth: nothing for nothing gets nothing.

I'm here to understand why cocaine is so violent. And if a sicario can't make me see, who can? Head high, Cachote strolls in, surveying all. Sicarios have that spatial awareness, weighing who is who, where is the best exit. He's dressed in a camouflage tracksuit, large black Gucci sunglasses tipped in gold, white Nike trainers; a small gold chain hangs off his neck. A few of the faithful take him in. They may not be able to explain how they know what Cachote is, but know they do. Maybe it's the flow of ghosts in his wake.

In front of the statue, Cachote utters the Assassin's Prayer. It feels sacrilegious.

"This shrine was built by Pablo Escobar for us, the sicarios, so we can be closer to God, so the Virgin Mary can forgive us and help us to stay free."

Legend has Escobar, vocal Catholic and loud philanthropist, paying for this shrine in the side of a mountain. Since the 1980s, this shrine has been known as the Virgin of the Assassins, where killers and drug traffickers pray for favor and forgiveness. The smart, the chancers ask for forgiveness *before* the sin.

"We sicarios come to ask for help. We perform our rituals and bless our bullets. If anyone has any curse against us or bullets meant for us, now they won't work."

The other pilgrims disperse, a few taking a final glance over their shoulders at Cachote. A grandmother gives him *the look*, the withering stare. She's close to the end, she doesn't care.

Cachote is twenty-five years old, small but with a gymed-out physique. He has a swollen head, short torso, and long arms that swing down like an ape's. He sits with his back to the wall, his gaze clocking who comes, who goes. He's not cursed with an abundance of smarts, but he's got the malice and the balls to do this job.

"If God didn't want me to kill them, then he would stop me. He would send some sign that would stop me from killing a person," he tells me. "And because he doesn't stop me, it means that person was supposed to die; they had done something to die."

Of course, in the madness of this bloodshed, the sicarios find the truly responsible: God. Does he feel guilty for killing people he didn't know?

He pauses and removes his sunglasses, and his eyes shock. There's eternal darkness in the gaze. Eyes that have returned from lands we'll never see with things we'll never believe.

"No—maybe they haven't done anything to me, but they've done something to someone. We're all guilty. And maybe what I'm being paid to kill him for isn't enough for someone to die, but he must have done something to someone in the past. And now it's catching up with him."

Killing for God on the streets of Medellin, one blessed bullet at a time. Cachote has absolved himself of any justice in the universe, riding those outer edges where there's madness in the logic. Or a logic in the madness.

There's one power Cachote knows he won't escape—the laws of cocaine. When Cachote prays, he prays to the Virgin and the White Goddess.

The kilo pays Cachote's wages. The killings are on the side; his main job is bodyguard for his *patrón,* a drug trafficker named Alex. He accompanies Alex across Colombia and the world, arranging cocaine deals. Murdering for hire has taken a kid from the slums to luxury hotels in Miami, Madrid, Panama. See the world, meet interesting people, and kill them.

Some die because they owe money on a cocaine deal. Steal the kilo and as a matter of policy it will be ugly.

"You have to make an example of those who steal the merchandise."

Live dismemberment, plastic bags over the head. A single, merciful bullet becomes something to offer in negotiations with the man tied to a chair, when all know the conversation has stopped being "if" and is now "how" and "when."

Sometimes he doesn't know why people are ordered to die by his hand. Ask why and the next bullet may be his. The trick of moving through cocaine is knowing what info will save you and what will kill you.

"If they call me for Monday morning, the normal procedure is to send me photos, addresses. . . . I can't go crazy and go kill someone, exposing myself to danger—no. As a sicario, I have to be intelligent." He wants me to know: he's a hard worker who enjoys what he does. The merry killer.

"If they tell me the person has to die Friday, that person dies Friday. Because if that person doesn't die, I may die."

His is a bland face as void of emotion as a sheet of plastic. I wonder how many people's last sight of this world was this face. I can't resist: How many have you killed?

Pause.

"There have been a lot. And with one after another after another, you lose track of who you've killed," he says. He trusts me, but some questions are too incriminating. He's agreed to an interview, not to send himself to prison. We don't speak about individual cases.

So why kill for money? For the money.

"I like money. This allows me to buy the things I want. There's no other job where I can make this money. I'm good at it and my boss pays well."

Every time I meet him, he has a shopping bag of a purchase that day—Tommy Hilfiger shirt, Hugo Boss sunglasses, Calvin Klein underwear.

"If it's a public figure, or a heavy narco, then I'm going to charge more. . . . If it's for a nobody, I could do it for 250,000, 300,000 pesos [$100]."

That's how murder becomes normalized. Five minutes ago, I was asking how he can do it. Now we're discussing prices.

Businessmen, top narcos, politicians can net a sicario tens of thousands of dollars.

"If it's a public person, that's going to require more money because those people are always protected by bodyguards—so I have to go in ready to die or kill everyone who's there."

The biggest jobs offer the biggest money. But you're not coming home. There's a long history of contract killers being hired to kill presidential candidates, senators, and drug lords and then being murdered by their handlers. There's even a name for the sicarios on one-way missions: "suizos" (Swiss, but from the word for "suicide"). Money is saved and loose ends tied up, all for the cost of one more bullet. Killers killing killers for killing.

You can hear these stories and be overly understanding. The bad childhoods, the poverty, the lack of opportunity. It's a mistake. Millions grow up poor. They don't kill for a living. Cachote decided to be a killer. But in a society that offered the job up as a profession.

We're done for the day and as Cachote walks away, I feel hundreds of ghosts leaving with him.

Later that night, I go through my wallet. There are three

one-hundred-dollar bills. I realize I could have anyone I know in Colombia killed for these notes. They say life is worth nothing here. That's not true—it's worth three pieces of paper.

A RANDOM WEEK, MARCH 5 to March 11, 2019. The killings of sicarios alone in Medellin:

Saturday morning: An unidentified man in his early twenties is found shot to death. Neighbors say that he picked up trash to recycle. His killing ends an unexpected stretch of peace—Medellin had gone 81 hours and 32 minutes without a homicide.

Monday: Seven men on motorbikes arrive at an apartment in the Medellin neighborhood of Bello at 4 P.M. They enter Ana's home, pushing an unnamed woman and Ana's children into a room while they speak with Ana. Ana, in her early thirties, is shot to death with a silencer. Her brother-in-law, fifty-four-year-old Luis, hears the ruckus from the street and goes up to the apartment. He is shot to death.

Tuesday: Juan, twenty years old and known for rescuing stray animals, walks his dog with a friend. He is shot to death. This occurs in a community park that has yet to be officially opened. "But has already become the scene of a murder," reports *Q'hubo*.

Tuesday: Raider, a seventeen-year-old Venezuelan who has sought a new life in Colombia, is shot to death by a sicario while walking next to a nursery.

Wednesday: Today seven people will be murdered.

Wednesday: Cristian is nineteen years old and works in a garage. Two men arrive at the workshop in a taxi. They

walk in shooting 9 mm handguns. Cristian is fixing a
motorbike when he falls dead. Police will find forty-five
bullet holes in him.

Wednesday: Steven picks up his best friend, Miguel, from
the barbershop where he works. The two men, twenty-
three and twenty-four, are riding a motorbike through a
major avenue when another motorbike rides alongside.
The men open fire, killing them both. The police blame
the gang the Agony for the killings. Miguel leaves behind
two sons, one and two years old.

Wednesday: Luis, twenty-five years old, is found in a Dodge
100. He's dead, with twenty-one bullet holes in him.
Neighbors heard all the gunshots but didn't dare venture
out, fearing they too would be caught in the shooting.

Friday: Esteban, twenty-seven years old, is walking when
two sicarios shoot him. Injured, he runs, escaping into a
house whose door is open. The sicarios follow him in and
end his life.

Friday: Yuridia Arboleda is convicted in a court case of
hiring a sicario to kill her husband. The thirty-seven-year
old is sentenced to twenty years for the killing, which was
aimed at taking over the properties of her husband for her
and her lover. The husband was murdered as he drove
to work at 6 A.M. on his motorbike. The alleged sicario is
thought to have been involved in multiple killings.

Saturday: Passersby discover a set of plastic bags that
contain different parts of a man. Police say this is the
third dismembered body they have found in two months.

PLATO ASKED: IF A RING could turn you invisible, would you stay
honest? How many live honestly only out of fear of the law? A

functioning government holds back our worst impulses. Most of us need never face what we're truly capable of.

No Colombian alive has ever known a functioning Colombian government. Impunity is so high in Colombia, it's Plato's experience writ large. One attorney general guesses that impunity runs at 99 percent. When you know you can get away with it, the crimes become that much more tempting. In the chaos, men and women like Cachote grow.

And that's why the most honest people I've ever met are those in Colombia who had every chance to live dishonorably, yet lived true.

POVERTY, COCAINE, IMPUNITY, THEY ALL sharpen the blade, but Colombia was birthed in violence: a bloody conquest of indigenous lands, followed by a violent revolution and war to expel the Spanish. Squabbling elites plunged the country into countless civil wars over the next centuries. Whenever the tiny oligarchy has been asked to share some of its riches, it has replied with savage violence. Banana workers asking for higher wages? Order the army to slaughter them by the hundreds. Workers trying to organize? Make Colombia the deadliest country in the world for trade union officials. Activists campaigning for the 1 percent to share some of the 80 percent of the productive land they own? Slaughter them by the dozens. Political power and wealth are to be kept in the same hands as always.

Colombia's sicarios trace their spiritual grandfathers to the biggest names in the civil war so horrific it's known as "the Violence." Red liberals or blue conservatives, bandits became famous "triggermen," roaming the country for political opponents to slaughter. "Black Blood" and "Black Soul" earned their fame as much as any American West outlaw. These men understood violence—deeply. To be effective, bloodshed must be a spectacle. When death rains, to stand out the murder must be theatrical. Black Blood popularized the so-called Colombian necktie, a throat slit and the tongue pulled out the open bloody gash. Decades later, theater would be made with the chain saw, the machete, the rock.

The Violence subsided and so did the need for full-time killers. In the 1970s, the Americans rediscovered cocaine and the cartels were born. They introduced this new job into the slums—sicario. The job flourished across the city, a recognizable profession, a career. The city hummed to the sound of young men on motorbikes amid the drumbeat of gunshots.

As the Americans dug deeper and snorted more cocaine, there was more money to fight over in Colombia. At the height of his power, Pablo Escobar opened a collection office, the Office of Envigado. Staffed by young killers, the job of the Office of Envigado was to collect money owed to Escobar and other debts incurred in cocaine. Escobar set up a school for killers. An instructor taught young men how to kill, using a motorbike. The final exam was to kill a stranger on the street, their execution judged on speed and effectiveness. For high-profile murders, they sometimes carried out dry runs, killing a stranger on the street in order to see any problems with the plan. The school was eventually shut down and the instructor was murdered—by two young men on the back of a motorbike. Everyone assumes the killers were former students. Cocaine has a sense of humor.

As the narco culture spread across the country, so did collection offices. A tool of the cocaine business, contract killing went mainstream. Need a cheating husband removed? A business partner stiffed you on a deal? Do like thousands of others have and call the local assassination outfit. Paid killings now occur daily for the weakest of offenses.

Unlucky sicarios are caught. A vast reserve of young men is ready to take their place. And those who order the killings, the "intellectual authors," are rarely bothered by the law.

Cachote has seen civilians order killings.

"They get the dead body they paid for. But here's the thing—now you're involved. And you didn't kill them, but you're the intellectual killer and now you've got the thoughts 'I sent that man to his death.'"

As he talks, I wonder if he's a psychopath. No, I've met psychopaths, and you know it. The hairs on the back of the arm stand up, a knot in your gut, you pick up on some invisible vibe that tells you this man was born wrong. It's an evolutionary trick humans have learned to protect ourselves from psychos. Like the deep red on a frog tells you it's poisonous. They call it aposematism—when nature warns you something is dangerous.

No, Cachote is scarier than that. A psychopath is nature's error. We made Cachote.

RANDOM MURDER HAS BECOME CRUELLY normal. Sicarios have felled presidential candidates, housewives, the country's most famous comedian, models, actresses, policemen, grandmothers, football players, priests, and children. A constellation of corpses and we look for the pattern.

In the confusion of the bloodshed, sometimes the only thing that made sense is to blame the victim. As if the world makes a little more sense if this killing can be explained away. Common to hear at a murder scene as the body cools is "Must have done something . . ."

Of course, everyone wants the murders to end. But it would be a lie to say it doesn't fascinate. Teenagers laughingly share videos of shoot-outs on WhatsApp. Taxi drivers slap little bullet holes stickers on their cabs. One Sunday afternoon I spent with the indigenous Paez community, everyone watching a firefight between rebels and soldiers on a mountainside just 150 feet ahead of us. Everyone was drinking beer, whooping it up, and laughing with the volleys of machine gun fire. Every grenade set off more laughter.

"You have your Hollywood, we have this," an old indigenous man said. I grabbed a beer and joined them.

The rich have paid for high walls and small armies of bodyguards to keep them safe. Now no longer threatened, the wealthy consider murder quite distasteful. Highbrow newspapers followed suit, ceasing to report the daily murders that plague every Colombian city, every day. Lawyers and doctors breezily declare murders as a thing of the past. The poor live among the murderers and the murdered; they know better.

On sale at street corners in the city centers are the daily roundup of the drug war: the tabloids. Big letters, short words, these papers are the city's id in black, white, and red all over. Front pages splash the latest, strangest murders: color close-ups of corpses in the gutter, deep red pools of blood to go with your morning coffee. And on the back, a full-page color photo of a sex kitten in lingerie winking at you—just you! An espresso shot of sex and murder to start the day.

The old joke is that these tabloids don't stain hands ink black but blood-red. The tabloids are always on the lookout for that perfect Colombian story: deeply weird and bloody. The half-naked woman dancing in the river's shallows next to the floating corpse. The gay priest lovers with terminal AIDS who hired a hit man to kill them before the disease would. Bodies dismembered for reasons of the occult. Every crime reporter, every detective has their favorite case to be shared over rums.

Colombia fears, despises its sicarios. Yet, man, how they fascinate. Rueda Rocha, El Arete, Tyson, La Quica, all became household names. Their murders, their lives inspire songs, soap operas, movies, books, documentaries (sooo many documentaries).

What does an old, retired sicario do? He becomes a YouTuber. Jhon Jario Velasquez is better known as "Popeye" and claims to have killed hundreds on the orders of Pablo Escobar. Popeye is a dislikable character, who was imprisoned for twenty-two years on charges of terrorism, drug trafficking, extortion, and murder. Once freed, he became a YouTuber, with more than a million subscribers the world over. He rants about communists, reminisces over Escobar, and spouts off his hard-right politics, like a drunk uncle thumping the dinner table. Colombian gangsters' politics are always hard-right. The mafia thinks of itself as entrepreneurs of the underworld. They consider the world a brutal battlefield where the weak are to be stomped and the strong adored, and compassion is a personal failing.

Popeye lasted four years on the outside making documentaries, selling his life story, which was turned into a telenovela. He's now back in prison awaiting trial for extortion.

CACHOTE INVITES ME TO THE San Pedro cemetery. The graveyard is a graceful circle, decked out with palm trees and an elegant white church. It looks a pleasant place to spend the afterlife.

"All of mine have ended up here—I don't leave anyone alive. When I execute my order, no one's left alive. They'll end up here—or in another cemetery," he says, wearing a Hugo Boss baseball cap, a Superdry T-shirt, and gold-colored trainers.

A coca picker carries his sack of coca leaves through a field of the bush in Catatumbo, northeast Colombia. They are paid by the quantity of leaves they pick. *Photo by Nicoló Filippo Rosso*

A coca picker moves through a coca field, collecting leaves. This field is in Catatumbo, alongside the border with Venezuela. *Photo by Nicoló Filippo Rosso*

A coca picker shows off his hands. Ripping leaves from coca branches leaves the pickers' hands with nicks and cuts, so they cover them to protect their fingers. *Photo by Nicoló Filippo Rosso*

A coca picker prepares to weigh his sack of coca in a makeshift laboratory. There the coca leaves are turned into paste, the first stage in the production of cocaine. *Photo by Nicoló Filippo Rosso*

The Catatumbo is a land of jungles and mountains where the government is largely absent, leaving the small farmers to struggle to survive. Warring narco-militias are ever present. *Photo by Toby Muse*

Antinarcotic police launch blitz missions into territories where narco-militias oversee cocaine production. The police spend a few hours fumigating the coca bushes and then fly out before the militias can launch an attack. The fields, such as this one in Tumaco, southwest Colombia, are littered with landmines sewn to slow down eradication efforts. *Photo by Toby Muse*

An antinarcotics Black Hawk helicopter flies over a field of coca in Tumaco, southwest Colombia. Hidden in the cluster of trees, in the photo's center, is a small coca laboratory used to turn the leaves into coca paste.
Photo by Toby Muse

Captain Max Perez of the antinarcotics police turns away as a helicopter takes off from a field of coca. They are here to destroy the coca crops in Tumaco, southwest Colombia.
Photo by Toby Muse

This is Manuela, a kinkajou who was being held by an animal trafficker. Often called honey bears, they are native to the jungles of Catatumbo. We gave her to a kindly store owner who was devoted to animals.
Photo by Toby Muse

A coca laboratory in the jungles of Catatumbo. Gasoline, ammonia, and sulfuric acid all are ingredients used to make coca paste and cocaine. The farmers dump the residual waste into nearby streams. *Photo by Nicoló Filippo Rosso*

A fire rages in the jungles of Tumaco. Farmers often slash and burn rain forests to plant coca. What looks to be two coca laboratories can be seen. *Photo by Toby Muse*

Gocho, a bomb dog with the antinarcotics police, prepares for another mission in Tumaco. Landmines are strewn through the coca fields, meant to slow down the police by causing as much damage as possible. The dogs are vital in detecting the explosives. *Photo by Toby Muse*

The city of Tumaco seen from a Black Hawk helicopter on its way out to a mission in the jungles. *Photo by Toby Muse*

A woman walks into a brothel in Catatumbo. When coca establishes itself in a region, prostitutes come to profit from the coca boom. *Photo by Nicoló Filippo Rosso*

A couple dance in a brothel in Catatumbo. *Photo by Nicoló Filippo Rosso*

A man crosses the road a block away from police searching for clues to a homicide carried out by a killer for hire. *Photo by Toby Muse*

Cachote, a hired assassin, lays out five bullets to be blessed. *Photo by Simone Bruno*

Cachote recites the Assassin's Prayer before a statue of the Virgin Mary. *Photo by Simone Bruno*

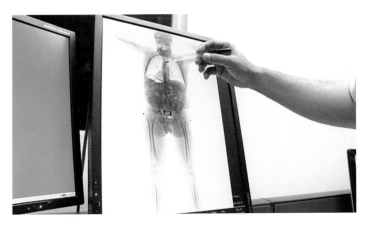

A police agent points to an X-ray that shows a drug mule's stomach filled with cocaine capsules in Bogota's El Dorado airport. Mules are caught at Colombia's airports daily, and in recent years more foreigners are being caught with cocaine. The average drug mule carries around one kilo and will be paid about $5,000. *Photo by Toby Muse*

Airport workers and police search for drugs in packages before they are sent abroad. This warehouse is part of Bogota's El Dorado airport.
Photo by Nicoló Filippo Rosso

US Coast Guard sailors stack bales of cocaine on the deck of the cutter *James*. The Coast Guard patrol the eastern Pacific Ocean, the most important cocaine transit route on the planet. These 600 kilos of cocaine were found floating in the middle of the Pacific Ocean. The Coast Guard estimates the worth of the haul at $18 million. *Photo by Toby Muse*

An American teenager is taken out of Bogota's El Dorado airport after the police found four kilos of cocaine in his luggage as he tried to board a plane destined for Madrid, Spain. Drug mules typically spend five years in Colombia's violent prisons. *Photo by Toby Muse*

Sombra ("Shadow") the police dog prepares for another day searching for cocaine in Bogota's airport. A recipient of multiple awards, Sombra has detected tons and tons of cocaine. One trafficker was so enraged by her discoveries along the Caribbean coast that he offered money to have the dog killed. She was brought to Bogota and lives under heavy police guard. *Photo by Nicoló Filippo Rosso.*

In the Colombian naval base Malaga Bay there is a graveyard of vessels that have been seized from smugglers as they tried to take cocaine out across the Pacific Ocean. *Photo by Toby Muse*

This is a semi-sub. Called "narco-subs," they move stealthily through the ocean, virtually all of the ship beneath the waves. These vessels are constructed in clandestine factories and cost a minimum of a million dollars to make. *Photo by Toby Muse*

US Coast Guard sailors receive guns as they prepare for a mission to find cocaine in the eastern Pacific Ocean. *Photo by Toby Muse*

An empty boat floats on the eastern Pacific Ocean with the Coast Guard cutter *James* far in the background. They found 400 kilos of cocaine on the boat after her crew tried to outrun the Coast Guard and was stopped only when a sharpshooter blew out the boat's engines. The Coast Guard then set fire to the boat, sinking it to the ocean floor. *Photo by Toby Muse*

The US Coast Guard returns from another mission with hundreds more kilos of cocaine. *Photo by Toby Muse*

Sailors of the Coast Guard form a human chain to transport the sometimes tons of cocaine captured in these operations. *Photo by Toby Muse*

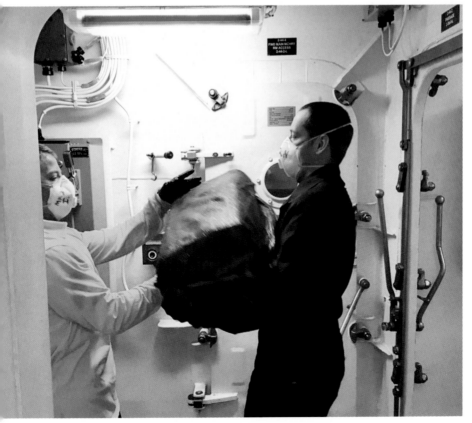

The Coast Guard prepares the sleeping spaces for those captured. The detained eat the same food as the sailors and are given daily showers, but their ankles remain shackled most of the day.
Photo by Toby Muse

In this operation, the Coast Guard seized two tons of cocaine from a speedboat designed to ride low in the waves and hide from the authorities. Traffickers put different stamps on the bricks of cocaine to mark out the kilos' ownership.
Photo by Toby Muse

A line of detained Ecuadorian fishermen prepare to be transferred off a US Coast Guard cutter and handed over to Ecuador's navy. Thirty-one fishermen were captured in the operation. *Photo by Toby Muse*

The Ecuadorian fishermen were found with 1.6 tons of cocaine at a rough estimate of $50 million. No Coast Guard sailor could remember an operation that detained so many. *Photo by Toby Muse*

A boat on which the Coast Guard found 400 kilos floats aflame on the Pacific Ocean. The Coast Guard set it on fire, as they don't have the capacity to drag all of them to shore and leaving them afloat would be dangerous to ocean traffic. *Photo by Toby Muse*

The eastern Pacific Ocean is the loneliest spot on earth, home to shivers of sharks and pods of whales. The Coast Guard's five cutters must patrol six million square miles. It's also the world's most important cocaine corridor, connecting the producer countries and the biggest market: the US. *Photo by Toby Muse*

"I'm here to see a friend. . . . Who knows? Maybe tomorrow they'll be coming to see me. . . ."

We pass through the beautiful white sculptures. Cachote knows his way well around this cemetery. The tombs are the homes of this "Necropolis," a city of the dead. Today it's busy. Families walk slowly through the rows of graves. A gorgeous woman in black and sunglasses walks through the tombs, an entourage of friends and employees trailing behind her. High heels, a short black skirt, and a tight black blouse—from head to toe a drug lord's widow.

In front of another tomb stand young men from a combo. A kid tosses some trash on the ground. Cachote stops and tells the boy to pick it up. The teenager knows what Cachote is and quickly picks it up.

"People have to respect this city. I tell people to keep it clean."

He strides the stairs to a huge curved open-air corridor. Along a long handsome white wall stand hundreds of vaults, tombs stacked six high. Walking with him doesn't inspire confidence. There's not a successful sicario out there who isn't on someone's hit list. People want Cachote dead. "Heating up," that's what people call it when you're hanging out with a friend in the crosshairs. I keep an eye on those around us.

He arrives at his friend's tomb. He leans in, his forehead resting on the vault. Flowers have wilted in a plastic cup.

"Friend, God bless you. God keep you in his kingdom. That he forgive your sins. And blessings to you wherever you are," he whispers. He raps his knuckles four times on the tomb.

This is Blondie, the man who brought Cachote into the business.

The tomb looks abandoned. Only sicarios mourn sicarios.

THESE YOUNG MEN AND WOMEN grow up on the mountainside slums. Every day, they look down on the shopping centers, the nightclubs, the car showrooms. There's a whole glittering world out there beyond their grasp. It forges a materialism burned with rage.

"When I dreamed as a child, when I dreamed of being someone in this life, I always wanted to be a good Colombian. I wanted to be a pharmacy manager. I've always been interested in medicine." There's nothing smaller, humbler than the childhood dreams of crooks. And as tiny as they are, these dreams are impossible in a country where the poor are as disposable as trash.

"Our economic situation was always bad. My parents were not able to give me a lot," and in the misery, he drifted. Why go to school if it will only earn you a slum job? Why go legal if your reward is to be a nobody all your life? That's the thing: everyone wants to be somebody. And there is no way that will happen following the right path. In the neighborhood's narrow, dark alleys, he started smoking weed. There he met "Blondie," a slum kid on the rise.

"I remember him with the best motorbike, the best clothing, the finest pussy. The best hit men have the best women, the nicest chains. . . . I learned everything from him. He inspired me."

Blondie put Cachote in touch with the men who hire the killers. And they gave him a contract.

"It was so tough. It was with a knife. I had to stab a lot of times, around fifteen times. I tried to slit his throat, but the man raised his hand to his throat, he wouldn't die. I took advantage that he couldn't run and stabbed him in other parts . . . his chest, his heart . . . I threw up. I looked like a crazy man."

He was fifteen—still a virgin, now a murderer. That same day, shaking and vomiting, Cachote swore he would never do it again. But he knew—there was no way back.

"I couldn't stop thinking about it and it drove me mad. How I had murdered this man. But the money . . . the money murdered all those thoughts."

The elder crooks could see Cachote had a future in killing. An older sicario told Cachote he wasn't like other boys; he was special—he had the gift of killing.

"They train you. It's not like you're ordered to kill and then you're straight off killing. They train you in shooting ranges. They make you kill dogs to see if you've got—as they say vulgarly—the balls to kill someone, because this ain't easy."

Cachote joined a collection office in Medellin, working alongside his buddy Blondie. Blondie kept training Cachote, how to handle different weapons, the tools of the trade.

"Everyone knew he was evil, but he was always so happy, always looking out for his friends. But at the same time, he was soulless; he would kill his friends if he needed to."

One night, Blondie blasted a friend in the head while he cleaned his gun.

"He didn't do it on purpose. But once he saw that his friend was dead, he didn't care."

Cachote had made it—he was someone in the slum. Feared, respected. His new high-powered Japanese motorbike roared through the city. The old slum-wear was discarded for imported high-end brand names and shiny new cell phones. Like every good slum sicario, he spoils his mother: presents every month, he's helped pay for a new house. Every homicide cop in Medellin dreads Mother's Day. The murder rate always spikes as sicarios go out killing to earn money to buy nice presents for their mothers.

A RISING TRAFFICKER OFFERED CACHOTE and Blondie jobs as body-guards. Alex's name was ricocheting through the underworld as someone smart, ferocious, and more sophisticated than the average narco.

Now Cachote is making more money than ever. But like everyone in cocaine, he never saves—why bother? Someone will always need killing and no one is retiring out of this. Cachote knows reaching thirty is an ambitious goal.

The blood money goes quickly in the nightclubs of Medellin. Nights stretch into three-day benders of cocaine, the hallucinogenic drug 2C-B, and whiskey. Party today, die tomorrow. The nihilism of cocaine. Cachote parties and loves as much as life will give him before the inevitable end, an end almost certain to come via another sicario's bullet.

"I like the parties to distract me from all I did. But other times I like to be alone, so I can think on what's happened. Analyze it and get over it: I killed him, now is time to move on with my life. I calm down, I go shopping." No one is more materialistic than those of the underworld.

Cachote is bisexual, partying along Medellin's "Street of Sin." The city's small gay scene crams into a handful of clubs. Sicarios dance and leave with lawyers, doctors, men whose lives would never intersect save on a gay dance floor, a court trial, or a hospital emergency room.

Cachote's sexuality is a secret in the underworld. His boss, Alex, knows and doesn't care. But he's ordered him to keep it quiet—he's not going to be mocked or tested by other traffickers for having a bisexual bodyguard. Cocaine doesn't really care about race or sexuality. Medellin does. It's a conservative city, with the spirit of the shopkeeper, the religion of the devout.

Cachote tells me a story: This drug lord fell in love with a handsome young sicario. The sicario was hetero and popular with women. Jealous, the trafficker ordered the killing of the sicario's girlfriend. When the sicario found a new girlfriend, he had her killed, too. The sicario went through five girlfriends in a year. He couldn't understand why his girlfriends kept dying of bullets. Convinced he was cursed, the sicario found his only relief by putting a gun in his mouth and pulling the trigger.

"And the trafficker found a new man to obsess over."

Cachote finishes the story and looks at me like only an idiot wouldn't understand the moral of the tale.

"I WENT ON ONE JOB but didn't realize that the target was with his bodyguard. And he lit me up with his bullets. So, I couldn't commit the homicide. I went back to my *patrón*. Alex told me that now my life was on the line: I had to finish the job. The target was now forewarned. It was going to be a tough job so I had to ask the favor of Blondie in order to get it done."

The target was killed and Blondie had saved Cachote's life. To make more money, Blondie was taking outside work, killing for money off the books. Alex heard of the other killings and Blondie was warned. The reason: every boss is responsible for his men's murders. Blondie took another job without permission and killed another man—a close friend of a high-ranking trafficker. Questions were asked and the underworld quickly discovered that Blondie was the killer (the police never discovered who committed the crime). The trafficker asks Alex: Did Blondie kill my friend on your orders? Peace in Medellin is on the edge.

"That's when the big powers got involved."

Once it reached this stage, there was only ever going to be one solution. Alex was going to kill his own star killer.

"He didn't follow the rules. And sadly, now he's in San Pedro cemetery. . . . He was my best friend. It hurt when he was killed. But it was the same corporation that I work for that killed him. I couldn't do anything. I couldn't even cry. I saw him there on the ground, and I couldn't cry. Why? Because all those who killed him were there in the crowd looking at his body, waiting to see if anyone was going to say something. That's the law. If the dead man is your best friend, you can't say anything because it's done, they killed him."

Any bitterness? Even the idea is dangerous.

"It was my *patrón* that gave the order. It's over. . . . He's dead and I'm alive. We sicarios pay the price. They can send my best friend to kill me—and he'll do it if the money is right."

We leave the cemetery. Cachote says he can go for months without a killing. The city hasn't had an all-out drug war for a decade now.

"Something is in the air. You can feel it. A war is coming," he says. And he smiles.

"COLOMBIA, BROTHER, IT'S JUST ONE big graveyard," a forensic investigator says.

We're on a break from searching for hundreds of murdered corpses. The place is called La Escombrera, on the city's outskirts. Families believe the combos and cartels have been dumping hundreds of bodies in the huge rubbish dump for decades. Finally, the local government is digging it up to search for the corpses. The workers have gone home; the diggers have shut down. It's the end of another day, and still no bodies. We're looking at the same mountains: I see the greens of the forests, a sinking sunset, a modern metropolis beneath us. The investigator sees clandestine mass graves and ghosts.

Killers like Cachote have dotted the country with home-made graves, shallow and mass. Victims are dumped into rivers, buried in forests, stuffed into dirt holes at the city limits. These are Colombia's 85,000 "disappeared." Far-right death squads and the security forces disappeared left-wing political activists, who threw around those dangerous words of "reform," "change," and "organize." Graffiti paints the cities with a philosophical maxim changed to a brutal Colombian reality: "I think therefore I disappear."

No body. What's to investigate? And the victims' families are left in perpetual torment. To really understand these forced disappearances, sit and listen to the families left behind—it's a lit cigarette on your nerve endings.

She's in her early forties and welcomes me into her humble home. Her living room is covered in framed, faded photos of her and her husband. Her husband was . . . I catch myself, *is* a trade union activist and was disappeared twenty years earlier. Years of tears. Endless questions, no answers. Did he suffer? How did they kill him? Is he really dead? Is he alive somewhere out there?

Then hope! Someone's seen him in a distant town. She's giddy. Then confirmation: not him. Another false hope. Another crash. The wounds ripped open like the first day again. It never stops being the first day of pain. Everyone else moves on. She's stuck in that moment he disappeared. Seasons come and go. Friends and families grow older. They resent her for not overcoming the pain. She resents them for moving on. It's the love of her life? How can she *not* obsess over his face?

No closure. Her worst enemy could not torment her more. Her grief is her worst enemy.

I ask the horrible question: Do you believe—after all this time!—he could still be alive?

I instantly regret it. Through her tears, she smiles dementedly: "Yes!" That crazed glint in her eyes comes from *that* question. This grief is a pain so large it has snapped her mind.

"Every day I think: he's going to walk through the front door," and she points to the door as if he might complete the sentence.

He does not walk in. He will never walk in. He is not beyond that door. Beyond that door are men who murdered her husband and disappeared his body. They know the agony it causes her. Their souls will rot in hell.

Only her own death will close this case. Endless torment. Eternal peace denied.

Yet in cruelty and despair, sometimes a divine madness emerges and murder creates beauty.

IMPERIAL AND FEMININE, THE MAGDALENA River roils through the country, slicing Colombia in half. Boating its clean, green waters, you imagine the indigenous in canoes a thousand years ago, Spanish conquistadores five hundred years later navigating the treacherous currents, chasing gold and genocide.

The Magdalena is the river of Colombia. Poems, songs, and stories are dedicated to her. She takes, she gives, feeding millions a day. Angered, her floods kill by the hundreds.

Pablo Escobar appreciated the river. He built his farm, Hacienda Napoles, just off the Magdalena where he lived the template for traffickers for decades to come. Decadent parties mixed fashion models with the world's most ferocious drug lords. Pablo's toys were speedboats, four-by-four trucks, buggies, helicopters, and small planes. A private airstrip was used to fly cocaine in and out. Pablo's zoo received animals from across the planet. Hippos, zebras, lions. And when Escobar was killed, the hippos were left to fend for themselves. In this tropical climate, they thrived. The first four multiplied into forty and they live and frolic along the Magdalena River. Colombia now has the largest population of wild hippos outside of Africa.

Hippos, Escobar . . . just one of the Magdalena's stories. These roiling waters birth legends and myths. Five hundred years ago, an indigenous princess ran away with a Spanish invader, giving birth to one of the world's first mestizos. As punishment for disobeying him, the indigenous chief drowned his daughter in the Magdalena's waters. Now as the Water Mother she lives under the river's waves, luring, beckoning fishermen to their watery dooms.

Along the river's banks, long-bearded, hairy Mohan stomps. An indigenous giant, he hunts men to torment and women to seduce. His eyes glow yellow in the dark. Ever stumbling, drunk, he carries the moon on his shoulders. Wandering men are butchered. Women washing clothes at the river's edge are grabbed by a massive fist that shoots from the waters. Mohan drags the women to his palace at the bottom of a lake, where they will live among his hoarded treasures in huge, brightly lit halls.

La Llorona (the Crier) wanders the shores of the Magdalena, screeching when the moon is bright. Her face is a skull, two throbbing flames for eyes. When there are too many fireflies, the wise peasant knows the Llorona is near. After an affair, she gave birth to a baby. But her lover shunned her and the babe. Enraged, distraught, crazed, she drowned her new-born in the Magdalena. Grief-struck, she returned to search for her baby. But it was gone. And now, when the moon is out, she screams out: "Here, I left him! . . . Here, I left him! Where will I find him?" One twist on the tale is that she carries her dead baby even as she frantically searches for him.

Amid the dank and dark forests at the river's edge roam the old gods. This was the Magdalena everyone knew. And then the body parts started floating by and all remembered that the real monsters wield chain saws and talk in kilos.

In the middle of the Magdalena, in the middle of these myths, sits Puerto Berrio. It's dusty and the short white buildings blind you in the midday sun. The town is lethargic in the heat. It's not hot, the locals tell you, it's five minutes from hell hot. And damn if it doesn't feel hotter than that. The town mixes conservative religious beliefs with the bartering culture of a port town.

The Magdalena Medio is Colombia's center. And that wasn't good for the locals. Drug traffickers, leftist guerrillas, far-right death squads all fought over these strategically valuable hills and rivers. Coca crops and cocaine rocketed. From the 1980s to the 2000s, massacres to control these cocaine tons and routes were commonplace.

"They all did their parties here. Five dead, ten dead. A party here, a party there. A good Christian didn't know what would happen every time he left his house," Franco, a taxi driver, says. I nod along. Only later do I realize "party" means massacre.

Guerrillas, drug traffickers, far-right death squads all tossed their victims into the Magdalena. A good chunk of those 85,000 disappeared floated down the Magdalena in pieces.

Down the river these bodies drifted, every witness turning their back on the horror. After countless bodies floated by Puerto Berrio, someone made a decision. No one remembers who, but a tradition was born. The town decided that it would fish out the floating bodies. Firemen boated out and dragged out the floating, swelling corpses. The authorities would give a quick review of the bodies. In the avalanche of the death, there was little time for a full investigation to discover the dead's names. Forms were signed, stamped, and with the bureaucracy satisfied, the John and Jane Does were laid to eternal rest.

In a ratty corner of Puerto Berrio's cemetery, they started burying the anonymous dead, known here as NN. The bodies kept floating, the firemen kept fishing them out, and the wall of tombs of the NNs grew larger. And then—again, no one knows who, why, or when—the people of Puerto Berrio collectively decided to start a tradition of charity and solidarity. The people of the town started adopting the individual tombs of the disappeared. They tended the abandoned tombs. And in return, they prayed to the souls of the disappeared, asking for favors.

And it worked.

The dead shall have their day. In Puerto Berrio, Monday is the Day of Dead, when the locals and the spirits mix. The grave digger is a cheerful, talkative sort. Ramon Morales's job is digging graves and handling corpses. He's a bulldog of a man: short, squat, and shiny bald. He has reflector glasses and three chains around his exposed neck, a crucifix, a ring with a large black rock, and a medallion made of an old one-peso coin. He looks like the graveyard's bouncer, manning the velvet rope for the one club where everyone gets in sooner or later.

"People believe that those who go to the beyond, their souls can intercede for us left behind here in this vale of tears, because that's where we're living, in the vale of tears."

We wander through the graveyard, passing through pleasing white gravestones, on to the NN section of the graveyard. Ramon dabs the sweat from his forehead with his poncho. It's a wall of vaults, five tombs high. The wall thankfully offers us some shade.

"It's not that you go to any old tomb and start praying. The belief is that those souls who are not doing well, less protected, who don't have any family, they will help you more. These people who are buried and forgotten, their families don't know where they are; these souls will work harder to make the prayers come true," says Ramon.

Across the wall are the plaques of thanks the devotees have paid for. Engraved in gray marble is a portrait of Jesus praying. Sketched into the rock, it reads: "To someone I never met, I consider you a friend because you were at my side when I needed you," signed "G.D." People ask the spirits of the disappeared for work, health, or help with relationship trouble.

"These people have got jobs; they've won lotteries and chances. They've got opportunities for work and to study, to improve the situation in their homes."

I like this deal: the locals treat the souls like the family they no longer have, and wait to be helped out. Along the wall, there are touching plaques. "Thank you for the favors received," with a plastic cup of fresh flowers on the tomb's shelf. The locals compete for the dead souls.

Janet goes to her tomb, touches it, crosses herself. Unlocking the glass door she paid to install, she cleans the tomb's face. Her tomb is the nicest tomb here. She has heavy indigenous features, gold hoops, black hair pulled back. She's a jolly woman in her late twenties. In her tomb, she's set up four little statues: three of the Virgin Mary, one of Jesus on the cross.

Janet asks me not to use her second name. That's common enough, but her reason is a new one: she and her two older sisters all converted to the evangelical church and they don't know she's returned to the Catholic Church.

"I've always loved coming to cemeteries. And here I didn't have anyone, so one day I came here. This tomb was very dirty, ugly. So I chose it. Now I had someone to visit, so I took it." She laughs. "I chose someone who didn't have anyone to care for them, to visit them. And after all there is a human being buried there. And an abandoned tomb looks ugly.

"In other towns, when you go to the NNs section, it's so sad. It's like they dug a hole for an animal. It's sad to think there's a person buried there. They just throw dirt over them and that's it!

"And I started thinking: What should I call him? Jesus and Mary, that's it! Then I thought, what if he doesn't like the name?" And she laughs again. "Well, I'll name him that anyway!"

She doesn't know anything about her soul, except that he is a friend. And a lucky charm. She played the local lottery with all she knows of her friend—05-03-05, the date he was buried. Jesus Mary didn't let her down.

She won $2,500.

I SPEAK TO THE LOCAL priest of Puerto Berrio, Father Juan Jose Cardenas.

"In this situation of the violence, many people lost their loved ones. They haven't found their loved ones they're searching for, so what do they find? An NN that was floating down the river, fished out, and buried. So they adopt them at once. Now they have someone to pray for, to speak to, and to have some sort of consolation."

You can split the priests of Colombia in two: dullards whose weekly highlight is the Sunday lunch at the local rich man's house, and fascinating analysts of Colombian society, intellectuals who drink whiskey and chat. Cardenas was the smart type.

"An NN in itself is an act of violence. An act of violence, a victim of violence who they want to eliminate. And to avoid any judicial consequences, they throw them into the river and so they rub out any trace of this person. So the person is silenced and forgotten. And the crime is unpunished. So what do the people do? As a form of social resistance to this violence, they adopt the victims. The killers want to wipe this person from the face of the earth and the people are bringing the victim back, making sure they're never forgotten."

"When you see people praying for people who have been forgotten, to pray for people who have been disappeared, it's an expression of charity."

Elizabeth Gonzalez sweeps the cemetery under a midday sun that hugs like a blanket of lava. She cleans the cemetery and is Ramon's wife. She has the look of an Italian grandmother; graying hair pulled back, glasses.

"I chose a NN and cleaned it up. . . . I asked that my husband do well in his job as the grave digger. And that we get our daily bread.

"That night I dreamt of the NN. I saw him all black, all skinny, and I got scared. He spoke to me but I didn't reply. He was ugly, ugly, ugly. I woke up in the middle of the night and thought, I can't keep on with this . . . to think of little me here alone with the NN, I couldn't." She smiles at the thought that this is ridiculous. "I never returned to his tomb.

"Obviously, it's not the dead you should fear. It's the living."

I RETURN TO MEDELLIN TO see Cachote. His face tells of some sour months. Once smooth as plastic, now his face is gaunt. Black bags line black eyes. His small apartment is sparse, as if he moved in hours earlier. There is a sofa, a stereo, and on the wall a crucifix. A thick cloud of sweet-smelling *cripy* marijuana smoke hangs in the air. A life of killing ain't brought him much.

His only people outside of cocaine, his friends and lovers in the gay scene are falling one by one to AIDS. His own dead are catching up on him.

"It's constant. My deaths terrorize me constantly."

He's taking regular tugs on his joint. Something in this apartment feels like the end.

"I have a lot of nightmares. Because all your dead, all the deaths you possess, they haunt you. They're always there."

I can't see them, but I know they're there: a whirlwind of ghosts swirling around him. The joint burns down. There's not much left.

"I can be good, fine. And then the dreams begin. Images come back to me of people saying: 'Please don't do it!' or just the blood. . . ."

Empty baggies, residued with white powder, litter the table in front of him.

"Every time I commit my murder, I take drugs to get away from everything I just did. Well . . . the drugs bring on depression," he tells me.

He's trapped in a hellish circle: murder, three days of drugs, partying, and sex to dull the senses. Is he killing because he's trapped in the cartel system? Or is he killing so he can afford three days of nonstop partying? I can no longer tell.

He takes the last tug on the joint. A dreamy look passes over his face.

"If I could go back, I would be a different person. Now there's no time."

The full comedown of a life of cocaine. The life has been lived, now the bill is arriving. There is a realization that doors are closed behind you, that there is no way back. Cachote knows that his boss, Alex, will never let him go free. No drug lord who has ordered hits lets an assassin retire, not with all those potential witness testimonies remembered.

I ask about the future. It's a dumb question. There's a real simple answer to what Cachote will be doing when he's thirty-five—he'll be dead. That's his future. He knows it and lives accordingly: a frontloaded life of all the sex and partying he can endure and not a penny saved.

He shakes his head at the question. The joint has run out. He stubs it out in the ashtray.

"I missed out on a lot in my childhood, playing around, sharing time with the family because of ambition. When the ambition touched me, I wanted to have everything in my hands immediately and that's how I became who I am."

What is left but the self-pity? No one else will pity him. He chose this. He can justify it all he wants, but the end feels close. This is a man who sees the end is approaching and notes the room is getting hotter.

"I do believe there is heaven and there is hell. But right now, we're here on earth. The real hell is here on earth." His eyes keep flicking to his door.

"If I stay in this business, sooner or later, death will arrive.

I can't expect anything good if I stay in this. And life returns to you what you give. Sadly, for me, life returns to you what you've given."

There's nothing left to say. I leave him in his apartment, sitting alone, his back to the wall, those eyes fixed on his own front door, waiting.

THE TAXI BOMBS THROUGH MEDELLIN'S narrow streets. The kilo of cocaine is ready to move on and I'm on my way to see it move. The taxi slams to a stop in a traffic jam. A crowd stands in the middle of the road, craning its neck, snarling traffic. I climb out of the taxi and know what's beyond the line of people.

On the sidewalk, the man lies on his back. His face is fixed on the clean blue sky above us. He's around thirty and a thin stream of dark red blood flows from his head to the gutter. Next to him is the bag of chips he was eating when his killer shot him in the head. The police have cordoned off the block. We stand behind the plastic yellow lines, staring at the corpse, waiting for him to do something. He does nothing. Investigators scour the street for clues. He's been dead for thirty minutes. The shock is gone. Young men take selfies with the corpse behind them.

I ask around and no one knows what happens—or they don't want to tell the foreigner. A homeless man is playing the sage of the street. We've all got a role to play.

"My fourth dead man this month. Someone sent this man to see the devil. You know, he must have done something."

Men in white jumpsuits arrive and wrap the corpse in plastic. He's loaded into the meat wagon.

CHAPTER 8

THE CAPO

THE KILO'S TIME IN MEDELLIN IS COMING to an end. It's time to move on and abroad. The kilo's owner, the drug trafficker, will make the decision where.

At the center of this storm of money and murder sits Alex. An ex–police officer, he is one of hundreds of drug traffickers who export cocaine. The kilo is ready to move, to be shipped abroad. And it is Alex who will decide where it goes. Alex is a master of cocaine, if anyone can be said to control something as anarchic as cocaine. He sits at the center of this industry like a spider in a web. He bridges the coca farmer in the mountains with the consumer in the United States, Europe, and the rest of the world. His orders move the kilo forward. On his orders, the kilo's obstacles are removed, through bribery or murder.

"You know what we really need?" he asks me.

Alex leans over the table, a face solemn as if ready to share the secret of the universe.

"War!"

And he laughs like a burst of gunfire.

"War is what we need," he says, now all smiles. "Get rid of all these small traffickers. There's too much chaos, too much confusion. We need order.

"War," he grins.

We're breakfasting in his favorite spot, an expensive hotel on the outskirts of Medellin. Waiters glide with silver trays of scrambled eggs and plates of fruit. It's one of those gorgeous mornings when you think the people of Medellin may be right to boast they have the finest weather in the world. And yet, here we talk of war.

"War is constant for us. This peace we're living in is not normal. And it's brought its own problems. I'm sick of it," he says. "When we had Pablo Escobar, there were rules and it ran smoother," he says. Behind him, at another table, are his two bodyguards. Silent, they sit and stare at us. "There has to be rules. Can't have people doing whatever they want."

Peace has allowed too many traffickers to rise in power. The cartels are the business giants, but in their shadows operate hundreds of independent traffickers. A proliferation of drug lords is pulling the industry in every different direction, causing chaos. The clarity of war will sweep away the weak, leaving only those strong enough to be a drug lord. Alex is searching for order in the chaotic world of cocaine.

"If there are rules, well . . . then the world is yours."

Today, his look is of the international businessman: Salvatore Ferragamo loafers, dark Hugo Boss jeans, a white Armani short-sleeve shirt, capped with Gucci glasses. He's wearing his black hair longer than when I last saw him. Each time I see Alex, he looks different. Changing his appearance is one way to stay ahead of his enemies. On the table, he's laid out his two iPhones.

"There is so much cocaine out there. Anyone can grab a few kilos, send them abroad. And now they're walking around telling people they're traffickers," he says.

Medellin hasn't had a drug war for a decade. Like recessions, drug wars come around every decade or so. No one wants them, but still they come on time anyway. No one, that is, except men like Alex. There are always men who find the meaning in life in war. Perhaps he wants a new drug war just for the thrill of it, a time to show his mettle. Maybe somewhere out in the endless jungles when he was a police officer, he got stuck on the thrill of hunting men and dodging death. Some get the war bug and never lose it. Daily life can be difficult and gray after the psychedelic rainbow of a life at the extreme. War becomes all that matters.

Alex hopes a single leader, a king of cocaine, will impose order on the chaos. Alex is smart and convincing—I have little doubt that he'll get what he wants.

And, I think: Man, these traffickers are fucking insane.

What I don't know is that he has an even bolder plan.

ALEX IS A RICH MAN. He is a man of violence. A man of some charm. A man who believes himself above the world in which he operates. A man who aims to succeed. His morality is practical. What needs to be done is done—what's left to be said? A man who knows the cocaine business will kill him before he reaches old age. Live a life of riches at 200 miles per hour and die young. That's the deal with cocaine and he's happy with it.

He sits atop a small criminal empire. Dozens of people across the country work for him: men, women who travel to towns like La Gabarra to buy the kilo, those who transport it, those who protect it, and those who send it abroad. He has neighborhoods in the city of Medellin, run by combos that answer to him. The secret to Alex's longevity is that he is never in the same room as a kilo of cocaine. His power comes by pulling strings from afar, knowing where to buy the kilos of cocaine and where to sell them.

Men like Alex are the shadow power in Colombia, the leaders of an alternate society that runs parallel to the legal one. They are some of the wealthiest men on the continent and wield the power of life and death over all around them. For all the riches, it's a precarious life. Authorities and rivals are always around the corner, waiting to send Alex to prison or to the grave.

Alex is the new generation of traffickers, who live in the shadows, thriving in the low profile. The InSight Crime Foundation calls the new traffickers "the Invisibles." This new generation of drug lords look like graduates of business school: yuppie psychopaths. Their money flows through the legal economy, building shopping malls and funding start-ups. His cocaine ends up in Europe and North America. Like all good businessmen, he dreams of expanding into China. Cocaine always chases the money.

And like a good business school alumnus, Alex has his self-help bible: *The 48 Laws of Power,* by Robert Greene. It's a series of aphorisms, drawing on Machiavelli, Sun Tzu, and others. "Win through your actions, never through argument," "Crush your enemy totally," and "Keep others in suspended terror: Cultivate an air of unpredictability."

ALEX'S NAME HAD LONG PRECEDED my meeting him. Sicarios and combo members had all described this man on the rise. His employees described him in awestruck terms: smart, classy. A gentleman. A man to be respected for who he was, not just for the injury he could inflict. Murdering enemies, dating actresses. A man of taste and violence. An aristocratic delinquent.

It was a night of drinks and dancing. A friend, Marcus, got off the phone and said stonily, "Alex wants to meet you."

"Leave it. Let's see him another day." I was with another reporter and we were relaxing after a day shooting a documentary. We were having fun. To meet Alex would mean that heavy orbit of violence and death that surround these men.

"A man like Alex . . . you don't get another chance to meet him," he said. This was not an invitation; Alex needed to meet me to ensure I was who I said I was.

On the ride over, Marcus stressed at the taxi's slow pace through the night traffic. He snorted drugs to calm himself. The taxi driver looked at him and turned his eyes back to the road.

"Why do the fucking cars of this city move so slow? The police ought to arrest these drunk drivers clogging up the roads," he said.

Finally the taxi arrived at a gas station in the San Diego neighborhood of Medellin.

To one side, a black sports car idled. A well-built man with a short military haircut got out. He jabbed his hand out for a crushing handshake. He flashed a prince's smile, confident that all those around him will aim to please him.

In the car, his girlfriend Diana waved sweetly from the passenger seat. On the driver's seat was his Glock handgun. Techno drifted out of the car.

"Do you know who I am?"

I nodded.

He sized me up for a moment. And now that I saw him up

close, I caught a mad, jolly glint in his eyes. This man was capable of anything.

"Whatever you need in Medellin, just ask." He offered me the city as if it were his to give. We shook hands again and he got back into his car. It roared off into that orange glow that is Medellin at night.

And I exhaled.

"SONS OF BITCHES," GROWLS CARLOS as we drive past a parked police car.

Carlos is suspicious of me; he keeps looking at me in the rearview mirror. That's his job: to suspect everyone who comes close to Alex. He is Alex's right-hand man. And he has the habit of muttering "hijueputas" ("sons of bitches") every time we see the police.

Carlos is driving Alex's white sports car. In the back is Katia, a sometime prostitute, and Marcus, who finds women for Alex. And in the middle, myself.

"We have Mexican friends coming in tomorrow. We're going to give them a welcome party. Marcus—three women for each. We'll eat and then go to a club," says Alex.

I wince. Now I know something I don't want to know. And if anything goes wrong, any arrests, any piece of bad luck, I could be blamed.

"Yes, I'll get some beauties. Katia, you've got two friends ready, right?"

Katia, beautiful, blond, nods.

"I'll get the others," Marcus says. "Find some girls that like to party, take 2C-B, and fuck."

2C-B is the narcotic of choice of Colombia's narcos. 2,5-dimethoxy-4-bromophenethylamine. Synthetic, it's sometimes called "pink cocaine." Imagine the "Fuck yeah!" of cocaine mixed with a light psychedelia of LSD. Here in Colombia, 2C-B is the drug of success. A gram of cocaine is three dollars. A gram of 2C-B is thirty dollars.

Carlos turns to face Marcus: "Look, I don't give a fuck if they like to party and snort 2C-B. Just make sure they're ready to fuck."

Chastised, Marcus replies: "Sí, señor."

Later, Marcus tells me: "It's a big deal they're working on. That's a celebration!"

I WAKE UP THE NEXT day and scan the headlines. It's bad. The newspaper reports Mexicans have been arrested arriving at Bogota's El Dorado airport. The police say they belong to the Sinaloa Cartel.

Options: If I flee the city, it's a sure sign of guilt, and my only hope would be to keep going until I'm out of the country. If my guilt has already been decided, they'll have someone watching my hotel. The long ride to the airport is an easy stretch to kill someone. If I'm wrong and no one suspects me, an erratic mad dash out of the city will be suspicious. I wait and see.

It's a strangely silent day. No one calls. I stay in my hotel room. As the sun sets, it starts to rain, a tropical Medellin downpour. Lightning strikes and thunder booms around the city.

At 9 P.M., my phone rings in between the thunder. It's Marcus. He introduced me to Alex, so if I'm a snitch, according to underworld law he is responsible—"He who introduces, pays." Marcus doesn't have a chance to escape punishment, but the mafia may make him believe he can survive if he makes it right.

I've known him for ten years. His voice is strained like I've never heard.

"I need to see you. It's urgent," he says.

I need time to think. Somewhere public.

"Tomorrow in the Juan Valdez, El Poblado?"

"No, now. I'm outside your hotel."

There's no escape.

"Okay, coming down."

I hang up. I grab my small knife and pocket it. The blade is short and fat and a rapid throat jab will kill. I slowly walk out of my room, composing myself with each step. My hand is wrapped around the sheathed knife in my pocket. I know enough of what happens in torture sessions that they'll have to kill me cleanly out here on the road. I'm not going to a warehouse.

I look out the window from the seventh floor. In the sheets of rain, I see a taxi, its lights flashing. I walk down the hotel's stairs. My heart beats crazily. I regret ever doing this story. I had a whole world to report on, and I chose the cartels. I'm a fool.

I step out into the rain. I look all around for men on motorbikes. My hand is clammy, gripping the knife.

Marcus is in the front seat of a taxi. There are two other men with him I don't know. With my thumb, I gently ease the small knife out of the sheath, keeping it in my pocket.

"Hello," says Marcus, his voice different. "I've got the flu."

My fist clenches around the knife.

"Can you lend me a hundred dollars?"

With my free hand, I take my wallet out of my pocket, and single-handedly open it and pluck out the bills. I'm not letting go of this knife. I say good-bye and walk backward to the hotel. I return to my room soaked by the rain. I had misunderstood—a friend wanted to borrow some money. Hanging with these criminals has me on edge. My heart continues to hammer.

I never ask about the Mexicans.

THE DIRTY SECRET OF THE drug war in Latin America is how many drug lords start off as police and soldiers. Fighting cocaine, they're exposed to her, seduced by her. It's the perfect training ground for future traffickers—they see how the business works up close, learning the chinks in the security forces' armor.

Alex doesn't talk about his time in the police. What's there to say? He was out there in the mountains and jungles killing guerrillas and trying not to get aced himself. But unlike so many in cocaine, he had options in life. That's what makes him different: he doesn't need to do this. He wanted it.

Colombia's long-running civil conflict birthed in him— and the country—a deep cynicism. He doesn't believe in the peace process.

"Colombia will never know peace. That's not in us, not in our blood."

Of course, if you believe that everyone is evil, that war is permanent, that justifies going out to kill whenever needed. Get your vengeance in first, as they said in Northern Ireland.

As he progressed in the police, he met people in the underworld. He had something they wanted—access to intelligence. Within a few years, Alex began working with the Gulf Clan cartel. Then he began working for himself.

Like all these traffickers, Alex's politics are hard-right. The mafia considers themselves brave entrepreneurs. The widow of the trafficker known as "Jabon," a truly bloodthirsty monster, passes her time on Facebook criticizing left-wing politicians for trying to ruin the country "for those of us who work so hard to get ahead." The most bloodthirsty drug lord in a decade was her work. One drug trafficker launched a campaign against a left-wing political party, a war that would lead to the political genocide of up to five thousand party members. Two presidential candidates were murdered in one year alone. And look at the ranks of the most right-wing politicians in the country and you see family relations to organized crime: the senator whose father was a famous trafficker, the close presidential advisor and cousin of Pablo Escobar.

It's unsurprising: cocaine is capitalism, stripped of any veneer of respectability. It's the law of the market wrapped in blood and claws.

I meet his girlfriend Diana one morning. We grab a coffee. She is stunning, with a gym-firm body, caramel skin, and beautiful long hair.

"He was never a *carranga resusicitada* [slum boy who became rich] who came from the slums, who killed people and extorts and does bad things to get ahead," she says. "He wanted to be the bad boy, but really isn't."

"He came from the best family. He had everything in life. And maybe that created a hole in him—having everything in life, he likes to get money the easiest way," said Diana.

Why does Alex speak with me? I never ask. I believe he enjoys our chats. He has an unusual interest in the world beyond cocaine. He asks about America, life in England. He is more curious about the rest of the world than normal in the conversations of the underworld. Our chats are a way for a man to understand how he arrived at this very peculiar juncture in life.

Does he see me as a lifeline if things suddenly turn bad?

Maybe he considers me an ace up the sleeve to serve as a bridge to the Colombian government or the United States in case of an urgent surrender. In the underworld, there's always an angle.

Still, the interviews are delicate. If, after a talk, the trafficker regrets anything he has said to me, he'll have me killed. It's that simple. Even being around them stretches the risk. If Alex is arrested while I'm in the city, he may assume I am the *sapo* (snitch) and will kill me. I am trusted, but no one excels in cocaine by trusting too much.

So, I don't want to hear anything about current shipments—some secrets are too dangerous to know. He speaks in general terms about the necessity of murder in the business, but never specific cases. These interviews aren't meant to be tickets to prison cells. Just because we don't speak of it, I cannot forget them. Cocaine promises glamour but it's a business built on murder.

One hit man fresh out of prison says of Alex: "He killed those who needed it."

Behind the charm, this was a man who killed people.

Alex's most important asset in cocaine is the routes. These are the pathways from Colombia to the rest of the world to sell the cocaine. It's the knowledge of where the cocaine should travel, who needs to be bribed along the way. The routes fund everything else. The crew, the sicarios, are paid from the sale of cocaine abroad. Alex's routes go to Italy and Mexico. Alex deals directly with Italy's mafia and those of Mexico. In the deals, they agree on the quantity and price of the kilos to be sent. If it's for Italy, it goes through Venezuela. If it goes to Mexico, it will go via the Pacific Ocean. When traffickers negotiate their surrender, it's the routes they hand over to authorities.

The shipments of cocaine vary by size. How much cash does he have to spare at the moment? Each ton costs Alex about a million dollars. For big shipments, traffickers may seek investors. At times, Alex works with the Gulf Clan, investing in their shipments.

As much as traffickers spend thinking about exporting the cocaine, they spend time thinking on how to import all the cash. Some use human couriers bringing back suitcases rammed with bricks of cash from Europe and Mexico. A ton of cocaine can cost $10 million in Mexico. That's 100,000 $100 bills to bring back. Narcos launder their money through properties and businesses. Alex has properties in Europe, Mexico, and throughout Colombia. Still, the language of cocaine is cash. Alex keeps large amounts of cash on him for emergencies and also because when he needs to buy more cocaine, it's always in cash. Narcos hide their cash around the country in so-called *caletas,* secret compartments stuffed with cash. Police found $80 million from one narco, nickname Lollipop, alone in a few of his apartments and houses. The police believe this was a fraction of the cash he stored.

FARC guerrillas buried many of their millions from cocaine in the jungle. On a mission, an elite unit of troops found around $15 million of the guerrillas' money. The 145 soldiers took the money and went wild, hiring prostitutes and paying them with motorbikes. The army realized something was up when grunts who earn $200 a month arrived at the army base driving new trucks and wearing gold chains around their necks. Half were caught, tried, and convicted. The other half escaped with many on the run today.

Drug traffickers are as obsessed by the glamour of the underworld as anyone. Alex loves the films *The Godfather* and *Scarface,* frequently quoting the latter's line, "The world is yours!" He orders the kids in his combos to watch the movie. He calls himself a *bandido* (bandit), tapping into a romantic ideal in Latin America of men and women who are forced into lives of crime by corrupted societies. Breaking the law is the only path for an honorable man in a rotten society. But Alex knows it's not true. The dirty secret of organized crime is that it is impossible to traffic without help from the authorities. Police, soldiers, port inspectors, politicians, customs officers, coast guards, there's usually someone who is paid off to get cocaine out of Colombia. One trafficker bribed a US agent with Immigration and Custom Enforcement who was working on a large operation targeting Colombian drug lords. For $20,000 in cash and prostitution, the agent got the drug lord's indictment dismissed and helped him enter the United States. Cocaine, the ultimate corruptor.

"The authorities never lose. When you think about it, we're the suckers. They work with us and they get rich. And if we go down, then they take the credit for our capture and then they make deals with any trafficker who will replace us," says Alex, with a laugh that says the joke is not funny.

COCAINE AND SEX. THE SEXIEST of drugs. From cocaine's beginnings, sex was on everyone's mind.

"Woe to you, my Princess, when I come. I will kiss you quite red and feed you till you are plump. And if you are forward, you shall see who is the stronger, a gentle little girl who doesn't eat enough, or a big wild man who has cocaine in his body." That was Sigmund Freud laying it down in a letter to his fiancée.

Sex is a prime mover in cocaine. It's not a perk of the job;

it's why the young men sell their souls to traffic the drug. When the young men dream of lives in cocaine, they conjure images of rivers of money, power, and an endless line of beautiful women. Alex is no different. With his charm, Alex is a man whom a woman could introduce to her family and with a straight face say he is a "businessman."

"Alex loves his guns, the exotic ones, the ones in gold, with ivory, the rare ones," says Marcus. "But he got into this for the women. He is sick for women."

It's one of Colombia's open secrets how many models and actresses end up with narcos. These are men of power, wealth and violence, so attractive to many women (it's common to see the richest sons of executives and politicians acting as if they were narcos). Narcos like things that sparkle, and beaming through the nation's television screens catches their attention. The country's top news anchor had an affair with Pablo Escobar. Some models charge by the night with the narcos for $15,000, $20,000, $30,000, confirming the narcos' sense that everyone has their price.

Marcus gets models and actresses for Alex, earning his spot in the ecosystem of cocaine.

"He'll call me and say: 'I'm here at this club or restaurant, come!' And I'll phone two women he might like and we'll all arrive there."

Alex has tried to teach Marcus to be more correct.

"He's always telling you to read his book, *The 48 Rules of Power*. He keeps asking me: How far are you on the book?"

He likes Alex a lot, a real friend. But he knows how these men are.

"I've dealt with these men all my life. Trust me: not one, not one, not one, has an ounce of goodness in him. These are men motivated by evil. It's like when an appliance burns up because there was a short in the electricity. These men are born with the short. They're born bad."

THE MUSIC VIDEO IS BEING filmed in a garage. It's so dingy for a second, I fear it's a snuff movie and I'm the star. The director films Carlos singing. He comes from one of the most ferocious slums of the city. He hopes his way out is singing reggaetón. In a low voice, his arm swings, taking in the set, and in a low voice he says: "The mafia is paying for all this."

Carlos is starting out. I don't know if he has talent; the voice is all modified. He's handsome and has the look of a heart-wrenched young man, pining for his woman. The mafia pay for various careers in music and modeling. If Carlos becomes a hit, they can launder money through his career. It also keeps the drug lords in the orbits of the models and actresses.

Carlos lip-synchs his song into the camera. He's giving that hands clasped over his chest, doe-eyed look. Behind him dance three beautiful women. Laura's body curves and releases with the beats. She's dressed in black stockings, a see-through mesh shirt, and black masking tape crossed over her breasts. She thrusts her waist. She draws her hands over her breasts. Her back arches.

The director calls cut for a break and the sex drains from her face. A flick of the switch and she is back to normal. She's faking it and every man here knows it, but right now each man would kill for her if so ordered. Laura comes over and sits next to me. Laura is a model, dancer, and part-time prostitute. Marcus introduced Laura to Alex.

"Alex is different," she says. "He's funny. And he has a

charm to him. I never imagined he was involved in drug trafficking. I learned that later"

Their first meeting was in a bar.

"We talked about my cell phone and I mentioned it was broken. He immediately took out of his pocket three hundred dollars and told me to buy a new one," she says. That's more than a monthly wage for half the country. "We moved on to the hotel."

"I wanted to be a singer. But I never had the voice." She looks at me quickly and laughs. She's revealed a dream too personal, opened herself up too much. "It's nice to work in the industry somehow."

As the narcos have lowered their profiles, so have their women. The old-style narcos liked their women impossible. The mythology is that the first Colombian cocaine traffickers made deals in Texas strip clubs in the late 1970s. The men were awed by these giant Texan strippers, their large breasts. Business cemented, the traffickers returned home and demanded their women be operated to get the exact same body specs placed on their tiny Andean bodies.

"Lady Tits" was the perfect woman of the underworld, a constant sight at the city's top clubs. Blond, industrial-sized tits, a titanic ass, and a tiny, elf-sized waist. Nothing looked natural and nothing was supposed to. She flitted from narco to narco. Each relationship she earned more and more in "maintenance" and the narcos kept paying for ever more surgery. By the time I met her, she had ceased to look human; grotesque, twisted into fake curves, false arches, a body crudely contorted by crude men's desires. The clubs were filled with these women.

When around the narcos, she always wore a smile. As soon as the narcos left, Lady's smile would vanish and she would rub the top of her back. Her breasts were causing her constant, aching back pain.

But the Invisibles have their own taste in women. Their taste is for what they call "fitness," lean bodies of hours spent in the gym. Six-packs. And Lady Tits dropped out of favor like last year's fashions. No one could benefit from her, so the invitations stopped. I asked her friends after her only to have the question breezily waved away. The last I heard she had lost her mind, wandering the streets in her bathrobe, muttering to strangers, complaining of her never-ending back pain that, now poor, she is doomed to carry around with her forever.

She's twenty-eight.

ALEX USED TO TELL FRIENDS that he didn't want to live until fifty. Then he met Diana. She studies and models on the side. Alex won her over in their first nights by filling a jacuzzi with thirty-five bottles of champagne, at a thousand dollars a bottle. Here was something he could spend his money on.

Affairs in cocaine are transactional—the meter whirs with every kiss and caress. One narco's girlfriend told me she spends $50,000 of her boyfriend's money a month on clothes. She's received seven cars in her lifetime. She's twenty-four. Every day, she's in the gym, working on the tool that earns her money. She's working hard to make sure the trafficker stays with her—there are a lot of women out there ready to lure him away.

These women have a coldness to them, a hardness to their eyes. It's a strange look: beautiful faces, tight bodies, and the eyes of the dead.

She posts pictures of herself on Instagram daily—where

she shows off her body and provides an easy way for narcos to get in touch. Under each photo is a platitude about being her "best self" or some other nonsense.

Diana is different. She and Alex act like lovers, partners. Every time I meet Diana I can't believe she's with a trafficker. Her beauty is complete, the type that pauses a room when she enters. A beauty that makes her the center of any gathering. The beauty of the lonely.

This is a woman who can do anything in life; every door will be open to her brilliant smile. Behind the model's smile, there is a sharp intelligence.

Alex met her where the traffickers congregate: the city's clubs.

DARK TECHNO MUSIC HAMMERS THROUGHOUT the nightclub. The narco party is in full swing. Drug traffickers and their women dominate the dance floor. Costly bottles of whiskey are pushed into hands, drug-dazed faces are illuminated by the club's flashing lights, and the dust of the purest narcotics in the world hangs in the air.

This is the glamour of cocaine. It's here that the trafficker feels they've reached the summit. It's in the nightclubs where the traffickers show off all they've won—the new actress girl-friend, the expensive car parked outside, the costly Swiss watch. It's a chance to provoke envy. These traffickers can't make it half an hour without one of the seven deadly sins.

The clubs feel like the center of this business of dreams. Cocaine has that nervous energy of a casino where everyone keeps winning money, sex is everywhere, and at any moment, someone might step up and put a bullet in your head. That's the deal in cocaine and people are happy to take it.

Step carefully here. Bump into someone, spill a drink, it could be fatal. An aura of repressed violence pulses through the air, a spring compressed, a cobra coiled. There are no good people here tonight. Anyone who stepped in here by mistake, looking for a normal night out, felt the vibe and left immediately. A heavy mafia mood is what hangs in this air.

The second floor is the VIP section. There drug traffickers celebrate; brothers hug, champagne pops, narcotics are snorted, and lovers kiss. Like an electrical current, rumors flow through the club that these traffickers are celebrating a narco deal.

The girlfriends look down on the dance floor smiling, mouths curved in sex and cruelty. Dancing, they writhe as if casting spells with their bodies. Stunning, the women are dressed in expensive dresses, their bodies sculpted to the millimeter by the finest surgeons. Pupils swelled by drugs, they look like mad queens surveying their subjects.

In a corner, killers for hire share jokes and a snort.

The techno hammers hard and the men dance like punches. The dance of the damned. All know their ends are coming sooner, not later. Prison, murder, extradition to the United States. It's coming. Enjoy tonight because tomorrow never comes: the philosophy of a life in cocaine.

The DJ lets the track fade away. Silence. Something's coming.

"Bring it!" a woman in a skintight silver dress screams.

The bars of the next song tinkle in.

The club explodes. Everyone is on their feet, hands in their air, bodies dancing, faces tilted upward, eyes half-closed by the drugs.

A woman's sultry voice comes over the speakers. It's the Assassins' prayer. And the music blasts in. The whole club dances now, even the barmen serving the drinks. A congregation united in ecstasy.

"Fuck," says Marcus. "Whenever I hear this song, I think someone is going to get shot."

Dancing wildly, her arms curling above her head like two serpents, is Dalia. She's one of the most beautiful women in the club. Also one of the deadliest.

"That girl breathes bullets," says Marcus, his phrase for the dangerous. He introduced me to Dalia some years ago—when she was killing for money. Dalia's specialty was to approach men in clubs and poison them. Her boyfriend used to ride the motorbike and kill with the gun.

Dalia got smart and realized she could make more money dating rich men. Now Dalia is a social media model. She posts an unstoppable flow of photos of herself, along with inspirational quotes from intellectuals like Gandhi, Einstein, and Justin Bieber. It's online that she meets her boyfriends, who pay to maintain her. Dalia divides her times between dating musicians and narcos. If she's here, I'm guessing she's back to narcos.

Dalia loves her 2C-B and tonight she's drugged to the eyeballs. Dalia will make the party go for three days. I say hello to her, and she hugs me. It's hard to talk in the club. I step back. A narco steps over and starts whispering in her ear. She ignores him, closing her eyes and dancing again. He looks at her insistently. She keeps dancing to herself. He walks away. If there's anyone who can handle themselves here, it's Dalia.

These are the intense parties, becoming vortexes for many. When the nightclub shuts, the crowds bundle into chauffeured trucks and it's out to the farms that surround the city. Parties with no rules that run for days. Sex everywhere, trios, foursomes, drugged-up orgies. Arguments that end in shoot-outs. Bodies buried in shallow graves. Lives on the edge find catharsis through the most savage delights.

The sensory overload, the sheer voltage of it all.

Alex lost himself in the parties. The 2C-B became daily; a snort to begin the day that starts at 3 P.M. and bumps throughout the day to keep going. Diana would talk of children and Alex would vigorously nod even as he snorted more 2C-B. "I had to suffer. He didn't go to a clinic. For him it was breakfast, lunch, and dinner."

Diana laid it out clearly: her or 2C-B.

"I told him that if he didn't stop, he would pass those bad habits on to his children. He stopped immediately."

NARCOS ARE ECCENTRIC AND SUPERSTITIOUS. Believing in nothing, they believe in anything. Alex consults witches for protection help shipping out the kilos. When the kilo will move, Alex will pay Danilo for a spell to be cast.

Danilo needs a black cat. In a week's time, he will take a cat to a mountaintop outside of Medellin . . . and he will perform a ritual. If it's successful, the ritual will help shipments of cocaine avoid detection as they leave Colombia. The cat will not survive.

Aged around thirty, Danilo has a shaved head, sweatpants, and an Armani T-shirt.

Colombia is a melting pot of gods—Catholics pray next to singing Protestants alongside spirits brought over from Africa by slaves. Throughout the jungles stalk the old gods of the indigenous. When normal life is one of chaos and violence, superstitions become rational, the eternal striving to understand the chaos.

"The jobs people ask for are different. There are jobs to win back a loved one, to have someone fall in love with you, to sweeten a spouse. These are the 'good jobs,' you know what I mean? There are 'bad jobs,' too. Like wishing evil on someone, make it so someone doesn't get ahead in life, to split up a couple, or even killing someone with a disease," he says.

He says women come by every month to request a spell for making drug traffickers fall in love with them.

"I don't take on jobs like that. You don't want to be casting spells like that on those men and they find out," he says. In the supernatural, every action has a reaction.

"If I perform a job to make someone fall in love with you, that person won't act as they normally do because they'll have spirits controlling her. The spirits will follow her, changing how she behaves," he says. "She won't be the same person."

Danilo's is an eclectic set of beliefs. He mentions the devil, angels, the four elements (water, earth, fire, air), and after a while, I am lost. Some pay Danilo to cast a curse over others.

"They can be pursued by shadows that torment them. These shadows whisper to the person: 'If you don't kill yourself, we'll kill your family.'"

The narcos come calling for their own spells. The black cat is to be used for a ceremony he'll be performing this weekend.

"It's a spell for invisibility. . . . It's not real invisibility, it just means that things are harder to spot. A shipment will go through customs undetected by the police. The narcos like that."

He doesn't like casting this spell—as part of it, he'll have to kill the black cat. The cat will be cooked alive. Its bones will go with the shipment to make it invisible.

"Poor little cat," he says to himself.

"The underworld I see is a hell. These people have to live in this hell because in their past lives they were bad, they were killers," he says. "To escape this hell, they need to evolve their souls."

No trafficker has ever paid Danilo to evolve their soul.

LAW 47: "DO NOT GO past the mark you aimed for; In victory, learn when to stop." So instructs *The 48 Laws of Power.*

Alex has a bold plan that will allow him to realize the traffickers' dream: to retire from the business with money stashed away. Step off the ride on your terms, before you're forced off. He's made his money, he's had his fun. He wants to raise a family with Diana. He and she have been going to a clinic for treatment to help them conceive.

Alex wants traffickers to hand themselves over to the authorities, a coordinated surrender for a sweetheart deal: short prison sentences, million-dollar fines, their records wiped clean, and being allowed to keep the rest of their fortunes. The Gulf Clan wants such a deal. Otoniel publishes two videos, one for the Colombian people, one addressed to the pope.

Otoniel appears dressed in military fatigues. Overweight, his belly rolls forward. He wears the rubber boots of the countryside and stands before a plastic camouflage sheet (background vegetation can give away the location of where it was filmed). He reads from his piece of paper like a child reading his essay to the class, stumbling over every other sentence. He's aging badly, looking much older than his mid-forties. His face is gray, as if he never sees the sun, hiding from the CIA satellites in the sky. He wears a holster on each side.

"We want to be part of the end of the conflict, to achieve the total disarmament of all the armed groups in the country," he reads. There's the roar of the insects behind him and the regular cluck of a chicken.

"We want to go to Colombian justice with the guarantees that will lead to a national reconciliation." (He stumbles over "reconciliation," quickly looking up at the camera.) With the guarantees, "we're prepared to suspend all the illegal actions of the organization."

To the pope he says: "I'm a small farmer who has been forced for more than thirty years to carry arms. . . . I am convinced that the only exit for this conflict is dialogue. To this end, I humbly ask for your prayers so that this may become reality."

He calls his men "men of God."

These handovers have a complicated history. The Cali Cartel wanted to hand themselves over in the 1990s. They said: we've made enough money, let's negotiate and end the threat of a forever prison cell that hangs above us. This angered a generation of traffickers who had yet to make their fortunes. The old men had grown fat and complacent and the young wolves were hungry. A war broke out that effectively ended the Cali Cartel. The new cartel took over.

Medellin is in a more combustible situation—with no single king and countless traffickers out there working for themselves, working outside the cartel system. Like Alex himself. There are too many drug traffickers. It will be impossible to get them all to agree—some have just got their first taste of the business, the women, the riches. No way they'll give that up. It has to be all traffickers or it won't work. Alex knows a partial surrender of the drug lords will be suicide. Those who surrender will be picked off by those still in the business. This is why it needs to be war—clear out all those who won't agree to a surrender.

There's no guarantee that the government will go for this. The standard government line is that the government doesn't negotiate with cartels.

So Alex has a plan to reach peace: war.

AROUND THE TABLE, THREE COCAINE traffickers and a mass killer enjoy their ice creams. Alex is welcoming "Bunny," who is just out of prison.

"It's time for another war," says Bunny, the mass killer.

He looks for a reaction from the other men. They keep licking their ice creams. He shrugs and returns to his ice cream.

We're in the city's luxury shopping mall. Around us walk wealthy teenagers and pampered housewives.

Everyone here knows these men are traffickers—they exude it. The expensive clothing, the hair cut short, the granite in the eye. The shoppers don't look twice; it's as normal as a pit bull on the street—just don't get close enough for the bite.

But Bunny is something more—and everyone senses it. A scarier something.

Concentrating on her toy cell phone, a young girl of perhaps six years old walks into Bunny's chair. He lays his large hand on her hair, tousling her hair. Annoyed, she's perplexed as to why a big man and his chair were in her path. I catch the mother's look: her eyes are wide open, her fear behind a brittle smile. The pit bull has its paw on her baby girl.

"A beautiful girl," Bunny says, looking up at the mother. She nods. "Thank you," she says, taking her daughter's hand and walking off.

It's the small details, by themselves inconsequential, that tell everyone that Bunny is something to steer clear of. In this group he looks out of place: Alex and the others wear two-hundred dollar jeans, brand-name T-shirts, and expensive sneakers. Bunny is rocking supermarket jeans and heavy workmen boots. His skin is darker, more indigenous than the lighter-skinned traffickers. He's bulky, a physique of a life of manual labor, not toned in the gym under a trainer's guidance. All of these tiny clues tell that mother and everyone else that Bunny is from the countryside. And someone from the countryside sitting with traffickers means violence.

The reason why the notoriously racist Medellin traffickers accept Bunny is that he is a master of violence. Sicarios like Cachote are fine for gunning down a man in the center of Medellin. Men like Bunny have memories of destroying towns.

In the drug war, the city's violence has been functional, detached. The city kills with bombs and shootings. In the fight to control coca, the countryside has passed through a blood frenzy, massacres of impalings, chain saws, and rocks. The murders are as macabre as possible.

Bunny fought through this whirlwind of blood, only to emerge the other side eager for more. Formerly he was with the far-right death squads. He was finally captured and sentenced for homicides.

Then, just thirty days ago, he was released. On probation, Bunny went to straight to Alex for a job. And here he is, eating ice cream and itching to kill and be paid.

Alex says: "Bunny, business is good right now. But . . . Yes, at some point something may need to be done."

Bunny nods and stabs his ice cream with his spoon.

"Someone will break the truce. . . . And then war," says Bunny.

In a car thirty minutes later, Alex and Carlos talk. It's racing through the streets; traffic laws and rules are for everyday stiffs.

"Bunny's not going to do something stupid, is he?" Alex asks.

"He better not," replies Carlos.

Alex wants the war, but he's not ready. And he's not powerful enough to launch the war himself. Alex is, after all, a junior trafficker. He wants a larger trafficker to begin the fighting and consolidate the underworld. The car is moving up Calle 10, the heart of Medellin's tourist zone.

"You've got some hot women where you come from," Carlos says, turning to me in the back. He points at a group of three women who look to be Swedish backpackers: weighed down with a monstrous backpack, a guidebook in hand, and a look of confusion on their faces.

"I love that natural blond hair. Their faces are beautiful. But man, they've got no tits or asses. Your women don't get surgery, do they?"

Surgery isn't so prevalent in Europe, I say.

"Yeah, I can see that," he says, his eyes on the Swedish. "We've got it in our DNA now—we need them to have big tits and a big ass. If they're not born with it, we'll pay for it. One girlfriend I had, her grandmother bought her and her two sisters all the surgeries they wanted when they were fifteen: tits, ass, nose job, lips." He looks out the window. "None were very smart, so I guess she figured they'd need all the help they could get."

Alex chuckles and turns to me.

"The thing about Bunny is that he was in prison for years. Now he's out and he's wants to work. But there's less work in killing now. There's peace. For now."

"Did anyone send him money when he was inside?" Carlos asks.

"Yeah, for a few years, but . . . you know people forget

about all you did for them when you're down," says Alex. "So he wants to make money again. But right now, the work's not there."

"We'll have to keep an eye on him," says Carlos. "Be nice to enjoy the peace a little longer."

A police van drives past.

"Hijueputas!"

ALEX HAS ALWAYS TOLD PEOPLE that he'll die a bandit. Now, in Diana, he's found a reason to live. And this hastens his plan to retire. Alex hopes he can outrun the traditional fate of the narco.

Over lunch, I want to know—why don't traffickers leave after they've made so much money, their grandchildren don't need to work? Why not just stop trafficking and retire?

"You can't leave," Alex says. "No one trusts that you won't deal with the authorities or the gringos."

If he tries to leave by himself, today's friends would be the first to kill him tomorrow. Those at the top of cocaine are as trapped as anyone in this world. As long as he makes money, Alex is untouchable. The moment he steps down, cocaine will turn on him. He'll be food for the wolves. Riding the tiger.

A trafficker named the Chemist was captured and sent to the United States, where he bargained for a reduced sentence. More than thirty members of his family and close friends, civilians all, were slaughtered in the narcos' rage. Decapitations, dismembered while still alive, many tossed in the river, their bodies to drifting to oblivion. Organized violence in Colombia is always a punishment and a message to others. Rat on us and all you love will die.

Alex has his own questions. He wants to know about the

legalization of marijuana in the United States and Europe. Is it reversible? he asks. I tell him that this is irreversible. He broods.

"We don't want drugs legalized. The money to be made is because it's illegal. We take the risk, we earn the money. More risk, more money," he says. "The police have their job, to stop us. And we have our job, to get the drugs abroad. It's simple. Why do people have to fuck this up?"

I laugh out loud. Alex looks directly and sharply. People do not laugh around him in jokes that he doesn't get. Drug traffickers and those pushing the war on drugs unite in their desire to keep cocaine illegal.

Since the beginning, most drug lords have ended up in prison cells or in early graves. When starting out, they all accept that as their fate. But now that he's been in the world for a few years, and those possible endings are a lot closer than they once were, he figures he'll try to cheat fate. Alex wants to be one of the few to make it out alive at the end. Alex is still trying to figure out this plan to hand themselves over. Alex is hopeful he can break the drug lord's curse—that he can make the money and get out of cocaine alive. He has his crew and Diana, whom he trusts.

Alex and Diana move in together as they get more serious. He's moved her into a fully furnished $3,000-a-month apartment in Medellin's nicest neighborhood, El Poblado.

"He's too focused on Diana. He needs to watch out," says Marcus.

I am out of the city for months. But still the rumors reach me. One of Alex's shipments is seized by the police. The underworld shares the gossip that Alex is out $2.5 million.

A few traffickers are hearing of Alex's plan. Will he reveal too much? Will he rat on those who keep trafficking? A major trafficker sends Alex a message via Marcus: "People are un-happy with you."

Alex laughs and gives him three hundred dollars.

"Don't worry about me. I'll be fine."

Two weeks later, Alex and his bodyguard are driving along a road. A motorbike pulls up alongside and the shooter opens up, covering the SUV with bullets. Luckily, it's bulletproof. The SUV drives in a building's courtyard and the assassins keep riding on.

Alex doesn't tell me any of this. To know that someone tried to kill you weakens you.

Things are happening that people cannot explain. People notice an electricity in the air, like before a thunderstorm or a night of violence. A pressure is building and no one can explain exactly why the city feels on edge. Friends tell me: "It's very heavy right now in the city. I'm getting out." It's not the actual violence but the suspense, the tension in the air. The city is a balloon and everyone is squeezing, squeezing, squeezing.

There are grumblings in the underworld about Alex. Some-thing is wrong. Gossip says that he ripped off some Italians for $3 million. They are crying to other traffickers demand-ing justice. The Italians are powerless to act by themselves in Colombia. Another rumor says that there's a piddling debt of $10,000 that hasn't been paid.

And the stability of the Pax Mafioso trembles every day, adding to the mood of chaos. There are plans to kill Medel-lin's mayor. One plan involves killing policemen in order to bring the mayor to a certain part of the city and kill him there. The mayor vows not to be intimidated.

The Pax Mafioso delivered a falling murder rate. Colom-bia's largest cities are seeing their murder rate fall in the last few years. Not Medellin. Homicides are on the rise and no one is exactly sure why. Analysts are wheeled out to news programs to offer explanations. Tectonic plates are moving in the underworld and everyone feels it and no one seems able to stop it.

The leader of the Office of Envigado, "Tom," celebrates his fiftieth birthday and is arrested by police. Tom had a $2 million bounty laid on his head by the United States. Among the guests are Popeye and Botija, a longtime trafficker. Popeye and Botija are questioned but released.

Tom's arrest sets off a series of killings among midrange traffickers of the Office as they move to control the organization. Days later, Botija drives through El Poblado at midnight in his black truck. Two assassins on a motorbike ride up alongside and open fire. Hit, Botija speeds up his truck, loses control, and slams into a tree. The motorbike pulls up, the shooter jumps off, and he delivers the final shots. The killing was caught on closed-circuit TV.

Tom's second in command, "Pichi," is arrested after a heavy night partying out on the Caribbean coast. Handcuffed and surrounded by twenty policemen must make it the worst hangover of his life.

An "Invisible" is arrested: Sebastian Murillo Echeverri. He had married a famous television presenter and was a fixture on Colombia's celebrity scene where he claimed to be a successful businessman. Police say he was a leading associate of the Office of Envigado. That sound you heard that day was the sound of Colombia's actors and singers deleting their Instagram photos alongside him. *Semana* magazine reported that Murillo, in his t-shirt and boxers, asked the policeman filming the early-morning operation: "Can I ask a favor: Can we repeat the filming where you guys enter my apartment and you arrest me? Look at how I am, I can't be seen like this." He will be sentenced to eighteen years in prison for his role in the killing of a former member of the Medellin cartel.

A stash of the mafia's money of $6.5 million is stolen and a trail of bodies appears across the city.

And still Alex tries to sell his dream of a war. Forge the new world of the mafia through steel and blood. A leaner, sharper mafia will emerge from the chaos and the bloodshed. And with the chaotic independents out of the way, Alex can go with his plan for a mass handover to Colombian authorities. Still none take the decision.

Meanwhile, the famous peace of the combos is fraying at the edge. Combos battle in different parts of the city. It's not enough to call it a war. But those paying attention look to the sporadic flareups and wonder: We will look back on this and say, yes, that was the beginning of the city-wide war? Is anyone still in control? Does anyone have the power to impose a necessary peace to keep the cocaine flowing? Alex says the only solution is his plan: war and a mass handover.

"And the world is yours!"

DEAL OR NO DEAL, PEACE or no peace, the business has to keep moving. Two to three tons of cocaine leave Colombia every day. That's a lot of work to keep the world well stocked in cocaine. Alex will sell the kilo to the Mexican mafia. The kilo is on the move out into the world.

CHAPTER 9

THE HUNTING
OF THEBEAST

BENEATH A SKY THE COLOR OF SUICIDE, the passenger makes their way to the airport. A dismal gray Bogota, when one and all dream of hopping on a plane. The traveler enters the main entrance of the El Dorado international airport as the lightning and thunder crack and lash above. They walk across the polished floors to the check-in counter, rolling their suitcase behind them. They may even think to themselves: I can turn around. I still have time.

At the counter, the passenger hands over their passport and checks in for the ten-hour flight to Madrid, with a connection to London. The flight leaves at 17:50. They hand over their suitcase. It weighs in at twenty-two kilos. Eighteen of those kilos are clothes, shoes, sneakers. Four kilos are cocaine. When this is cut and sold on the streets, this will be worth close to a million dollars in London. The drug mule will travel in seat 23C. Has the mule left a scent? Because here men are on the hunt.

THE KILO IS ON THE move, the invisible thread of demand pulling it toward the first world. Cocaine runs along the grooves of globalization. Flight routes, shipping lanes, and highways are designed and built by decent women and men for honest ends. Hijacked, they're corridors for cocaine to reach every corner of the planet and achieve its destiny: sold and consumed.

The El Dorado airport is one piece of the global infrastructure cocaine needs. It's named for the indigenous chief, who covered himself in gold flecks and jewels and would bathe in the freezing lake in the Andes Mountains. El Dorado, the Golden, the greedy Spanish called him. For hundreds of years, Europeans searched for these riches, all ending in failure and despair. And the golden chief laughs in the forests and streams where his spirit roams. El Dorado, as elusive as victory in the war on drugs.

Today, April Fools' Day, the airport sits at the western edge of the chaotic capital. An uninterrupted line of planes take off, swallowed by fat gray clouds.

The blur of the airport. Transience and the transients. Seas of people flow through the concourse. Muffled voices over PA systems deliver incomprehensible orders. It's the perfect spot to people-watch, to enjoy the human zoo. The young couples so in love that each second apart aches, young children bouncing off the walls after eating four donuts, the old man who is people-watching you.

Amid the glass and the steel, this is the scene of a hunt. Policemen hunting "beasts."

In their small office, the police gather around. Second Lieutenant Oscar Tarquino holds up three colored balls. Slowly, so all can see, he puts each ball in a black bag.

"Green ball, Lufthansa-Frankfurt. Red, Avianca-Barcelona . . ."

He offers the bag to the policemen, who rummage around before retrieving a ball from the bag. This is how policemen are randomly assigned to check the different flights. It's played as a game. But it's a recognition of cocaine's power to corrupt anyone. All a corrupt cop has to do is *not* see something. Ain't much easier in this world than that.

Patrolman Roger Farias pulls the blue ball: his flight is the 17:50 Iberia flight to Madrid, IB6586. Farias has the look that suggests a smile would crack his face. He's quiet, possessed of dark eyes that take in everything. The other officers say he can root out mules, or as the police call them "beasts." He is able to see the drug mule invisible to everyone else. A good hunter.

"What we see in the best profilers is an interest . . . a desire to be a person who picks up on everything. Someone who can see beyond the details, who learns how to read the behavior of people," says Captain Miguel Angel Godoy, the head of the antinarcotics police here in the airport.

He trails off . . . Hunting is so primordial, it's outlived language. People can't put it into words what makes a good hunter—it's that ability to see the trail left behind, to see the invisible, to see what should be there but is not.

We have time to kill before a raft of night flights to Europe. Farias drinks a tinto. He looks off into nothing. Other police show off old X-rays of captured mules. Black-and-white outlines of people, stomachs bursting with fat slugs, the pellets of cocaine. Another X-ray shows an obese man's stomach jammed with balls of condoms filled with cocaine, like a bag of fish eggs. Mules pregnant with ecstasy, thousands of highs—in their bellies, they carry sex, death, glamour, money, violence. All these dreams will be shit out an ocean away.

THE TRAFFICKERS STARTED THE DRUG mules way back in the 1980s, recruiting those in need. Pay them three thousand dollars and they swallowed a kilo, carried it in their suitcase. The mules were easy to spot, men and women straight from the countryside, first time on a plane, faces carved of desperate need. Once the police understood the game, it was easy sport, easy prey for the hunter.

As ever, cocaine learned from her mistakes and evolved. The mule wranglers got smart and started recruiting from all walks of life. Today the mules could be anyone—the nun, the child, dogs, you. Even beyond appearances, though, now it's a numbers game. Send fifty mules to London, a kilo each, and if two get through, you're in profit. And those caught? The mules rarely know much about their handlers, but it's enough to know their families will be killed if they cooperate with the police.

Drug mules have democratized cocaine trafficking. Escobar needed fleets of boats and planes to get the narcotics to the United States. Now a freelancer needs the price of a plane ticket and the dollars for a kilo and the nerve to swallow it. At Colombia's international airports, cocaine mules are a daily business; vaginas distended by kilos of cocaine, bellies rounded out, anuses jammed with drugs, false-bottomed suitcases. And countries across the world all have drug mules who have flown from South America with cocaine in the belly.

It sounds like easy money. But if it were easy, everyone

would do it. When swallowing the cocaine, most mules aim for one kilo. They break the kilo into dozens of pellets and practice swallowing dozens of grapes, widening the throat, loosening the gullet. Then they painfully swallow all fifty pellets. If any of those pellets crack open . . . it's a fatal over-dose.

How does it feel? You're dodging clouds at 37,000 feet, riding the air currents, and you feel something, maybe in your stomach? Is it a sudden burn, your skin and face on fire? Your heart now pumping like crazy? The feeling is of a tsunami of cocaine coursing through your veins, heading straight to the heart.

Ask Udo N., a forty-two-year-old Japanese man. He's flying from Colombia back to Japan when his convulsions begin. "Is there a doctor on board?" the stewardess calls over the intercom. No luck. The pilot takes the plane down for an emergency landing in Mexico. The convulsions stop before touchdown. The paramedics board to make it official—declared dead at 02:25, one Friday morning. Midflight, dropped dead by cocaine. The autopsy shows that Udo had 246 packets of cocaine in his stomach. Cause of death was a brain swollen by cocaine. Why did he do it? He was set to earn hundreds of thousands of dollars for this kilo in Japan.

That's always why people keep swallowing the pellets.

And still the mules keep evolving. The new mule doesn't look like the old mule, the peasant down from the mountains. The new mule may not even speak Spanish and carries an American passport. It's the flip side of Colombia's booming tourism—the more visitors who come, the more see how cheap the cocaine is.

"Over recent years, we've noticed that the crime of drug trafficking has been hurting not just our country, but also those foreigners, who come to our country to make money," says Godoy in his tactful way. What he means is that greedy American and Europeans are becoming beasts. A third of the mules in Bogota's prisons are foreigners now.

Once foreigners realize just how cheap cocaine is in Colombia, their eyes glaze over as they daydream about smuggling themselves a kilo. It's $2,000 for a kilo in the cities. Get that kilo to Miami, wholesale you'll get $25,000. New York? $40,000. London? $60,000. Wholesale. Get this to New Zealand, a gram there costs $235. Sell the kilo retail and you're tripling these figures. That's life-changing money.

Some foreigners work by themselves, but few have the connections to buy a kilo. Most are recruited by Colombian friends. The foreigner is told the fix is in, the police are paid off, the scanners don't work, the X-rays are broken. It's easy to con someone whose eyes are dazzled by dollars. You can't con an honest man.

"Malicia indigena"—that's what the police use to find the mules. This is a central tenet of Colombia—*malicia indigena*. It's a shifting, vague term, but essentially means outwitting the person in front of you, not letting the person take advantage of you. It's become a byword for Colombia's incredible ingenuity for malevolence. The police take that natural wisdom for bad and turn it back on the mules.

Godoy knows this. "I've always said that if we Colombians and the drug traffickers among us used our creativity for good, you can bet we would be far more advanced. . . . We would be a great power here in Colombia."

The police look for telltale signs, sweaty hands, a nervous look. Short visits to Colombia are red flags. The police ask the travelers where they've been, what hotels they stayed in, what tourist attractions they visited. They don't have the answers, but they're watching the reactions. They look for what doesn't make sense. A man says he's a businessman, and he's in a suit, but his shoes are cheap. A woman says she is an executive but doesn't have any credit cards. If the traveler stumbles, it's a trip to the X-ray machine. Because once the police focus on you, you lose. The only hope is to slip by unnoticed.

"Today we might find a foreigner with drugs hidden in their shoes. And tomorrow the traffickers may say: 'They've realized how we pack the cocaine or heroin in the shoes. Let's invent a way to hide it in our jackets.' Every day they're inventing. Every day they invent something new. This is a game of cat and mouse."

The police love sharing these stories of the endlessly inventive drug mules.

"The business of drug trafficking is evolving every single day. . . . We can't get stuck saying: 'Only these types of people swallow the drug.' No, every day we see that drug traffickers are always looking for new ways to get the drug to the international market."

A pregnant twenty-eight-year-old Tabitha walks through Bogota's airport, on her way home to Toronto. A pregnant hippy, she has a shawl over her shoulders, a bulging belly beneath her T-shirt, and sandals. She passes through the police control, showing her passport and boarding pass. A policewoman kindly leans in and asks her how long until the baby. The Canadian snaps at the policewoman. Mistake. Now she has all the policewoman's attention. The policewoman reaches out and touches her belly—and feels that it's hard, cold and latex.

The Canadian blurts out: "I'm seven months pregnant."

Too late. Now she's on her way to the back room where

our mother will deliver twins—two death-white blocks of cocaine. She's in Bogota's women's prison, the Good Shepherd, for her five-to-seven stretch.

Paola, a twenty-two-year-old attractive Honduran, stands in the security line. Her hair is tied back; her curves burst through her clothes. She looks nervous enough to make a policeman curious. In the back room, it takes only a few questions to confess that her large breasts are augmented—with cocaine. In a grimy garage, a man cut open her chest and inserted a tied-up latex glove filled with liquid cocaine in each breast. At a Bogota hospital, doctors extract 1.5 kilos of liquid cocaine. Paola is now a neighbor of Tabitha in the chilly Good Shepherd prison.

A veterinary student cuts open puppies and inserts bags of liquid narcotics, before sewing them up and sending them to the United States. The police raid the farm and the vet goes on the run. He's finally found and tried in the United States, where he's sentenced to six years. As always, the dogs laugh last—one of the rescued puppies is raised to become a drug detector for the police.

Many of the drug mules end up in La Modelo prison, where the air fizzes with the tension of barely constrained violence. Mules have looks of constant regret. They got greedy, they got caught, and now they live among thieves, murderers, rapists, and child abusers.

Trying to get by is Rafael, a polite young man from Spain who once owned a business. He has broken the law once in his life.

"What a fool I've been." And so he begins his story as we sit in the prison garden.

"I was living in Spain. I started a business and it went under because of the economic crisis. Someone proposed this idea for me to recover all my money. I thought it sounded easy."

Drug traffickers love men and women in need. His friends offer ten thousand euros to bring cocaine from Colombia to Spain. They tell him they have developed new, unbreakable pellets, invisible to X-rays. Safe and sure. He's given a pellet and told to stomp on it. It doesn't break.

Rafael is pleasant and kind, but a little slow. He swallows the capsules, a kilo and a half rattling around his belly. As he passes through the police control, the police ask him to come for an X-ray.

"I don't know why they called on me. I wasn't nervous," he tells me.

He steps into the X-ray machine with his trusted childhood friend's words in his ears: "The machines can't detect this plastic."

As he steps out of the X-ray machine, a policeman arrests him. "What are you doing?" Rafael asks the police.

"We found drugs in you," the policeman replies.

Convinced of his friend's words, Rafael is outraged.

"'Your X-ray is broken. Let's do it again!' I told them," he says. And now he shrugs with the wry smile of a man who trusted the wrong man.

They repeat the X-ray. The policemen take him to the computer screen to show him an X-ray of his belly filled with pellets. What did he feel in that moment? A pause. "Shit," he says. "That was all I could think."

He got four years in Bogota's infamous La Modelo prison.

"Foreigners come and think they're in a cocaine paradise. But here in prison, they realize the truth. It was here I realized it."

Rafael hasn't spoken to his mother back in Spain for more than a year. I record a video message for his mother.

"Mama, I'm doing good. Don't worry about me. Again, I'm sorry for what I did to you."

He tells her he is counting the days until he can return home.

Later in the day, I send it via email. The mother replies twenty minutes later thanking me and telling me what a good boy Rafael is.

But as always, there are those who never learn. In the Good Shepherd prison, three American women sit around a table and talk about how they'll work their drug convictions once they get back home. "We're going on Oprah, bitches!" one calls out and the others nod their heads and high-five. An immensely obese woman says she's been in prison for around a year and hadn't had the chance to tell her mother. I ask: "The last your mother knew was that you were coming to Colombia?" "No, I didn't tell her. I don't know what she must be thinking." Her mother's anguish didn't seem to perturb her.

WHEN TRAFFICKERS SEND LARGE AMOUNTS of cocaine, they may hire various mules. One will carry a small amount, the others the heavy loads. Traffickers may tip off the police for the light mule, the "bait." As the police concentrate their forces on the unlucky mule, dozens more sail through. Betrayal is constant in cocaine. One policeman tells me of a family that came through.

"We had one case that I'll never forget. It was a family going through the last checkpoint: a husband, his wife, and their teenage daughter. We do a random check and it turns out we find drugs in a bag of lollipops. There was over a kilo there in little balls of cocaine stuffed into each sucker. The father was carrying it. When we stopped them, the father was super calm, but the mother and the daughter were stressed. The father couldn't believe it when we told him. He kept shouting there had to be a mistake, shouting to his wife to tell them where she had bought them. She said nothing. Then as we handcuffed him he suddenly went silent. He just stared at his wife. As we took him away, he never said another word, just kept staring at his wife and his daughter. Your own family? I went home that night and looked at my wife real hard."

The betrayal occurs on the other side, too. No one knows how widespread corruption is in the airports and ports. Police officers admit it's a huge problem, but only in private, off the record. That's the hypocrisy of the drug war. In formal interviews, officers point out how well they're doing, the positive results. And as soon as the interview is over, and the recorder stops, they sit back and tell you what's really happening. They tell you of constant problems of corruption, how the war is unwinnable, how the only solution is legalization. In private, to state that the war on cocaine can be won would make you look like an idiot. To admit the war is unwinnable in public is to end a career.

The endless power to corrupt means every cop is looking at every other cop, peering over their shoulders, keeping their buddies honest.

"The traffickers will send messages via friends, families, a cousin. It will be an offer: you don't have to do anything, just ignore a certain shipment. How difficult is that? Not to do anything. And we'll pay you enough to buy a home," says one police officer at a different airport.

That is the power of cocaine.

Some cops do it once and then never again. I ask: Doesn't that leave them vulnerable to being blackmailed by the cartels? The cop shakes his head, telling me I don't get it.

"That's not how it works. If they tried to expose a cop, no cop would ever work with them again. And all cops would come after the trafficker."

Over two years, the police got rid of 2,500 officers suspected of corruption and working with cartels. Two chiefs of security for the president have been convicted and imprisoned for working with drug traffickers. Narcos paid off a unit of soldiers to slaughter an elite ten-strong unit of antinarcotics officers while on a mission.

PATROLMAN FARIAS TAKES ME OUT onto the concourse. The time is 16:30. The radio cackles. I feel the nervous energy.

"We may have one," he says. The X-rays have spotted something suspicious in three suitcases that are being loaded onto the night flight to Madrid. At the gate, there's the buzz of families preparing for the flight. Children run in circles. Business executives read their books. Backpackers stare at the sunset, one last look at this magical country. The sigh of departure. The excitement of arrival. It's 16:50. The PA system calls out three names, asking them to pass to the corridor that leads to the plane.

I wonder: Now does the mule think "It's too late"?

One by one, the three come through the door into the corridor. The first is a tall, skinny, young American man, with cornrows that reach his shoulders. Next through the door is a nervous young Englishwoman, who flashes a brittle smile at everyone she sees. The third is a middle-aged, bespectacled Spanish man who deliberately exudes irritation.

The three listen as Tarquino explains that their luggage has been flagged for an additional check.

Just minutes earlier, I was excited to watch a mule caught. Now I look at these three faces. Someone's life could be about to change forever.

Beneath the airport's fluorescent lights, Farias cracks open the Spanish man's luggage. He rifles through the clothes. The Spanish man huffs and glares at Farias, who ignores him. Finally, Farias finishes. He thanks the man for his cooperation.

Two left.

The Englishwoman hands her suitcase to Farias. She's not more than twenty-one. I guess she's a student backpacker finishing her jaunt through Colombia. As Farias opens her case, she smiles that very English nervous smile that says: don't hurt me, I'm harmless.

Passengers begin to board, walking by and staring at the woman as Farias goes through her suitcase. Blushing, she pretends to concentrate on her bag.

Farias thanks her. She smiles again and repacks. Ordeal over, it will become a funny story to tell of her last day in crazy Colombia.

One left. He's skinny, much taller than Farias, who stands next to him. He looks like a teenager and has large sunglasses perched on his head.

Farias opens the suitcase. He removes clothing.

"Where do you come from?" asks Farias.

"Manhattan, New York."

Farias returns to the suitcase. A pair of white trainers, a bag of clothing, folded jeans. Farias takes a long inhale of it all. He looks bestial, taking in the scent.

Farias takes out a bag of macaroni. His eyebrows knot in confusion. Who packs food for Spain? Now a pack of spaghetti. Does this kid know that pasta is available in Spain? Then a jumbo pack of Salsa Rosada, pink sauce, mayonnaise mixed with ketchup. Farias takes the pack out, views it from every angle, like he's weighing up a used car. He looks at the kid straight on.

Farias removes the cap and inhales. His face is blank. Out of his pocket, he takes a chopstick-sized toothpick. He pushes it into the pack, deep. It comes out with pink gunk. He sniffs it again. His face is blank. Farias hasn't looked back at the kid.

Tarquino and other police are watching Farias silently. Farias tastes the gunk. Tarquino leans in. Nothing. Farias pushes the wooden stick in again, deeper now. I've stopped breathing. His face is a rock of concentration. He pulls out the stick. He sniffs it. Nothing. He puts it in his mouth. He looks at Tarquino. He nods.

Immediately the policemen surround the kids.

"What's in there?" the kid asks.

"Drugs," replies Tarquino.

Farias screws up his face at the bitterness of the cocaine he's tasted, shaking his head. He administers the field test to determine if it's cocaine. The sample turns blue—it's cocaine.

"Can I see your passport and ticket," asks Tarquino. The kid hands over his passport and his boarding pass. Seat 23C.

"How old are you?"

"Sixteen." He corrects himself: "Eighteen."

"You're not sixteen. You've already told your first lie," says Tarquino.

Farias pulls out two more packs. Tarquino reads him his rights.

"I can tell you where I bought these," says the kid. "I bought them. I bought them."

"You're going to accompany us and we're going to do an inspection," says Tarquino.

"What about my flight?"

"Let me tell you: you're not traveling. You're not going anywhere."

And from behind us, we hear the slam of the plane door.

A GREAT RECKONING IN A little office. The police sit the American teenager down and handcuff him. Along his arm runs the tattoo "Money $Talks." Tarquino asks for his passport. The teenager shakes his head. Tarquino and Farias huddle to figure out where the passport is. Farias starts to leave the office to return to the lounge to look for it.

The American hears the word "passport."

"Passport? I've got it here."

Tarquino is pissed.

"Screwing around. Apart from the charge of drug trafficking, this is what you're doing. Sixteen . . . no eighteen. Hiding the passport, we call that obstruction of justice."

They fill out more forms. The teenager sits there. It is a strange mix of tremendous emotion and boring paperwork.

"What else do you have in your pockets?" asks Tarquino.

"Money."

He shows the bills. Tarquino explains that the money will stay with him and that at no moment will it be confiscated.

"Take my advice, hold on to it, because where you're going, it can disappear—easily."

The kid sits down, a look of fear across his face. The room shrinks as the enormity of his predicament grows.

"What if I tell you the name of the store where I bought this?" He points at the packs.

"All of that, you need to explain to your lawyer, who will then communicate it to the prosecutor and the judge," says Tarquino, filling out the form. No store sells kilos of cocaine in bags of ketchup and pink sauce. And everyone knows it.

Farias lays out the three "jumbo packs": "Twelve hundred grams—an extra two hundred grams free!"

Farias carries out tests to confirm that it is cocaine inside. It comes up blue.

"The test is confirming that there are drugs inside," says Tarquino.

"What's inside?"

"Cocaine."

The kid is playing dumb. The police wrap up the packets.

"Do you have family here in Colombia?"

"Friends."

Tarquino asks if he wants to phone his parents in America. The kid shakes his head. Now it is clear: he's not too bright. A dumb kid, easy to fool with promises of riches and far-fetched tales of easy passage. And here he is, eighteen and heading for a Colombian prison.

His foot fidgets, tap, tap, tap, tap, tap. He asks if he can have a cigarette.

"There's no smoking area here."

Farias and Tarquino fill out forms, calcifying the kid's life. A future decided in a dark room.

"Right now you need to give us a number, so you can phone someone and tell them that you are under arrest. I imagine someone is waiting for you there. If you don't call now, it'll be more difficult where we're taking you."

The kid deflates. He shakes his head. We all feel it: he can't face the shame of telling his family. But he has no idea of the hell of Colombia's prisons. Tarquino tries again. He speaks slowly, trying to convince the kid that this is very important and to take the advice.

"Someone abroad needs to know that you've been arrested. At some point, you're going to need someone to bring you food, clothing; there'll be some sort of situation. It's better if someone knows," says Tarquino.

He stares at the kid for ten seconds. The kid is silent.

"Okay," Tarquino says. And he turns away. He tried.

The kid is heading to prison. Gangs run the prisons, extorting, raping, and murdering other prisoners. One prison couldn't account for prisoners who kept disappearing—they were being murdered, cut to pieces, and stuffed down the building's plumbing. No one realized for years. Life in prison, an existence of tedium interrupted by thunderclaps of savagery. Even the bare minimum of life in prison costs money—a bed, food, safety. The lowest of the low are the foreigners who have no friends and family to drop off money regularly. This is what Tarquino wants to say. But he can't.

They weigh the three packs: 4.2 kilograms of cocaine.

These blocks have reached the end of the line and will be delivered over to the specialized department of the antinarcotics police and incinerated in an industrial oven.

A mule was caught yesterday. A mule will be caught tomorrow. Victories to be celebrated by a patrolman, while the general sees the war is being lost. Evolution has its own dead ends. Cocaine has a long game plan. Lose a couple of kilos, but the trade gets smarter, leaner. More efficient. Deadlier, it returns.

After a couple of hours, the last form is filled out. Farias and Tarquino escort the teenager through the airport. He walks with his head high, his handcuffed hands dragging his suitcase. Still, he avoids eye contact with everyone. He walks past the Juan Valdez, past the luxury leather bag store, the grinning family, past the bookstore. For the first time, I notice that the back of his shirt says: "Freedom." He passes a store where a woman behind a counter looks at him, smiles, sees the handcuffs as he passes, turns to her friend, and shakes her head. Duty-free shops, perfumes, booze, cigarettes, headphones, coffee, rum, vodka, beautiful women. Life. Liberty. Happiness. All of it is passing him by.

They exit the airport. It's night now and chilly. A police van waits. Finally, he gets his cigarette. I light it for him. I can't imagine how much he's needed it. He smokes like a child— exaggerated inhalations, his cheeks puffing out with smoke.

"What's going to happen to me?" his voice cracks, his American accent now clear.

I'm stumped. What else is there to say: "You're going to jail."

We have nothing else to say. He finishes his cigarette in silence. He's helped into the back of the van. The door closes and clicks firmly. He looks out from behind the barred back window, his eyes wide.

And that's it—he'll arrive at jail tonight, a night that might not end for five to nine years.

CHAPTER 10

TO KILL A SHADOW

IF THE KILO IS TO MAKE IT out, it needs to get by Shadow. Shadow might be the sanest one I ever met in the drug war. And she chews on rocks. Shadow is a handsome German shepherd police dog who trots through airports finding cocaine shipments. She's so good at her job, she won two medals for all the cocaine she's busted. She's so good at her job, the world's biggest cocaine trafficker offered thousands of dollars to kill her.

Traffickers ordering the murder of German shepherds. The madness is total.

Shadow now lives under twenty-four-hour police protection in the antinarcotics police's headquarters, surrounded by bases of the army and the air force. Every morning her handler, patrolman Misael Firacative, stops by the dog kennels, setting off an orchestra of barks. Thirty German shepherds, golden retrievers, and Labradors woof themselves into pandemonium.

The day starts with a run through the police garden, next to El Dorado airport in Bogota.

"She's special. She's very loving. She expresses her love to people like a person. It makes you think that you're interacting with another human being, not a dog," says Firacative, watching his partner run.

Her favorite game is to run up and drop her rock at my feet. She watches me, intelligent eyes. I reach for it, she snaps it back, and proudly trots off, convinced she's outsmarted me. She moves with that German shepherd elegance. As she bounds along with her favorite rock in her joyful innocence, all else seems grim and pointless.

It takes three months to train a dog to become a drug detector. The trainers make the dogs associate finding cocaine, marijuana, and heroin with rewards: find the drugs, get the toy.

"Their sense of smell is so well designed by Mother Nature that to try to match it would be near impossible," says Firacative. He takes a joint out of a plastic container. He walks the length of the garden. Shadow sits, her eyes following him as he walks. He hides the drugs and returns to her. He gives the sign and she bounds over to the hidden drugs. She sniffs around, then sits next to the spot. She looks at her handler to make sure he understands. He walks to where she sits and picks up the drugs. "Good girl," and he tosses the ball. She's off in a flash, her tail wagging. The ball was all she wanted.

She's warmed up for the day and ready to find some cocaine.

Shadow was working on the Caribbean coast, busting shipment after shipment. In the port of Santa Marta, she found a ton of cocaine, hidden in a Europe-bound shipment of sugar. Shadow became only the second dog ever to receive the police's Canine Medal. The bust cost the Gulf Clan $30 million. Police intelligence reported that an enraged Otoniel ordered the dog's murder. A police officer was approached with the offer to kill Shadow for $7,000. He alerted his bosses, who ordered Shadow be flown to Bogota under police protection.

The police knew they had an amazing story—a charismatic hero in the grim, never-ending drug war. Shadow was invited on to the biggest TV shows. TV hosts fussed and chattered over her, and Shadow remained dignified.

Today Shadow works in the cargo warehouse of Bogota's El Dorado airport. It's under heavy security, every person heavily checked every time they enter and leave the warehouse. It's an enormous warehouse, dusty, gloomy, and gray. This is where Colombia's exports come through before connecting to the rest of the world: coffee, emeralds, flowers. And cocaine.

"This job is a struggle not only to protect our country from the curse of drug trafficking, but to help our sister nations against this plague. . . . This job is not about one country, it's the whole world," says Firacative.

He guesses Shadow finds cocaine four times a week. The dogs work for only three to four hours a day; their focus and concentration fades after that. One policeman was caught deliberately working tired dogs who couldn't detect the drugs.

Shadow wears her yellow vest as she runs along a line of boxes ready to be sent abroad. She sniffs each box. Firacative points to a box and she inspects. She passes by twenty boxes in fifteen seconds. All clear.

"She loves what she does. For her, work is a game."

She is the queen in this warehouse—every worker decked out in gray overalls pats her, strokes her head, says hello. Shadow looks at everyone with that intelligent curiosity of the best dogs.

It's a game of chance. The narcos know the police can only check so much. And they're betting that theirs will get through. Shadow runs along a line of new packages. She stops by one package. She moves on, but then returns to the large cardboard box. She sniffs it and looks at Firacative. She's gone from trotting, with wagging tail, to sitting rigidly. It's the sign.

The box is taken to the metal cage in the middle of warehouse where suspicious packages are reviewed. In the package is an old-style hi-fi amplifier. The policeman opens the amp up, unscrewing the back and looks inside. The package is to be sent to New York—expensive postage for something this cheap and easily acquired over there. But he can't find anything. He looks all around, but nothing. He won't give up, but he can't find anything.

The policeman finally returns the amplifier to its box. But he's annoyed. It's a red flag, but he's found nothing. It's frustrating, because he's spent forty minutes checking it out. And while he focused on that, the unspoken question is: Did the cocaine slip by while he looked the other way? Just yesterday, this one warehouse found sixteen packages of cocaine. But how much got through?

Shadow stops by a large package. She sits down and looks at her handler. The package is taken into the metal cage. Inside are four enormous and heavy screws, a foot long each, the type that bind cruise liners and bridges. They pass them through the X-ray. They don't seem to be solid all the way through. But it's inconclusive.

An agent attempts to drill a hole in to one, but the bit breaks on the steel. A policeman goes for another drill bit. Firacative looks the screw over and over for any way to open it up. Nothing. The policeman returns with another drill head. This has been going on for thirty-five minutes. Shadow looks on. The drill squeals and whirls and this time breaks through the steel exterior.

There's a powder inside. Firacative tastes the powder. It's cocaine, destination: Madrid. These four kilos were going to make someone a nice profit.

"It tastes like electricity. It's unpleasant. It's a dry taste. Like an electrical shock on the tongue," he says. Yet, after a hit of the pure stuff, he's noticeably happier, jabbering, laughing, and smiling.

Four kilos is a small victory. Still, it's a victory.

Shadow has been sitting there all the while looking at Firacative. He turns to her and throws the ball and she's off. Traffickers tried to make a hefty little business and the police spent time and effort stopping them. A human drama. And all Shadow wanted was her ball.

Even dogs lead accelerated lives in cocaine. Shadow is six but is to be pensioned off in a matter of months.

"God willing, if the police approve it, I'll ask for her to be given to me, so she can pass out her days with me as a house dog," say Firacative. He already has a pug, a terrier, a pit bull, and another German shepherd.

First, Shadow will pass through the police dog retirement home in Guaymaral, north of Bogota. Imagine dog heaven.

"Behind every dog there's a story," says Yeimy Paola Bucuru, the antinarcotics police vet. There are around sixty elderly dogs in Guaymaral: Labradors, golden retrievers, Belgian shepherds, and German shepherds. It's total chaos, exactly as the dogs like it. They swarm in circles in a single mass, barking and pawing each other. Suddenly there's a blur of snarls, bites, barks. Two dogs start fighting and in a second every dog is involved, all taking sides and now twenty dogs are fighting each other. Like a pub in southeast London on a Monday night.

Yeimy strides into the middle to separate the main fighters.

Mara is a dog that helped to detect explosives in the jungle. Now she has contracted the flesh-eating tropical disease leishmaniasis. Chapolo is a small dog that yaps. He once belonged to the Gulf Clan's Otoniel. The cartel had trained him to bark whenever he saw men in uniforms, to alert the drug traffickers. The police raided a farm looking for Otoniel. There was Chapolo barking and swaggering around. The police took him and retrained him to be a rescue dog, those who search for bodies in accidents.

The police have stepped up security here after attempts to poison the dogs.

"Two officers arrived in a jeep. They said: 'We need Shadow and Chapolo.' I said sure, just show me the paperwork and I'll sign. Then they begin with: 'We don't have the paperwork, we need them urgently for a secret mission.' I told them, they can take the dogs out, but only with the paperwork," says an officer. No need to say the obvious: they wanted to abduct the dogs.

In the barking chaos, Jairo is happy. Playfully, the dogs nip him. Bounding, they slam their paws on his chest. He makes his way across the mass of solid dog, rubbing heads, scratching behind ears, and everyone gets a "Good dog." Tails wag and noses are wet. Jairo smiles. All the while trotting by his side is a brown Labrador, his snout white with age, Rocket.

Jairo is kindly. His skin is pale, a face hollowed out. Everyone knows Jairo is not well. The brittle smile highlights how spooked his eyes are, agape as if struck stuck by lightning.

"I served ten years in the jungle, living and working." He's proud. Those who know understand what that means: a decade-long hike through hell. For those ten years, Jairo—not his real name—was ripping out coca crops in the toughest spots of Colombia. Caquetá. Putumayo. Tumaco. Guaviare.

These are the names of places that haunt the nightmares of mothers when they hear their sons are to be transferred. Ten years fighting in the jungle will change anyone. Everyone knows that. Some men come back stone-cold lunatics, like they picked up something in the darkness and never let it go. Others return, their minds snapped in half by the violence, PTSD'd forever. Life, friends, work become impossible.

Jairo leaves the dog pen with Rocket (also not his real name). He received the chocolate Labrador when the dog was four and trained him to be a bomb dog, sniffing out the mines laid for them in the coca fields.

"Everywhere there are mines. They'll put three mines in a field."

In one of Rocket's first weeks, he detected a dozen mines. Life was eradicating coca to a sound track of firefights, exploding land mines, and guerrilla mortars raining down. He tells of walking next to policemen and them simply disappearing in an enemy mortar attack. All this fighting over coca.

He estimates the dog saved hundreds of lives in their slow, decade-long march through the jungles and coca. Bombs, coca, and war. Jairo tells me this as he plays with Rocket, throwing a tennis ball.

"Good boy. Are you happy? You're happy now," he says.

The brown dog still loves the ball, after all these years. He's not as fast as he once was. Neither is Jairo. The dog adores him.

"With all I've seen and lived, I can tell you: dogs are much more loyal than men."

Every three months he was sent home to be with his wife and two children. But he felt out of place in the city, in civilian life. He dreamed of the simplicity of life back in the jungle—just him and Rocket with a single mission: stay alive and rip out the coca. I've had a touch of the war crazies. Life is so simple out there—just do your job and stay alive. And you return to what passes for normal life and everything seems slightly off. Every loud noise reminds you of incoming artillery; surprises have you reacting in survival mode. And people obsess over nonsense that has nothing to with the purest question you can start your day: Today, will I live or die? And that's why we go back to war, time and time again. My war crazies cleared up after a couple of months. But I know that if you keep on out there, at the furthest edge of what the mind can take, it will break in half on you.

Jairo knew the war was twisting him up, but he couldn't escape it. His wife gave him an ultimatum: stay home or she and the children will leave.

Divorced, Jairo returned to the jungle, now his connection to the world, his hold on sanity was Rocket. In one field, Rocket failed to detect the land mine and an eradicator set it off, injuring himself and throwing Jairo into the air, blood streaming from his ears and nose. Jairo was sent to a clinic for fourteen days, and his only company was his dog.

Rocket was retired and sent here to the dog farm. Jairo saw a life out of the jungle, beyond the war. And he followed his best friend here. He took a course to become a vet for the police. And he put in a request to adopt Rocket.

"They gave their lives for us. Now we need to dedicate our lives to them. We need to help them," he says. "They're my friends. My colleagues."

Colombia doesn't really understand PTSD. Trauma is as common as air here, where every family has experienced the violence. The wealthy never sent their sons to the country's wars. It's the poor who return from the battlefield, weighed down with trauma they fall through the cracks. The city centers are filled with homeless vets, violent and drugged out. It feels like every other week there's another case of a policeman who kills his wife and turns the gun on himself. Sex, PTSD, cocaine all mixed together in a horrible cocktail. This war twists you around.

Jairo rubs Rocket's head, whose eyes are closed in bliss.

"I was in Guaviare and it was hail and lightning coming down. And that dog sat there, taking it all. He never left me. A man—he would seek shelter. Not Rocket."

He kneels down and holds Rocket's head in two hands. The dog looks back at him in total adoration.

"Are you happy? You're happy now," he says, his face inches from the dog's. He's not just talking to his dog.

CHAPTER 11

A GRAVEYARD OF KILOS

ON THE PACIFIC COAST, THERE IS A graveyard and in it lies the dreams of narcos. It holds a dozen or so semi-subs, seized by authorities in antinarcotics operations on the high seas, each one capable of carrying several tons of cocaine. Hundreds and hundreds of millions of dollars of cocaine were seized in the operations that took these semi-subs.

Shipping has always been the narcos' favored way of pushing the drugs to Europe and Mexico. Planes are too easily detected. Mules can get a kilo or five through. Pack the cocaine right in a container and now we're talking ten tons of the drug. Still, sometimes the containers get busted in the ports and the narcos boats are intercepted in the open sea by the Colombian navy and the US Coast Guard. So evolution makes her leap forward, and the narco tries to make the kilo invisible.

The semi-subs look like regular submarines, except that above the waves there's a small cockpit and pipes to bring in oxygen and expel exhaust. They can't descend to depths, so they move along the ocean's surface like a shark in chase. Inside the semi-subs, it feels like sitting in a missile. Men who have traveled inside these vessels describe them as metallic coffins that always feels one second away from sinking to the depths.

The vehicles are kept here in a museum inside Colombia's main naval base of Malaga Bay. Here it is raining, a torrential downpour that pounds and keeps going. The naval base is a small town carved out of the thick jungle along the coast. The base has its own supermarket, church, restaurant, and bar— all seen through a near constant torrent. Malaga Bay is the center of operations against the semi-subs leaving Colombia.

Here at the graveyard of semi-subs, the vehicles are sodden with emotion. Walking among them, you feel the hope and the greed as traffickers and semi-sub crews packed the cocaine on. How grand the eight tons of cocaine must have looked. You feel the men's fear, desperation as they are chased down at sea. And the crushing defeat as the semi-sub is captured, the jubilation of the navy as they've caught the vessels.

The museum director is a young lieutenant, Eduardo Otero. He may know more about semi-subs than anyone else on earth.

"This job isn't for everybody," he says, looking at these metallic hulks. "Someone who says: I'll trap myself inside a five-meter-long metal tube and go under the waves for days. Well, not everyone can do that. That's someone in dire need and they're doing it for the money."

No one can be sure of who invented the first semi-sub, but here the navy says it was commissioned by Pablo Escobar way back in 1993. It was a contraption to be dragged under water behind a boat. It was fittingly found on the tiny Caribbean island of La Providencia, once the base of the English pirate Henry Morgan.

Looking at all the different semi-subs captured over the past two decades is to watch evolution. Each vessel is slightly improved on its predecessor, cartel craftsmen perfecting these vessels: sleeker, more sophisticated, larger to carry more kilos of cocaine, more difficult to detect. Now the semi-subs are outfitted with advanced radar equipment, capable of covering their trail to give no hint they're in the water, with complex systems to bring in oxygen and expel carbon dioxide. What began as a novelty has now become a full-fledged enterprise.

A sleek whale-gray semi-sub stretches 20 meters and could carry seven tons of cocaine. Another is deep blue, 17 meters long and capable of carrying 5 tons. It hangs five meters beneath the surface. An iceberg of cocaine trafficking, it rides with just a fraction above the surface, pregnant with the narcotic below. Another monster is 30 meters long, capable of carrying eight tons of cocaine. This has a cockpit above the waves where the captain could sit and steer the ship, but a cockpit so small, it would avoid radar.

The price for these semi-subs, often made in makeshift factories in the swamps, starts at $1 million. When moving several tons of cocaine, that's a pittance; a single successful mission and the semi-sub has already paid for itself.

The up-front cost of building the semi-sub is the easy part. These are complex vehicles and the question is—who makes them? And this is one of those dirty secrets, the connection of the legal world and the underworld. As talented as drug traffickers are, they need the skills of legitimate engineers, welders, boatmakers. One prominent businessman was arrested along with his family for building these semi-subs. He promised to build one in four months for $2 million a ship. He was bringing in Italian motors to make the subs travel even faster, leaving less trace, making them harder to detect.

The pieces of sub are constructed in legal factories, and then transported to jungle factories, far from prying eyes, where they're welded together by professionals. And then they are gently eased into the ocean with tons and tons of cocaine on board. The miserable job belongs to the marines to trudge through the merciless swamps of the Pacific looking for these subs. It's a world of pounding rain, pissed-off snakes, and caimans watch your every move.

In his office, I meet Vice Admiral Orlando Romero Reyes. It's his job to stop the cocaine from leaving Colombia, a 1,300-kilometer coastline. Along much of the southern stretch of the coast, around Tumaco, the navy has installed a blockade, checking many of the boats leaving the port. It's paying off. In one month in 2018, they seized 21 tons of cocaine along the coast and at sea.

"What has happened because of the military campaigns? The drug traffickers have changed their corridors. The drug lords move it through Ecuador, because we have blocked that exit. Or they go through the south of the country or the east through Venezuela," he says.

Cocaine always adapts. But it feels like the cup scam: the con artist flashes the pea and puts it under one of three cups, which she moves to and fro, quickly passing the pea from spot to spot as we try to keep up. Nothing gets resolved, just pushed around the country.

He estimates that the Pacific Coast produces between 800 and 900 tons of cocaine, 900 tons of marijuana, and a ton and a half of heroin. (In 2006, the government invited the press to fly to a lonely mountain ridge to show them destroying the "last poppy bush" in Colombia. Another victory for the war on drugs.)

The admiral feels that he knows the limits of the iron rod to attack the problem of cocaine.

"There's more territory than state here," he says. "The only presence of the state is the military."

He looks out on a Pacific Coast mired in poverty, with not enough social programs.

How does this all end?

"There are some analysts that say that once and for all the decision should be taken to legalize drugs because so many resources are being used, the deaths of so many soldiers and the crops keeps growing, the economy is in trouble and high levels of violence. But I have to say that I am not a politician, I work for the government, but some analysts do say that it's time to think about legalizing drugs."

DARIO WORKS ON THE SEMI-SUBS. He's driving to the coast and I'm along for the ride. It's a journey through mountain passes, highways, countless villages, and hundreds and hundreds of miles of highway. And here's the deal: Dario needs to get to the coast in fourteen hours, but he won't tell me why.

We're half an hour into this journey when he takes out his first joint and lights it. He's not smooth with the wheel, and struggles to bring the lighter close to his mouth and focus his eyes on the flame meeting the joint's end. He draws heavily on the joint, pure *cripy* wrapped in cigar leaf. One hand is left on the wheel, but he's not watching the road ahead and the car slowly veers into the other lane.

Like every weedhead, he has his pat explanation: "Some people get sleepy with weed. Not me! It wakes me up!"

The car barrels down the small highway, passing hitchhikers and football fans who hang off the back doors of trucks. And we get to talking about life under water.

"Fear. So much fear," is how he describes these dangerous missions. Dario rides in the semi-subs twice a year. Tall for a Colombian, and ripped, I imagine him struggling in the claustrophobic tubes below. His job on board is the lowest of the low, to pack the cocaine on and off and do any odd jobs along the journey.

The semi-subs travel from Colombia's coast to Mexico, dropping off tons of cocaine. The trips last seven to eight days but sometimes stretch as long as two weeks.

"You hear sounds down there. Sometimes it's whales. They cry out to each other. The sounds come from all around you. It's strange."

Below the waves, whales occasionally nudge the vessel. "They're inspecting it, rather than aggressive." An unseen giant bumping you in the undersea gloom—how would it not freak you out?

Smoking weed is forbidden down there, so he nibbles on ecstasy pills to calm himself for the journey. Your meals are what you've brought: crackers, tins of sausages, and tuna. Physically, it's tough. It's hot down there and the vessels stink of the exhausts, gasoline, shit, piss. All to a soundtrack of the constant roar of the engines.

"Everyone knows it will be eight days of suffering."

No toilet down there, but there is a bucket.

"When we get the chance, we surface and get rid of the waste. But it stinks down there before that. You try your best to hold it in."

The vessel surfaces every five hours or so to eject the exhaust and the buckets of human waste.

"You need the air. And you need the air to remain sane. The pressure builds on your head. . . ."

But there are zones where the authorities have a heavier presence. And that's when everyone goes very quiet.

"One night, the captain told us we were passing through a heavily guarded zone. He said we couldn't surface as we moved through there. The captain told us not to breath too heavily. Imagine what that was like. We just sat there. Looking at each other. I was watching the other people. Making sure that they weren't breathing too much. And they were looking at me, too. And right then, I could imagine what would happen to us all if that boat sunk. We would attack each other in a second to survive. There's no loyalty in drugs."

Dario started on this because he got into debt. A cousin heard he needed money and he introduced him to a man organizing the trip. Others, he says, have their sailing courses paid for by narcos to build an army of semi-sub pilots.

As he speaks, ahead of us on the highway is a truck filled with chickens, packed into cages, stacked on top of each other. And amid the feathers, one chicken's head is stuck out looking at the mountains passing by. It feels like this life: watching the world pass by on our way to death. Dario's phone rings.

"Hello, my love, how are you?"

He's now driving at 70 miles per hour, a joint in one hand on the wheel and his phone in the other hand next to his ear. It's his girlfriend in France. She asks if he has deposited the money into the account of a travel agent to buy her a ticket back to Colombia.

"Love, I will do it in the next hour or so," he tells her, promising that when we pass a bank, he will send the money.

He hangs up and thankfully puts both hands back on the wheel.

Dario gets $20,000 per trip on the semi-sub; $10,000 is up front in case he is captured or disappears at sea, so his family has something.

Most of those who work on the semi-sub have little education and less sense in managing money. Money comes in, money goes out.

"There's the pressure that builds up under the water," and that blows up once the crew is back on land. "It's all parties for them. They burn through the money quickly in parties, women, and drugs."

When the money runs out, it's back to the semi-subs to earn some more. Because once the pilots and crewmen have a taste of this much money, a regular job will never compare.

As in all long Colombian journeys, we cross the Andean mountain range. We drive so high, so quickly, my ears pop. It's chilly and the mist blinds beyond thirty feet. Sometimes the mist clears and we are driving along mountain valleys so vast and beautiful, clouds are hundreds of feet beneath us. Here farmers wander in thick ponchos and hats, sometimes their cheeks rubbed red by mountain gusts. Forests grow on impossible inclines, and farmers plant fields at 45-degree angles. Along this narrow highway, curves are constant, as are the roadside memorials to lives lost in car accidents.

"I pray a lot. I feel the protection even down there."

He crosses himself every time we pass a statue of the Virgin Mary along the side of the highway. He crosses himself ten times during the trip.

He reaches for the second joint and I place my hand on his—to say no.

"It will be fine," he says, sparking it, the car veering across the yellow line that separates the lanes.

The sky darkens; clouds amass above us. We pass by tiny

Colombian villages that line the highway, one house deep, a couple of miles long. Children play just feet from the speeding cars and buses. We drive past five children who have set up football goals on each side of the highway; the ten-year-olds stand with the football in their hands waiting for the cars to pass. Mothers sit in laid-back chairs with babies on their laps, watching the cars roar past. Many will rarely leave their village, most will never see the capital. A life along the highway watching the voyages of others.

We pass through countless landslides that have been tidied to the side of the road. In one spot, half of the highway has collapsed down the mountainside, leaving a gaping chasm. All signs of the futile attempts to impose a nation on so savage a landscape. Colombia has always been too much to control, to tame. And our car hits the highway's potholes at 75 miles per hour, jolting us up and down, a reminder of the endemic corruption.

Around the corner, traffic is stationary. Dario slams on the brakes. The line of cars ahead of us stretches three hundred yards, ending in an accident of two big trucks.

We sit for twenty minutes. We look at each other. Neither of us wants to be late. Along these highways, passengers can wait twelve, fourteen hours for accidents to be cleared off the road. I feel an iron fist squeeze my stomach. And I know this world well enough—if anything goes wrong, they'll blame me for sure.

A motorbike drives up from the accident.

"Small cars can get through! Move it! Move it!"

Dario swings the car out of the line of cars and guns it to the accident site. The two trucks, one carrying timber, the other transporting cars, traverse the two-lane highway. Part of one truck has gone through the cabin of the other. I can't imagine someone surviving that. Locals stand around. There's no ambulance. God knows where the closest hospital is.

We're flying along the highway again and his girlfriend phones.

"Yes, my love," he answers. He explains the accident. She's not convinced, yet he assures her—he'll send the money shortly.

"Man, I have to deposit this money," he says.

He lights another joint.

Thick clouds have darkened now across the late afternoon sky. It starts to rain.

He overtakes a speeding truck as we approach a blind corner. The truck won't slow down and so we're racing parallel to it heading toward the curve. A car appears ahead of us, in our lane, heading straight to us. Dario doesn't react. Is he zoned out? Half a second passes. "Now," I say. No reaction and we're on course for a head-on crash, a smash of twisted metal, shards of glass and ripped off limbs.

"Now!" And he swerves. The other driver smashes the horn and flicks his high beams.

I tell him to get it together. He nods.

We've crossed the mountain range's peak and now the highway heads down. Point a bicycle down and let go, you'd glide for hours. When we leave the mountains, we drive by the river's edge, where children dive off bridges to cool off from the smothering heat and humidity.

Colombians themselves are astounded by the infinite beauty of their own country. Dario squeals with delight at each waterfall that passes us by. A country of such potential, such amazing people, but trapped in such hopeless circles.

We stop at a small town bank, he deposits the money. And we're off again.

"My love, it's done," he explains when she calls again. I can hear she is suspicious. He hangs up.

He tells me about her.

"We had a relationship for five years. And nothing. Last year, we broke up, but we got back together for a few nights last November. Then we broke up again," he says. She flew to France. And then three weeks ago, she called him up.

"She tells me she's pregnant. I'm going to be a father. And I want this in my life. She says it will be a girl," he says.

It's now August. I don't say anything.

"I want a baby to take care of. To kiss. To stroke," he says.

We're into the flatlands now. Enormous farms stretch out on each side of the highway. We drive looking out over these farms with no end in sight. Land is owned like fiefdoms in Colombia. The richest 1 percent of landholders own 81 percent of arable land.

We pass by an overturned bus that veered off the freeway into a ditch. It's the second accident we've seen and it feels like an omen. A young woman is on the phone crying. A man is crouched down, his head in his hands. The bus's lights are flashing in the night. Steam comes out of the bus, its underside naked to us. A mother comforts a hysterical child. Police stand around. An arriving ambulance wails.

The rain is coming down now. The lightning is so large, and hammers down on each side of the highway. One strike is so close, all I see is white for a millisecond.

"She sells sex, there in France," Dario says out of nowhere. He doesn't look at me, but straight ahead. "She says she wants to give birth here to the baby. Make it all Colombian. She tells me the girls there in France are in danger. They mistreat the Latin women who sell sex."

Hence the urgency of the ticket.

The only lights are those of our car and those of oncoming cars—there are no lights on the highway. An important stretch of highway in the country, connecting to a major port, but the local government hasn't installed any lights. Colombia is poor. But not that poor. Corruption is everywhere.

She phones back. He puts her on speakerphone.

"He says he hasn't received the money. You haven't done it yet!" she screams at him.

"Yes, I have!" he screams back.

I'm losing my mind: I'm stuck in a small car next to a couple screaming at each other in a cloud of stale weed smoke.

Dario shouts back, the rain is hard, the lightning smashes down all around our car. On a potholed and slippery highway, our car is moving too fast. We're leaving a trail of white marijuana smoke. Out of the darkness, through the rainy windshield, appear traffic cones and a large digger. And in the moment my brain registers what our car is hurtling toward, I'm already conscious that we're already that much closer to the digger's claws. He slams the brakes on. And we're sliding at a velocity that will be terminal. I'm thrown forward, my hands slamming on the dashboard. In the screaming and the lightning, I think: this is how I die.

We come to a stop less than a yard from the digger.

"Hang up the fucking phone on your fucking girlfriend!" I shout in his face.

Dario and his girlfriend are silent for a second.

"Now look what you've done! The gringo is pissed at me!" he screams into the phone and hangs up.

The rest of the journey is mostly in silence. The underworld doesn't get its first shot at the best of any generation. No, it's stuck with the no-hopers, men like Dario. You know when drug busts occur because someone did something stupid? Those are the Darios who keep police departments happy.

BUENAVENTURA IS THE CORPSE OF the dream of globalization. The people of Buenaventura live its failure every day. It's Colombia's biggest port, a gateway to trade with the rest of the world. Tens of billions of dollars pass through here each year, massive containers ferried across the Pacific Ocean to Central America, the United States, Europe, and Asia. In comes imports of televisions, cars, laptops. Out goes exports of coal, coffee, and cocaine. (Another example of Colombia's dire infrastructure—it costs less to send a container from Buenaventura to China, some ten thousand miles away, than it does to send that container by road from Buenaventura to the capital, Bogota.)

Yet this largely Afro-Colombian town sees none of these billions. Poverty here staggers. Slums stretch out on the sea. Entire neighborhoods are constructed on wooden stilts that sit atop the ocean. Wooden planks serve as pavements and corridors connecting each wooden shack. Bathrooms are a hole in the wooden floor that drops directly into the Pacific. Running water, stable electricity are dreams for many inhabitants here. Tsunami signs are all across the city. A big wave will kill thousands instantly.

Buenaventura receives almost no benefit for being a major transit zone for cocaine shipments—but it gets all the downsides. Different mafias fight to control this vital port: the Gulf Clan, La Empresa (the firm), narco-militias newly born in the post peace process chaos. The famous chopping houses started here in Buenaventura. Corruption is endemic. Police officers have sold snitches back to the mafia in the past. Four mayors have been arrested for corruption in Buenaventura in the past seven years.

When the occasional huge bust of cocaine is made by the police, the residents of Buenaventura know to expect a trail of dead bodies as the narcos work their way back, looking for the snitch. Better one hundred innocent men die than the guilty get off scot-free.

Traffickers showed the people of Buenaventura they were expendable. Under the reign of one trafficker, the ex-policeman known as "Jabon," the city became famous for bombs exploding simultaneously across the city: a supermarket, a police station, along a highway. The bombs weren't meant to kill dozens, just those unlucky enough to be standing next to them. It took months of these attacks before authorities realized they were a diversion: with everybody responding to the bombs, the narco-subs gently glided out to sea.

When the blood runs a little too freely through these half-built streets, the city militarizes itself, and marines patrol civilian neighborhoods, their fingers on the triggers. The cartels are wise to this. The violence tumbles as the combos and cartels wait it out. The game is always the same: militarize the city, murder rates plummet in Buenaventura, but explode in another spot along the Pacific Coast. The authorities proclaim victory in Buenaventura and move the marines to the new hot spot. And here the murder rate once again climbs. Someone once said, "Colombia is a tragedy with its own flag."

In the desperation, the bishop of Buenaventura suggests exorcising Buenaventura itself, performed by him from a helicopter.

"Some popes and saints have said that the main victory of the devil has been to make us believe he doesn't exist. It's not a devil with horns and a tail, but the evil there is in the world that shows itself through murder, corruption, robberies and extortion," he tells Caracol radio. "In Buenaventura, we need to kick out the devil so we can return this city to the peace it lost with so many crimes, so much corruption, so much evil and drug trafficking that invaded our port."

The city has an allure—sleazy and dangerous, but charming. An energy flows through its people. In front of their homes people sit slamming dominos while dancing in their chairs to the salsa songs blasting from six-foot-high speakers. The city has produced a succession of Colombia's greatest salsa acts.

Among the rows of shacks, the occasional three-story building with tremendous columns will appear and through the windows one can see the high-end stereo system and plasma television. That's the sign to his neighbors that the owner "crowned"—successfully delivered the drugs and got his money. What's the point of risking and earning big if you can't show off to the neighbors?

And lying alongside this city is the Pacific Ocean. The Pacific Coast off South America is not that of Tahiti, bone-white sand, blue skies, and crystal water. No, here the Pacific Coast is a lurching tumult of browns, of rain and black sand. It's not easy. In any sense. But once accepted, understood, its stunningly beautiful shorelines of sand are the only barrier between thick jungle and the ocean. The water is always chilly, the sky always overcast. One feels the storm's first raindrop and thirty-six-hours later you're still listening to the roar of the downpour.

For centuries, generations have relied on fishing. You see these men come in from the sea every day, carrying the catch. These men were schooled on the sea and not much else. This way of life is dying. Years of overfishing means the profession that once allowed a man to feed his family with dignity now provides a pittance. Huge Asian and European trawlers drag nets through the waters just outside Colombian territory, emptying the waters. With no care for sustainability, fish populations are destroyed. Entire stretches of the sea are now lifeless.

A Buenaventura fisherman is not going to learn to work in an office. He would think such work beneath him, a man proud to work with his hands, a job that requires courage, knowhow. From this pool do the cartels recruit their captains for the semi-subs.

UNDER COVER OF NIGHT, ARMED men oversee the packing of cocaine onto a speedboat. The crew is put onto the boat and told the route. The speedboat cranks its engines and sets off across the Pacific Ocean. The boat is jetting toward the border of Mexico and Guatemala. The aim is to do it in two days.

The technical name is a low-profile vessel, an LPV, made of fiberglass. It rides fast and low, in between the waves, dodging radars. It's fifty feet of speed and grace. It's the latest model, extra-wide to carry more cocaine. The entire front end is tightly packed with two tons of cocaine. Each kilo is marked with the logo of Corona Extra, a stamp to identify who owns the cocaine. The crew of three—Luis, Efren, and Alexis—all from Buenaventura's slums, all here for the money, sit on top of the bales of cocaine and the dozens of canisters of gasoline.

Luis is a fifty-five-year-old Afro-Colombian, with the large physique of a life lived laboring. He's a grandfather who was able to put his five children through school before fishing became impossible. He's in the boat because he owes money to Colombia's loan sharks, men called "drop by drop."

His wife of forty years was struck with paralysis, bedridden. Luis has no education, so when asked what she suffers from, he's unsure. A doctor gave him a list of medicine to buy. Luis was broke, but couldn't face the idea of his wife in such pain. He took out a loan of $1,200. The medicine worked and his wife slowly improved. She even started walking again. Luis's daughter looked after her mother full-time, while Luis tried to earn money to pay off the loan, the equivalent of five months' normal wages.

Luis worked where he could, doing whatever he could find. Still, he fell behind on the payments. Loan sharks are gun happy. It's part of the business plan to kill those who don't pay—let one client embarrass you and no one will ever pay you back.

So, they kick in the door of his shack at midnight and put a gun to his wife's head. Final warning.

For a man like Luis in Colombia, it is impossible to earn $1,200 in a short amount of time—legally. You might as well ask him to earn a billion. He knows how to earn money quickly. He asks around and someone puts him in touch with someone who needs a hand on a boat that will race across the Pacific.

It's risky and he knows it. In April 2009, Luis traveled on a semi-sub to Guatemala, where they unloaded tons of cocaine on the high sea onto small boat. Luis and the crew opened the holes and sank the semi-sub. They boarded the boat and went ashore. They traveled to the capital and flew back to Colombia. Three months later, Luis gets on another semi-sub: sixty feet long, a foot above the water's surface, seven feet beneath the surface. It's tight for the four men and the five tons of cocaine.

They were 350 miles off Costa Rica when the US Coast Guard spotted them. The crew worked quickly as the Coast Guard steamed toward them—life jackets on, board the life raft, and let the semi-sub sink. The Coast Guard picked them up. The United States didn't have the physical evidence of cocaine, but they had the video of the crew sinking the semi-sub, so they took it to court.

He pleaded guilty in his trial in Florida. The judge in the trial got a glimpse of Colombia's disorder.

JUDGE: What is your education background.
LUIS (THROUGH AN INTERPRETER): No. I haven't studied.
JUDGE: Can you read and write in Spanish?
LUIS: I can only sign my name.

IN COURT, LUIS SAID: "I would like to apologize to this country, to this constitution for the mistake that I committed. I committed this mistake because I am lacking in resources and that's why I was forced to make this mistake."

He's sentenced to 135 months in prison. Luis agreed to cooperate with the DEA, revealing all he knows about the man who recruited and paid him. That man is extradited and prosecuted in a US court. As thanks, Luis was given a reduced sentence, down to eighty-seven months.

He served his time, and returned to Colombia—in a brutal, merciless economy, he was a man without education, now in his fifties. Then his wife was struck ill. He looked out over the Pacific and got ready to do it again. He was paid $20,000 for the trip, half up front, so the loan sharks were paid off.

The other crewman is Efren. He doesn't speak much. He's in shorts, flip-flops, and a New York Yankees baseball cap.

The captain is thirty-nine-year-old Alexis, short black hair with a mustache. His is a life lived in Colombia's violence. He grew up in Tumaco, one of six brothers. His father abandoned them before he was born and his mother raised him to be a fisherman. Alexis married his childhood sweetheart and they had two children.

It was a poor but dignified life. But the catches were ever smaller as overfishing dried the oceans up. Alexis started working in a barbershop in Tumaco. One day as he cut a man's hair, a man from the FARC strode in and killed the man mid-haircut. The FARC sent Alexis death threats warning him not to testify. Alexis and his family fled to Buenaventura. He tried to make a life for him and his family, but poverty was the constant. A drug trafficker approached Alexis and asked him to captain the boat. Colombia produces these vast pools of men and women ready to risk their lives.

All three men have made their decisions and the vessel is now at sea. The LPV takes the route north, and then west. Colombia's coastline is behind it. Ahead is the Pacific Ocean, the vastest, loneliest stretch on earth. They'll hug the southern flank of Central America, passing Panama, Costa Rica, Nicaragua, El Salvador, Guatemala.

These are the wildest, loneliest waters on the planet, the eastern Pacific Ocean. Man was never meant to thrive on these waves. This is the world of below, a landscape of the endless, punctuated by whales and dolphins. Clumsy visitors, we stumble and drown in these sharks' playgrounds.

The kilo races west across the Pacific Ocean, chasing a never-ending sunset. Destination: the Guatemalan–Mexico border. The kilo is in her last stretch, a final 1,000-mile dash. If she can make it to Mexican waters, cocaine will be injected directly into the global economy's veins. Mexican cartels will receive the kilos, cut them, and then push them across the border into the market that craves cocaine the most: the United States of America.

As the speedboat tears west, the three men talk above the roar of the engine. Luis confesses this isn't his first time with cocaine: he has spent years in an American prison. Efren confesses the same. Alexis looks at them both. He's never broken the law. All three look at each other, and then one says it: Are we the bait? Is there a larger shipment taking an alternative route and these men are nothing more than a distraction? Have they lost before they started? Did they never have a chance?

There's nothing left to do. They've all taken the mafia's money. They must keep heading west and hope for the best.

CHAPTER 12

PLAYGROUND OF SHARKS

TO LOOK OUT OVER THE EASTERN PACIFIC Ocean is to see nothing: no land, no ship, not a soul. A dolphin's leap, a whale's surface, a shark's fin, the only disturbances to the rhythmic waves. Sky and sea. A landscape unchanged by millions of years. Look out and take in the void. But somewhere in that nothing, there's cocaine. In this infinity, the Coast Guard cutter the *James* must find the kilo.

The invisible thread of the US market's demand for cocaine has pulled the kilo through jungles, mountains, highways, and warehouses. Now it drags the brick of cocaine across the Pacific Ocean west toward the largest cocaine market on the planet. The war on drugs pushes the warship *James* east. And here, in the eastern Pacific, is where they two currents smash into each other. Up until now, they've been shadowboxing; the United States has donated funds and intelligence to stop cocaine, but always at a remove. Now the United States and cocaine clash head-on, on the high seas. The United States will bring the most technologically advanced tools to track and spot the cocaine. The traffickers will respond with their own ingenuity and the desperation of fishermen in need of money.

It's one of the last chances to stop the kilo.

THE COAST GUARD CUTTER *JAMES* imposes even as she rests. The 418-foot warship has powered down and sways gently with the waves. Sailors break for a smoke and a joke.

"I've got buddies who are cops back home. They get excited when they bust someone with a kilo," says one sailor. Already, his friends are laughing. "I'm like: Bro! You know how much we haul?"

A few yards behind us are stacked thousands of kilos of pure cocaine, worth tens and tens and tens of millions of dollars. It's freshly snatched coke from Colombian smugglers. These are good days here at the end of the world.

Sailors tally the seized cocaine and through the *James'* 120-crew, there's a collective smile. This is why they're here: to nab other people's cocaine. And today there is lots of it. Sailors keep tossing bales of coke on the boat's stern. The mound of kilos grows taller, fatter.

We're somewhere, nowhere in the middle of the eastern Pacific Ocean, a place sharks and whales call home. We're around 180 miles south of Costa Rica. Only empty seas and deserted horizons. This stretch of the eastern Pacific is the world's most important cocaine corridor.

Some of this flow of cocaine has ended here on the deck of the *James*. One hundred bales of cocaine in black, threaded plastic bags, stacked. To be precise, two tons of cocaine. Two million grams of cocaine. The Coast Guard estimates the haul at $60 million. That's cheap. Roll these two tons further along the chain up to New York City and these blocks are now worth more than $80 million. Wholesale. Retail? This is worth more than $200 million.

Maritime Enforcement Specialist First Class David Johnson cuts open one of the bales. He's a big man with a shaved head. He saws through the tough material with a thick knife. He reaches in and grabs one of the kilos and pulls it out. The brick of pure cocaine is tightly wrapped in yellow plastic, a big Corona Extra beer logo on its side. The logo identifies which trafficker owns this cocaine. Owned. It's the Coast Guard's now.

About five hundred feet off the Coast Guard cutter, across shark-infested water, sailors douse a speedboat, an LPV, in gasoline. Painted sea-gray, the boat is sharp and narrows like a bullet for speed. Out here it's the quick and the dead.

The crew is buzzed because they've never seen this boat's wide design before. The two tons of cocaine were packed so tightly in the fifty-foot ship, the sailors needed an electrical saw to cut open the boat's deck to get to the drugs. When finished, they bring back the sawed-out plate from the boat. War mementos.

The cocaine, the boat are the result of a twelve-hour operation that ran all night. Shortly a sailor will toss a match on the gasoline-covered speedboat and send it to the ocean bottom. The Coast Guard doesn't have the capacity to carry all the boats they find out here, and left floating they're a hazard to all sea traffic.

The speedboat was on a mad dash across the Pacific. The plan was to race the one thousand miles in forty-eight hours: gun the engines and no sleep. In the boat, there is only water, bags of crackers, and gasoline to get them to Mexico. It was spotted by a routine patrol aircraft plane and the *James* plotted a course that would intercept the boat. When they got close, two small boats and the helicopter launched from the *James* and the pursuit was afoot. The team was so stealthy they emerged from the dark night like lightning, surprising the smugglers into a quick surrender.

In the early morning, a little Coast Guard boat returns to the *James,* docking in the back of the warship. Aboard are the three Colombian smugglers. Coast Guard sailors offer their hands to help the traffickers off the boat. They're all dressed in T-shirts, shorts, and flip-flops. As one gets out of the small boat, he tilts his head back to take in the size of this warship. Now he can see the enormity of his doom, the giant that stalked them in the dark.

The three smugglers are escorted across the basketball-court-sized flight deck, taking in the massive warship in all its glory. They pass the orange helicopter that haunted them all last night. One of the men shakes his head, like "We never had a chance." Every step they take is one closer to the US prison cell they know awaits them. Yet they're surprisingly compliant. No one messes around—the Coast Guard is guiding the detainees with firmness and respect and the detainees are cooperating.

Walking the deck, the smugglers look east at the inferno on the water. That's their speedboat ablaze and alone on the Pacific horizon. They're transfixed by the black smoke that columns into the blue sky.

At the end of the deck, the Colombians arrive at the cutter's hangar. Two Coast Guard officials sit behind a table and register them. The men are frisked; their possessions, the cell phones and wallets, are put in a plastic Ziploc bag. They're handed a briefcase-sized whiteboard asking name, date of birth, nationality, and ID number. They dutifully fill them out. Letters and numbers—wholly insufficient to explain the life-and-death decision to race cocaine across the Pacific Ocean.

The three are from Buenaventura. There's nothing $60 million about them. The first is a gaunt fifty-five-year old Afro-Colombian, with a New York Yankees cap over his shaved head, shorts, and flip-flops. He stands before the table of Coast Guard women who register him. He doesn't know what to do with his hands. He gives his name: Efren. They give him his "welcome package," a Ziploc bag of toothpaste, toothbrush, deodorant, and soap. He's taken away for a shower and a medical checkup.

The second is a thirty-nine-year-old mestizo, Alexis. He shows them his passport. It's pristine, issued just three weeks earlier. First trip ever leaving Colombia and it's to smuggle cocaine. He tells them that he is the captain. He's shuffled off.

Third and last is a fifty-five-year-old man, with a massive chest and forearms, a lifetime of hard work under the Pacific sun. He struggles to write his name: Luis. I try to read his face (the Coast Guard won't allow any interviews with these men). I imagine it's the courage of the old man, closer to the end than the beginning, to risk more. And so he agreed to carry two tons of the cartel's cocaine to Mexico.

When they run the names, the Coast Guard see that Luis and Efren have been imprisoned before. If they're convicted—and how will they not be?—it's hard to imagine they'll see Colombia or their families again. Families of prisoners in Buenaventura don't have the money to visit the United States, which also isn't wild on handing out visas to the families of cocaine smugglers.

This is it. The end of the road. Decisions taken. Decisions paid for.

All this hangs in the air as they process the three men.

Luis's life is ending before our eyes. Across his eyes play regrets, sadness. Then a small stiffening of his back, his head stands higher. It's the pride of a man: I'll show you how a man from Buenaventura takes his blows!

It's a moment Luis will never forget. It's as intimate as watching someone lose their virginity. Or die.

The three men are taken for a shower and a medical checkup by the ship's doctor. When they return to the hangar, they're in the Coast Guard's burgundy scrubs and flip-flops. Along the hangar's floor are the yoga mats that will be their beds.

The Coast Guard offers them a prison Bible in Spanish: "Libre entre las rejas," "Free between the bars." None take it.

In the hangar, there are forty more detainees. None of the three speak. What's there to say? What good would words do? A moment for silence. Do they wonder? Were they the decoy? Did they ever have a chance? They'll never know the truth.

Alexis will be taken to the United States. He will accept a plea deal in a Florida court that will sentence him to fourteen years in prison. Efren will get the same. Luis will get seventeen and a half years. Luis is unlikely to ever return home. It is even more unlikely he will see his wife again, chronically sick as she is. The one reason he took this journey.

All of this awaits them. Now each man sits on his mat. A Coast Guard member points at Luis's foot and asks: Left or right? Luis nods at his right foot. The sailor closes the handcuffs through a metal cable that runs along the base of the mats and around the old man's right ankle. It shuts with a snap.

"ALL CREW TO THE DECK. Evidence detail," the intercom squawks, reaching every corner of the eight-decked boat.

The two tons of cocaine have to be stored, shifted from the boat's stern to a designated storage area. Dozens of crew members form a human chain that stretches four hundred feet through various decks of the warship. In chemical masks, the crew passes the hundred bales of cocaine, each weighing twenty kilos. Each bale is passed from the stern of the boat, through narrow metallic corridors, down steel stairs, and along the length of the boat.

It takes twenty-five minutes, and the crew is sweaty as the final bale moves along the chain. The cocaine is locked in a restricted area. All these sailors can tell their grandchildren about the day two tons of cocaine passed through their fingers. This cocaine will eventually be delivered over to the DEA and its incinerator back in the States.

Outside, the flames engulf the speedboat. It's the informal ritual after each of these busts for the crew to watch the sight of the fire on the ocean. The blazing boat upends. The back end, weighed down with the engines, always sinks first. The flaming boat stands in the air, the yellows and oranges dance against the rich blue sky. Twenty of the crew stand at the rails taking in the beautiful destruction. We fear death but nothing so pleases the human eye as annihilation. The boat is sinking and is soon to be sucked to the bottom of the Pacific, baffling sharks, whales, and giant squids as it descends.

Cameron Carrol, lieutenant junior grade, watches the boat go down. He shudders.

"It's just a very eerie feeling being a sailor, professional mariner, seeing any boat sink."

Spooky. The burning boat sinks and is gone, leaving only a cloud of black smoke of a fire that once existed.

"It's a great score. The boat is energized and ready for our next case," says Executive Officer James Jarnac. Everyone calls him XO. Both he and Captain Jeff Randall have been up all night, following the chase's progress. Now they're down on the deck to see the captured men and cocaine. Captain Randall nods his head. He tries to repress a smile, but he beams.

Taking down two tons of cocaine by repeat traffickers is a big win for the cutter *James,* its captain, and its crew. It's Sunday and it's the cap to a great week. Beneath them, plastered on the wall, is the ship's unofficial motto: "Own the Night."

By my count, the *James* now has picked up five tons of cocaine and forty-three detainees in less than two weeks patrolling the eastern Pacific. The boat can't move without capturing cocaine: 450 kilos and three fishermen. 700 kilos and three fishermen. 400 kilos and three fishermen. With cocaine raining down, everyone on the *James* is giddy.

These are the good times. They won't last.

THE COAST GUARD CUTTER *JAMES* is on a ninety-day counternarcotics mission in the eastern Pacific to stop the cocaine from Colombia from reaching Central America and Mexico.

The Coast Guard had told me that if I wanted action, the *James* was the boat. They told me to be in the Costa Rican town of Golfito on the thirteenth of October. The *James* would be there to resupply food and gasoline.

I fly into Costa Rica and take a bus down to Golfito, a sleepy fishing town on the Pacific Coast. The town is so small, a taxi driver tells me, it doesn't even have a disco. I wonder if I have the right town until I walk to the port and through the dense fog see the massive cutter *James.* In the mist that hangs over the water, the *James* looks like Godzilla. This half-a-billion-dollar warship dwarfs Golfito. At the front of the *James* is a massive cannon, the type of mechanized death that blows planes out of the sky. I'd bet on the *James* against Costa Rica itself.

Restocked, rested, and recreated, the *James* steams out of Golfito for the vastness of the eastern Pacific. By the end of the day—not twelve hours outside of port—it nabs a fishing boat with seven hundred kilos of cocaine and three Ecuadorian fishermen. Jesus Christ, we're going to be swimming in cocaine, I think. Then: Jesus Christ, how much cocaine is out here?

When I thought of the Coast Guard, I imagined men with bushy white beards, thick blue blazers, and a pint of rum in their hands, pointing to the coming storm with a "Ay, matey, it'll be a bad one."

I pictured them as an almost entirely volunteer organization dedicated to rescuing those stranded at sea. What I didn't know—and I'm guessing you didn't know, too—was that that was my grandfather's Coast Guard. The Coast Guard of the twenty-first century is a heavily armed police force for the high seas. And it's one of the biggest cocaine stompers out there, seizing hundreds of tons a year, more cocaine than all other US agencies combined.

LIFE ON THE *JAMES* IS strange: a floating village on a permanent voyage. The ship does not move toward a destination, but rather circles throughout the eastern Pacific, chasing down suspicious boats. Moving and living to the gentle sway of the sea becomes second nature.

It's a floating village with its gym, restaurant, study groups, common areas, Catholic mass, Bible meetups. The mess has the feeling of a school cafeteria. Dozens line up to get the meals. Sunday night steak. Taco Tuesday. Fish Friday. Sandwich Saturday. Sailors take their seat in the long benches. Two huge TV screens show AFN, the Armed Forces Network. It's mostly sports, interspersed with commercials inviting soldiers to dances in Kuwait and skiing in Germany, and offering help for those suffering depression.

Felicia DeCastro is the supply officer, the one who keeps the floating village floating. She oversees logistics, administration, medical, food, all with a booming laugh. "It takes a lot of patience and understanding because you live where you work." She gives a thick, throaty laugh to make sure you get exactly what she's saying. "You don't get to go home and leave it all behind you. It creates a family-like atmosphere."

The *James* is a monster—each anchor weighs 7,000 pounds and is at the end of 810-feet chains. A voracious monster, it guzzles $1 million in fuel over its three-month mission. Its crew gets through 15,000 eggs, a ton of beef, and 1.5 tons of chicken. It spends a quarter of a million dollars on food.

"Cooks are the biggest source of morale on board. If the food is bad, everyone is unhappy," she says.

She's found herself to be the sympathetic ear for people adjusting to ninety days in the empty eastern Pacific. The secret is that people have to be cool to live together. You need respect for those around you. Most of the crew share rooms, often four bunks in a room. Life is carried on throughout long steel corridors broken up with heavy doors that swing shut with a slam.

"We have a really decent crew. I've seen some people get in trouble under way—they've been out to sea for twenty-eight days or thirty days. That's a long time to go without seeing land and trees and birds"—throaty laugh—"and so they get a little crazy. For the most part, pretty well behaved."

She sees the beauty in the ocean as it goes by.

"It's funny how you don't realize what you take for granted until you don't have it. The simple things, like birds, trees, dirt." Laugh. "When you don't see that for days on end, it's like man, I miss that stuff. But when you're home, you're like whatever, it will always be there."

DeCastro believes in the mission.

"I don't think the end of the drug war is near. They will always find more creative ways and we have to find creative solutions in stopping them. It's going to be an ongoing thing. But every kilo counts. That's one less kilo on the streets in the cities my kids live in."

CAPTAIN JEFF RANDALL IS THE captain of the *James*. He's spent his time in the Coast Guard trying to figure out how to stop people committing crime, how traffickers think, and why they smuggle. That's how he will stop the cocaine arriving in the United States.

"I'm trying to think about how I can be ahead of my opponent here. It's somewhat like a chess game. I'm going to watch their move and I may make a countermove. Sometimes I might make an offensive move and sometimes I might make a defensive move."

Essentially, the captain has to choose the exact place and exact moment to be somewhere to nab the traffickers. All the traffickers need do is avoid that one spot at that one time and they'll make it. Battleship—plugging away at the map, guessing where the traffickers may be. The Associated Press estimates the Coast Guard's five cutters cover six million square miles "from the Caribbean and the Gulf of Mexico to the eastern Pacific Ocean—it's like having a few police cars watch over the entire lower 48 states."

Randall is a big guy, his still-dark hair brushed forward over his forehead. He has the pleasant habit of thinking on his words.

He's worked in Alaska, Hawaii, North Carolina, and now Charleston, South Carolina, where the *James* is permanently based. Randall has performed search and rescues, enforced fishing regulations, and helped out when Hurricane Maria slammed into Puerto Rico. He also sailed up to the Gulf of Mexico to aid in the rescue efforts in 2010's Deepwater Horizon disaster (an explosion on an oil rig killed eleven people and caused the largest oil spill ever in US waters).

"When we were on our way to Deepwater Horizon to respond to that oil spill, we were passing through this area off of Costa Rica and we actually took down a go-fast vessel."

Throughout his time in the Coast Guard, he's seen it become more militarized. Just like the rest of society, the 9/11 attacks militarized the Coast Guard.

"Prior to 2001, there was a lot of focus on saving lives and search and rescue because that's where a lot of our heritage lies," he says. "When 2001 happened, we had to fundamentally shift our mindset a little bit to becoming a more military and professional organization to counter the types of individuals who performed the acts of 2001."

The fear was what terrorists could bring into the United States from the sea. So the Coast Guard took a bigger role in searching the seas that surround the country, looking for contraband. Now the Coast Guard was a heavily armed agency, becoming a version of the police in the seas. And with that, it became their responsibility to hunt down the drugs.

Randall likes counternarcotics. He's read up on the industry, seen how cocaine destabilizes Colombia, Central America, and Mexico, financing the mafias there. He realizes that the smugglers they pick up are not the bosses.

"These are essentially the truck drivers driving down I-95, running loads to the distribution center in Mexico somewhere, Guatemala. They're supplying the distribution center."

These missions stop some of the cocaine and also accumulate evidence to be used in criminal cases against the Colombian cartels. He sees the relationship between cocaine, the chaos in Central America and Mexico, and the ongoing crisis of immigration.

"As drugs move into Mexico they create violence and destabilization. The legitimate governments have a tough time providing for basic security and as a result the people are trying to leave that situation and go to a better place and in this case it's America.

"When you stop it from reaching the shores or you stop it from reaching Central America and causing further destabilization of the legitimate governments, or when you are able to take out individuals that are connected to these criminal organizations and continue moving up to try to dismantle the organizations, you realize that you're contributing to something, that your work is part of something bigger that makes a difference and can make a difference in the collective society beyond just yourself.

"The downside is . . . it never ends."

He knows that is reducing demand is the key. But how?

"How do you tackle the demand piece . . ." There is a big sigh. "I think if I had an answer to that question, we'd have an answer to the drug problem."

THE PACIFIC OCEAN IS TOO much for one mind; its size fries the brain's circuits. The Pacific Ocean covers one-third of the earth's surface, larger than all the planet's combined landmass. It totals 63.8 million square miles. The earth's deepest point is in the Pacific, the Mariana Trench. It lies nearly seven miles beneath the ocean surface—imagine flying a 747 at cruising altitude, but beneath the waves—that's the depth of the trench. Imagine the monsters that dwell down there. It's called the Hadal zone, named after the Ancient Greeks' underworld Hades. This is 170,000,00 cubic miles of water. Numbers reach a certain level and they cease to make sense. Just swap the numbers for infinity and maybe they will become clearer.

"I never really believed the seventy-one percent of the earth's surface is covered with salt water until I flew over the Pacific," says astronaut Jerome "Jay" Apt, who gazed at the ocean from space. "Sometimes it took thirty-five minutes of our ninety-minute orbit to cross the Pacific."

The immensity inspires thoughts of gods and eternities. Pacific islanders believe gods live in these waves. Shark gods. Peru's Incas looked out and saw Mama Cocha, *Mother of Waters*. She is described as pale and beautiful. The indigenous would commune with her to calm violent waters, for abundant fishing.

Godlike, the Pacific Ocean was here before us and will outlast humanity. The sounds of the Pacific's waves feel like they hold within them our planet's history, if we just knew how to understand the notes. That rhythmic slap of the wave is one of the oldest noises on earth. When the sound of the waves finally ceases, so will earth. Because that will be when the earth's oldest sound, a wind, will be alone, whipping across an earth scorched red and too dried out for the Pacific Ocean.

Even this immensity must end. The ocean's eastern edge crashes up against South America. This stretch of the Pacific is a natural jewel. A natural sea corridor links islands off Ecuador, Colombia, and Costa Rica. Gorgona Island is here, named after the ancient Greek monstrosity whose hair was made of countless serpents, a nod to the island's inhabitants. Here are the Galapagos Islands, which inspired Charles Darwin's theory of evolution. If he had lived to see the cocaine industry, Darwin would have recognized the evolution.

Along this thousand-mile corridor roam pods of humpback whales and shivers of hammerhead sharks. Teeming with life beneath the waves, it is utterly desolate above the surface, one of the loneliest places on earth, an empty landscape. For thousands of miles there is nothing but open water. If you set off from the port of Buenaventura heading due west, the first landmass you'll hit will be Papua New Guinea, more than six thousand miles away. Sail south, and after thousands of miles, you reach Antarctica. Then what are you going to do?

Two fishermen were caught in a storm off Mexico that killed their engine. They drifted across the ocean. It took 438 days to reach the US Marshall Islands and only one was still alive.

Vast and empty, it is the perfect corridor for illegal narcotics. More cocaine passes along these waters than any other stretch of the world—connecting cocaine's producers to the largest consumer market. The Coast Guard estimates that 85 percent of the cocaine consumed in the United States will pass through the eastern Pacific Ocean.

And the *James* wants to stop it all.

DOTTED THROUGH THE *JAMES* ARE pictures of Joshua James himself. Now, he is *exactly* how you would imagine a Massachusetts coast guardsman: stern, serious, a man of purpose. In the era of *Moby-Dick,* he became a legendary rescuer of those in distress after witnessing the drowning of his mother and sister when he was ten. He entered the volunteer crew when he was fifteen and spent the next sixty years saving people as the weathers battered boats. In the Great Storm of 1888, over the course of forty-eight hours he led his crew to rescue twenty-nine men from six different shipwrecks. He sailed into storms and rough seas to save more than one thousand people in his life. In 1902, it was another day overseeing training. He sailed his boat ashore, stepped on to the beach, and collapsed. Staring into the sky, hearing the crashing of the waves, James's final words were "The tide is ebbing."

ON BOARD, THE TIGHTEST TEAM are the flyboys, the helicopter crew. In the sea of blue uniforms, the green jumpsuits of Tommy, Jerry, and Ty stand out. They're the eyes in the skies, buzzing through the Pacific in their orange helicopter looking for suspicious vessels. And every mission, they're in the sky as backup.

Ty is funny and has a contagious energy. He's the gunner who puts the bullets in the engines. The helicopter can out-run any boat out there, but it will also end the chase.

"The pilots are flying and they just get you in a safe area to take an effective shot. So, nothing's crazy, that gun target line where you put that round if you miss the motor, its's not going to strike any individual in the boat, it's going to hit the water. So they put you in a safe spot," says Ty. It's absurdly modest. We're talking about making a shot from a moving he-licopter hitting a racing speedboat, being slammed by waves, left, right, up, and down. At night.

The pilots better be skilled too, because for hundreds of miles around, there is one spot alone to land: the deck of the *James*. And in a storm, the ship will be moving, hard.

A common observation among many of the Coast Guard is how few people back home understand what they do in the eastern Pacific.

"You go to soccer games with your kids and other husbands talk about their day in the office. And you try to tell them what you did and they just don't understand," says Ty. "It's not until you actually get here and get put in the game where you're like: 'Oh my God!' It's nonstop, it's the real thing. Until you see that first vessel pulling drugs across a vast ocean, a couple of outboards, an open boat, you think to yourself this person on this boat running drugs across the ocean is crazy, crazier than I am trying to shoot out of this helicopter. Trying to explain that to a regular civilian . . . You can't. . . ."

The madness of the drug war is beyond words.

IT'S THURSDAY NIGHT AND THE flyboys are chasing down another go-fast speedboat. The pilot won't give up. Ty fires out the warning shots. The speedboat keeps slamming forward, diesel burning, all engines blazing. Ty shoulders the rifle and targets the speeding boat's engines. BOOM! The first engine is hit, disabled. The speedboat keeps going, ever deeper to the west. He targets the second engine. BOOM! Half the engine is blown away, dead. Two of the three engines are now dead. Like limbs amputated. The pilot gives up. Three more Ecuadorian fishermen and four hundred more kilos of pure cocaine into the hold.

Now it's Friday morning and someone's got to blow up the boat. Chief Damage Controlman Max Hermes and his demolition team load up on the LRI, or Long-Range Interceptor, a thirty-five-foot boat that is held at the back of the *James*. They're amped; they love their job. The boat slides into the Pacific and sails the mile and a quarter out to the speedboat.

The go-fast gently rocks empty and alone on the waves. It's a spooky sight, a *Mary Celeste* for cocaine. The thirty-foot-long speedboat is all there is on the horizon. A ghost ship. The sea gently slaps the side of the sea-blue boat, that rhythmic slap that never ends. There's nothing else around us: the go-fast, the *James*, and an ocean filled with sharks.

Hermes directs a sailor to jump on to the speedboat. The sailor drills holes at the fore of the vessel. Drilling and sawing, the sailor works his way to the boat's stern. The sailor steps over what the smugglers left behind; drinking water, a shopping bag filled with cookies, and gasoline. Dozens and dozens of twenty-gallon canisters filled with gasoline.

"A shit ton of fuel here—this thing is going to explode!" shouts the sailor gleefully.

To sleep, there was nowhere but to lie on the canisters of gasoline. Taking a shit was balancing on the edge of the boat and sticking your ass to the wind. This captain wasn't stopping.

Hermes looks the go-fast up and down and commends the men who made it. A wooden frame is covered in sheets of fiberglass.

"Locally made, very disposable," he says nodding in appreciation. There's always that grudging respect in the drug war for the professionalism of the adversary.

The sailor has drilled holes all throughout the boat and water slowly ebbs in. The sailor cracks open one of the gasoline canisters and douses the speedboat. He jumps back on to the LRI, which pulls out thirty feet. Hermes lights foot-long matches.

In quick succession, two flaming matches land in the boat. In fifteen seconds, the flames lick out belching black smoke. In ninety seconds, the whole boat is a ball of flame. An inferno on the water fueled by hundreds of gallons of gasoline. From a dense orange ball of fire, flames climb thirty, fifty feet into the sky. Thick smoke columns hundreds of yards into the blue sky. It's that dense smoke that looks like it'd give you immediate cancer with a single inhale.

"Sorry, ozone," says Hermes, with genuine sadness. "We'll pay for it later."

I wonder on the graveyard at the bottom of the Pacific, dozens and dozens of burnt-out boats, relics of unsuccessful runs and smuggler's dreams dashed.

We all sit back and enjoy the beauty of a blaze at sea. It's the most beautiful sight for hundreds of miles.

DAYS ARE FOR CHORES: SWEEPING, painting, fixing, sleeping. At night the boat awakens. There is a different energy when the sun sets: the crew are alert, focused, eagerly awaiting the next operation. This is what they signed up for: kicking in doors on the high seas.

Night is when they strike, arriving like lightning. The *James* has the self-consciousness of all giants, well aware she sticks out for miles in the daylight. Smugglers can see her on a Pacific horizon twenty miles away. But at night, steaming forward with all its lights off, it's a stealthy kraken.

When the sun sets, the lights inside the ship turn bright red, bulbs not so easily seen. In the blood-tinged gloom, silhouettes come in and out of focus as they pass through the corridor. Hellish red bulbs make every face seem demonic.

"LE level one, please prepare, Team Trident, Spear," pipes out the message. Another mission. The radar, the patrolling aircraft, satellites: something has picked up something suspicious.

The teams move to the stern of the boat and the armory is opened. Each sailor puts on their black flak jackets, helmets, life vests. Partners check each other's gear. From the armory, a sailor gives out SIG Sauer P226 handguns, M-16s, and shotguns. Lieutenant Junior Grade Simon Juul-Hindsgaul receives his handgun. He's young and blond as the Dane he is. He's also tall and skinny, a rare sight on a boat where many of the men spend hours a day lifting weights.

Mara Devros grabs her shotgun. She likes the power of the gun—and how it loads. It's also her spirit gun and goes to explain why she joined the Coast Guard.

"Shotgun versus sniper. I view myself as a shotgun. I can get the job done but you can bet your butt, I'm going to be all over the place versus a sniper—he can get his one job done, he can accurately get his job done."

She says the shotgun is the jack of all trades. Like the Coast Guard. She's a machinery technician, but she also carries out these missions to search and seize cocaine. The sniper knows one job—but one job alone. Like the military.

"Whenever we come out down in the East Pacific, I'm like, oh man, there's not a lot out here. . . . There's both feelings: There's the romantic feeling: 'Oh man, there's nothing out here.' And there's the 'Oh man, there's nothing out here!'

"It's that ominous feeling. Let's say if I was to go over right here, right now [into the Pacific]. . . . If I were to go over like this, no strobe light, nothing on me, no personal tracker, it's that ominous feeling of: would I be found?"

As the adrenaline slowly rises in the blood, the teams joke and banter in the darkness. Electricity flows through the air. Excitement. Anticipation. Times are good. They've been busting narcos every day. The order is given and Juul-Hindsgaul and his team move out onto the fantail of the boat, the final piece at the stern.

A glorious moon lays a perfect path of silver over the Pacific. It's chilly and the teams stomp their feet to keep warm as they wait. There's the taste of the sea in the breeze.

The crew of five climbs into the LRI, the boat that hangs at the back of the ship. The only lights are the red torches they all carry. Checks are carried out and one and all say they're ready. Now the *James*'s massive metal stern doors stretch open. Beyond is the black Pacific. The *James* slows down for the launch—but only a little. The LRI hangs there, attached by a cord alone.

"Pull the pin!"

The cord pulled, the LRI slides into the water, into the darkness.

From the small helicopter tower, permission is granted and the helicopter takes off into the sky, veering east toward the suspicious vessel. Flying at night in the Pacific when for hundreds of miles around there's only one spot to land takes teamwork.

"At night you tend to lose your references. You can get spatial disorientation quite easily, especially if you're focused on a moving target. . . . It's easy to lose your reference and try to fly the helicopter the wrong way, hopefully not down," says Tommy, the aircraft commander.

On the side of the *James,* another team, Hammer, board their small boat, the Mark 4. Mara Devros has her shotgun. Her buddy Zach has his M-16—they're the firepower in the boat. They're a good team: she's right-handed and he's left-handed, so they always sit opposite on the boat, ready to blow to kingdom come anyone who fires on their crew.

The boat sways in the air off the side of the *James,* hanging thirty feet above the sea.

Like everyone else in the boat, Devros is excited. And like everyone, there are the nerves.

"I get nervous because you have no idea what's out there."

Cranes and chains lower the boat into the Pacific. It touches down on the choppy waves. A sailor unhooks the metal cable at the front; another unhooks the cable at the back. For a moment the Mark 4 runs parallel with the *James,* then swerves off into the night.

Tonight it's a long ride and the waves are choppy. A bank of thick clouds appears and covers the moon so the boat sails blind. In the darkness, the boat jumps off every wave's crest and lands in every trough—hard. It's uncomfortable: the ups and downs slam their backs and knees. Comfort is not improved by the occasional face slap of cold Pacific salt water. But it's the job.

David Johnson, Maritime Enforcement Specialist First Class, is in charge of the Mark 4 where Devros is riding. He's going through his checklist as they approach the suspicious boat. He's making sure he's focused and alert to the mission. Too much adrenaline fizzles the brain.

"Once you get out on the boats and you're moving to make an approach, if you have too much adrenaline going, that's when mistakes get made. So it's better to have a lesser amount of adrenaline flowing so that you can actually focus on the task at hand: identifying who they are, what they are, and what they're doing," says Johnson.

They're looking for a fishing boat. Earlier that Friday, a US surveillance plane spotted a large fishing boat. And as is common out here, it was pulling a number of smaller fishing boats. What's regular is two or three small fishing boats, called pangas, behind it. This carried seven.

Juul-Hindsgaul is leading the LRI as it barrels full-speed through the night. What if when they arrive, all the pangas scatter, shooting off in different directions? It would be nearly impossible to catch them all. It's decided the two Coast Guard boats will come in like a pincer: Juul-Hindsgaul in the LRI will approach the main shipping vessel from the front and the Mark 4 boat will come in from behind to focus on the pangas.

It's been an hour and through his night-vision goggles Juul-Hindsgaul spots the boat. It's hauling ass, heading west; it's past 9 P.M. Most fishing boats rest at night.

It's a white boat, with the name *Ladi Mar I* (Lady Sea I) written on its side. Next to the name is a painting of a barracuda. The boat is nice by Ecuadorian standards, not the ratty floating bathtubs that the Coast Guard sometimes comes across. It's seventy feet long, two-tiered, with the bridge on the second deck.

Certain that the helicopter and the Mark 4 are in place, Juul-Hindsgaul orders the LRI to put on the flashing blue lights, like the policeman of the high sea. The Mark 4 hangs back, keeping an eye on the pangas trailing behind. The *Ladi Mar* slows down.

Everyone has their hands on their guns. Shoot-outs with these traffickers are so rare, no one can remember a case. Yet, smugglers are often armed against pirates and other smugglers.

The translator shouts to the crew of the *Ladi Mar*. Already a lot of figures are appearing. Five. Ten. Twelve. Sixteen, Juul-Hindsgaul counts.

Where are you going? Where are you heading? Nationality of the boat?

Fishing. Ecuador.

Juul-Hindsgaul orders all the boat's crew to the front of the boat. A large group of obvious fishermen—fishing trousers, rubber boots—move to the front and take a seat on the floor. Yet five men are hanging back at the boat's stern.

Juul-Hindsgaul has never seen so many men on a fishing vessel. Legal or illegal, why are there so many men on this ship?

One man tosses some papers overboard. Another tosses a cell phone. Juul-Hindsgaul radios back to the *James* outlining his suspicions that there may be drugs. He asks that the *James* ask Coast Guard headquarters to talk directly to Ecuador for permission to board and search.

Johnson spots one of the crew moving to the back of the *Ladi Mar* and cutting the line that holds all seven pangas together. Johnson barks to get back.

Johnson studies the pangas. He notices that there are ratchet straps passed around the middle of the pangas like a belt. Up in the helicopter, Ty the gunner is studying the pangas, too, with his heat-sensing infrared radar.

"On our sensor system, all of sudden I'm picking up these heat signatures in the back of these pangas, you know what I mean. You see them, then they go away. So, you're like: Am I really seeing this? . . . You see it again and it disappears and you think, what is going on?"

A blip in a panga. Gone. Another blip in a different panga. Gone.

The helicopter radios down: we think there are people in the pangas. Johnson's boat moves over and examines the first panga. They shine the spotlight over the pangas; they call out. Nothing.

The helicopter radios down: We just saw someone in the second panga. Johnson's boat moves up to the second boat, but again—just a regular panga with a tarpaulin cover.

Then the helicopter radios: Third panga! We've just seen someone else. The Mark 4 moves up to the third panga. In the darkness, Johnson sees a man sitting at the back of the panga. He shouts to him to put his hands in the air. He raises his hands.

The helicopter radios in more movement in the second panga. When the Mark 4 returns, this time Johnson spots a man there. "Hands in the air!"

Devros is looking at the seven pangas and finally realizes there's someone hiding in each fishing boat. In what is one of the loneliest spots on the planet, it's suddenly crowded with thirty-one people.

Up in the helicopter, Ty is getting the big-picture view of what's happening. And in one of the pangas, he sees a man release the ratchet strap.

"That was holding the contraband to the bottom of the pangas. Then all of a sudden a signal was put out and you see people from every panga do the same thing. And that all happened like that. It wasn't any buildup. It was like: Hey, we're here! Boom! Let's get weird."

Johnson sees these massive nine-feet-long packages floating in the water, wrapped in thick netting, all connected with a single rope. He realizes the packages were strapped to the underside of the pangas, and all tied together with the single line. For a moment the packages float free on the Pacific surface. And then gently, the first packages in line begin to sink into the black. As they go under, they start to drag the whole line of packages down. Whatever is in these packages, it's heading straight to the bottom of the Pacific Ocean.

Devros and Johnson quickly grab a boat hook and fish the rope out of the water. Johnson hurriedly ties the rope around the front of his boat to stop the packages sinking. His knife is in his hand, ready to cut the rope: he has no idea how much weight is sinking and if it's too much it will take him, his crew, and his boat to the bottom of the Pacific. The crew watches the line, a moment of tension. After thirty seconds, the whole hundred-yard-long line of packages resurfaces. The boat won't sink. At least not tonight.

Emergency averted, Johnson has a second to think: he's never seen this way of carrying drugs, strapped to the underside of the pangas trailing behind the larger fishing vessel. It's brilliant, really, because if the fishing vessel had more time, had seen the boats coming on the horizon, they easily could have ditched the drugs and had them sitting on the Pacific Ocean floor.

"I've been out in the eastern Pacific for the last four years . . . it's the first time I've ever seen anything like that," he says. "You know, once you're out here long enough really, nothing really surprises you anymore. You just kind of are always expecting the unexpected."

The packages are secured and the *Ladi Mar* is boarded. All the fishermen will be detained. No one's seen anything like it.

They pilot the *Ladi Mar,* the LRI, and the Mark 4 back to the *James.* Word has spread through the warship that thirty-one detainees are coming. The mother lode!

Once they arrive, in the early morning gloom, the *James*'s

cranes must lift the massive packages out of the water—each one weighs 200 kilos.

The loads are two to four meters long, with thick netting surrounding the packaging. As they're laid out on the *James,* Johnson kneels down and starts cutting through the nets. Minutes later, he's still sawing through. Finally, he pulls out a one-kilo brick. The brick is wrapped tightly in green plastic, with a yellow Apple logo. And other bricks are wrapped in red plastic with a psychedelic Apple logo.

Weighed, it's 1.6 tons of cocaine. The Coast Guard estimates that this is just under $50 million. This is a big bust and everyone is buzzing.

"I don't know why everyone is so excited—we've intercepted 1.6 tons of iPhones," jokes one sailor.

The new method of smuggling will be shared with the rest of the Coast Guard. But it leaves the sailors with an ominous thought.

"I've never seen anything like this. And for many of us we're thinking: wow, maybe we have seen this before but we didn't know what we were looking at," says XO.

THE MORNING SUN IS UP. It's a brand-new day here on the equator, just south of the Middle of Nowhere.

This is a win for the *James.* No one can laugh off the loss of a ton of cocaine. This would sting and annoy the largest traffickers. The biggest take the hit and keep going, though. A small trafficker could be put out of business with such a loss.

The message is piped throughout the *James:* "All hands on deck." Now they must process the detainees. They're ferried on board in groups of four. The first group arrives. Each fisherman is escorted across the flight deck by two Coast Guard crew members. These Ecuadorian fisherman measure about five foot two, five foot four, and are dwarfed by Coast Guard crew topping six foot six. The fishermen let themselves be led around.

In the hangar, the men are processed to be detained. The first man is around forty years old, with large moles coming out of his face. He's dressed in yellow rubber boots and red trousers. First Class Petty Officer Jamie Johnson sits behind a table to process them all. She hands him a whiteboard and ask him to fill out his name, nationality, and identification number and birth date.

He fills it out and hands it back to Johnson. She doesn't speak Spanish but smiles and says: "Gracias!"

Another sailor tells the fisherman/smuggler they need to take his photo. He quickly arranges his hair to make himself presentable and I think of a man stepping around a puddle on the way to the gallows. The man is given a welcome bag and then he's off for a medical check. And then the next man steps up to the table. They keep coming.

"I've never seen so many before in one go," says Johnson. "Some people think you might be a lucky charm."

I'll take it.

She gives each of the men a kind smile, to put them at ease. Smugglers or not, everyone is entitled to human warmth. Johnson joined the Coast Guard to give back to a country she believes has given her so much. She's a deep believer in the mission of stopping cocaine getting through to the United States, but the human cost of this battle, the detaining of these dirt-poor smugglers, "breaks my heart."

"I can't fathom what it would be like to have to sit there and make a decision of getting paid a couple of thousand dollars to not ask questions and take something from one place to another because maybe that's the only way my family is going to get food on the table. And maybe that's the most money I'll see at once in my lifetime."

It takes hours to process them all.

A few are around nineteen and twenty. One is sixteen years old. One misspells Ecuador. Others mess around, giving a single name or pretending to forget their ID number.

"They can call themselves Mickey Mouse, you're still going to jail," mutters the XO when he hears this.

With some of the younger ones, there's the smirk of the idiot, not understanding the weight of the moment. Another man, looking to be about thirty, has shaky legs and looks like he'll cry. He knows what's happening. Johnson gives him an extra-sympathetic smile.

It's clear many of these men are related—shared surnames, facial features. Some families back in Ecuador will be devastated.

Medic Dana Bennett comes out for some fresh air. He's been doing dozens of medical checkups of the men on the boat, many of whom haven't seen a doctor in years.

"I've been up since seven thirty yesterday morning. Get me an espresso. Or better yet, let espresso drip onto my face."

There is gossip that there's another panga puller on the horizon.

"Now I'm ready for you to get off the boat," jokes Ensign Nikki Nottingham, looking at me.

The Coast Guard keep processing them. And now the waft of bacon comes from the kitchen. You catch the Coast Guard smiling and shaking their heads—no one has ever seen so many people captured in one operation. And the line of them crossing the deck just never ends.

Johnson keeps smiling and taking down the details. But it's got her in a pensive mood. She knows the 1.6 tons of cocaine from this operation is sitting down below and will be destroyed so it will never reach a child's hands, but . . .

"Ever since I was young, middle school, we're talking fifteen, twenty years ago, the term 'war on drugs' came out . . . and here I am thirty-one years old and we're still talking about the war on drugs . . . so maybe it's helping, but I can't call this a victory. And that's my personal opinion, but what has changed? What has changed?"

THE HELICOPTER HANGAR HAS BEEN turned into a hold for the detainees. The helicopter is left on the flight deck. In the hangar, the Coast Guard has laid down dozens of yoga-style mats. At the end of each mat runs a metal cable to which each man will be cuffed by the ankle.

The detainees will spend the next three days living here, shackled except for a daily shower and trips to the bathroom. They are brought their breakfasts, lunches, dinners, eating what the Coast Guard eats. Some jibber-jabber, some are silent. Some play cards. Some look out watching the sea fade away. Anyone who wants a copy gets their prison Bible. Some lie back and stare at the ceiling. I stop by. It is stunningly boring for them.

The *Ladi Mar* and her seven pangas are commandeered by a team of the Coast Guard, but the boat's captain and engineer remain on board to pilot the ship. The *James* keeps in contact every thirty minutes and a code is set up that if anything goes wrong, the boat will veer off to the east.

Informed of the mass arrest of so many of its citizens, Ecuador decides it needs to do the right thing and take them back.

So, three days later, the Coast Guard of the United States and Ecuador's navy meet on the high seas, near the Galapagos Islands.

The United States will give Ecuador a sample of the drugs seized, just ten kilos, for any court cases. The rest is for the incinerator.

The detainees have been given white suits, like those used for crime scenes. In the hangar, they say good-bye to the other Ecuadorians and the Colombians who remain behind. There are handshakes, fist bumps, hugs. Those leaving keep the celebrations to a minimum. No one says it aloud, but these thirty-one are very lucky. If found guilty, if sentenced at home, they will receive a much more lenient sentence than the ones American judges hand out. And in prison, their families can visit every week, conjugal visits for the wives and lovers.

The other detainees watch them leave. They will stay on this ship possibly weeks longer, before being handed over to the US justice system, where they could face decades in prison and the possibility of never seeing their families again.

The detainees walk across the flight deck beneath a cloudy sky. They're ferried in the LRI to the Ecuadorian ship. As they sail away, the Ecuadorians wave back to the Coast Guard, smiling with thumbs up. The Coast Guard sailors halfheartedly wave back, uncomfortable waving to smugglers but unable to leave a wave unanswered. It's a very Latin American moment.

EVERY DAY A BENCH IS dragged out onto the flight deck. It's the surreal sight of an open-air gym as the Pacific Ocean flows by. Round the flight deck jogs Bennett the medic.

He's in his mid-thirties, with dirty blond hair.

"You couldn't pay me enough to take a boat out on the water and fly blind just with a GPS. . . . It's beautiful now. But we're talking about Mother Nature. We're one hurricane away from being in fourteen-, twenty-foot seas and getting tossed around."

He joined the Coast Guard fourteen years ago, feeling his life was aimless as he partied as a bartender in California.

"You hear that we're not winning it. I tend to think you know anytime you stop a boat with an amount of cocaine on board. That's a hit in the pocket. I don't care how rich the cartels are. That is a hit in their picket. I feel it is worthy."

He worked in a hospital in California, where he saw the bad results of when cocaine consumption goes wrong.

"I got to see firsthand a lot of the overdoses that would come in. I got to see firsthand even children coming from that background, where their parents are addicted. And they come in in filthy pajamas."

His job is to look after the health of the crew and the detainees.

"Sometimes these guys get on board and they realize what they've just done and they realize everything they've given up and they're not going home. Them being . . . secured to the deck with handcuffs by their ankle, I would say it keeps them from making a stupid decision and running and making a jump overboard. Some of these guys they come on here and they go through the stages of grief and denial and they just become overly sad."

Lawyers in the United States, when they take the cases of the detainees, complain about the treatment of their clients, kept shackled for hours at a time, kept detained for weeks on end. The Coast Guard says it holds the detainees as well as it can.

At the end of a hectic week, the *James* slows down and the crew breaks out the fishing rods. As the sun sets, lighting an orange burn to the horizon, the crew cast off the stern. The whole ship is in a good mood. The captain fishes off the back with the other sailors. They all bring out these huge three-feet-long mahi-mahis. The fish are laid out, their golden scales twinkling in the last of the sunlight.

"We're a fishing boat carrying tons of cocaine. We've become the enemy," jokes one officer.

Captain Randall fillets the fish for the whole boat and it has the feeling of a father overseeing a barbecue in the backyard. And everyone looks happy.

"WE'VE BEEN VERY BUSY IN the last week. Over six days, five interdictions," says Executive Officer Jim Jarnac. "We like to say 'we own the night' because when we operate at night, we level the playing field."

He's a twenty-seven-year veteran of the Coast Guard, gray-haired and wiry. He exudes energy and is loved by the crew. There's that Florida joviality, the type of man that calls you "brother." His job is to execute what the captain orders. Everything from the boat goes through him to the captain and everything from the captain to the boat goes through him.

He joined the Coast Guard because he wanted more structure in his life. He's happy working antinarcotics.

"Based on when I grew up in Miami, Florida, I saw some of the effects of cocaine. . . . The cocaine started to flow in the late seventies. It was in the news every night. It was in the newspaper every day. As I got older and went into middle school and high school, it was everywhere. . . . Even my classmates in school, to some degree, got caught up in cocaine. It was literally everywhere.

"They're constantly adapting. If we catch them doing this, they change their tactics. And then when we figure out what that tactic is, they're on to their next tactic. It's like squeezing a balloon. You get a good hold of it on one end and it pops out another place."

"Smuggling has been around for as long as we've been recording time. We're not smuggling cocaine, we'll be smuggling something else. Alcohol was illegal; we smuggled it."

Smugglers, the first globalizers.

"I feel good about every bust, every single one, based on my childhood and what I saw cocaine do to my city of Miami. It delivers instability, violence, corruption to states already struggling with their governance. Nothing good comes out of it. Any bit I get is a victory.

"I look at it. It's a cancer cell. . . . That's kind of how I see cocaine. It's a cancer cell and if I can stop that cancer cell from impacting someone else's life, how can I not feel good about it?"

Both his parents died of cancer.

IT'S THE WEEKLY QUARTERS MEETING, where all not on watch come and listen. It's the town hall meeting of the ship, where the captain can tell them what's occurring and hear any problems.

The whole crew waits in the mess hall, one hundred people taking over every possible seat, standing room only for late arrivals. Today everyone is buzzing, laughing, and joking. They know the ship is doing well. The senior officers are last to arrive.

The XO takes the microphone. And in a gentle, fading voice: "The coffee has worn off . . . NO IT HASN'T. AHOY, *JAMES!*"

"Ahoy, XO!" the ship roars back.

"Fantastic work. It's been seven or eight days since we left Costa Rica; that was our sixth case," XO tells them. "Fantastic work. It takes all hands. I'm tired. And I know I'm bouncing off the bulkheads and down the passageways and I see a lot of fatigue from the crew. I'm right there with you. Thank you for your efforts; it's been fantastic."

The crew beam back at him. XO passes the mic to the captain, who steps forward into the middle of the mess hall, eyes on him from 360 degrees.

"I'll tell you what: Somebody better buy this crew a Powerball ticket right now 'cause you got a hot hand. A really hot hand: 5,200 kilograms in under a week. Over $166 million street value of cocaine removed. New concealment methods found, effective LPV (low-profile vehicle) takedown last night, knocking down some pangas. It's been impressive."

Sailors smile at each, reveling in the praise. They've worked hard and their captain is telling them, good job.

"I'm proud of each and every one of you. It doesn't matter if you're washing dishes or pulling people out of the LPV, it takes a team effort and you guys have done a fantastic job over the last week delivering some fantastic mission execution. That said: I'll just let you know I got a note directly from the commandant about it, too, yesterday: he goes, man, you guys have got a hot hand. Keep knocking them dead. That's all it said, but he noticed. So, for what it's worth, people notice. Thank you!"

He wraps up.

"We'll continue doing other good things. Because they're already lining them up and there's more people to take down. And that's what we're out here for."

XO sends them to bed with encouragement to sleep on.

"You own the night! We own the night! Okay, don't ever forget that!"

The crew is smiling, wired and tired. And they're ready to do it again tomorrow and all the days to come.

Except the busts stop coming.

CHAPTER 13

THE VOID

TO KNOW THE KILOS ARE OUT THERE, to know they flow by. But not to get any of them. The daily frustration of the war on drugs.

No one on the *James* realizes the busts have stopped—at first. Suspicious blips on a radar, they keep coming. The teams keep going out on missions, checking boats. The *James* keeps steaming around the eastern Pacific. But now there's no cocaine to be had. No one believes they've hoovered up all the ocean's cocaine. No, they know it's out there and they're not getting any of it.

When you are standing on the bridge of the *James,* the vastness of the Pacific is magnified, a 180-degree view of the void. The human eye can see twelve miles deep into the horizon from up here. From here, the *James* is steered and piloted.

The bridge is filled with screens, radars showing red and green clusters. The screens are dimmed when strangers are present. Up here, the boat gently moves up and down, riding the waves. The young sailors monitor the screens constantly, sipping from huge cans of Monster energy drinks.

The helicopter takes off to investigate a go-fast heading west. The go-fast stops cold. Dead in the water. The helicopter hangs back. The LRI is on its way, but still thirty minutes out. The helicopter keeps its eyes on it, filming the boat. It's not throwing anything overboard yet. Prosecutors will still take cases if there is video of crews throwing merchandise over the side that looks like cocaine. Still, it's nothing more than a go-fast floating in the middle of the Pacific.

They see a flag on the boat and a registration number alongside. It's easier if they don't, as it means they can board. They contact the Ecuadorian government to request permission to board. XO is monitoring it.

"The men might be receiving orders. 'Travel to this position and wait.'"

Finally, Ecuador replies—the registration number is a fake. A spark passes the bridge—everyone is energized.

"Game on!" XO yells, grinning.

Outside, devil rays jump out of the water, their wings flapping.

XO tells of one go-fast that they found stocked with nothing but hundreds of gallons of gasoline. They suspected it was there waiting on the high seas for a cocaine-carrying vessel to restock its fuel, a floating gas station for cocaine. But there was nothing they could do—it's not illegal to be in the middle of the sea with gasoline.

The radio crackles. They've seen the men on the go-fast toss something over the side. It's not big enough to be cocaine. The LRI has arrived. They search for what was tossed overboard but can't find it.

There are ten people on the bridge focusing on what's coming across the radio. One sailor bites his nails. Some stare out the thirty-foot window at the horizon.

The crew of the LRI radio back. They have spoken to the boat. The captain says it is due to rendezvous with another fishing boat.

The radio crackles. The crew on the LRI recommend no further inspection—they're looking over the boat and they can't see anything.

"Shit!" says the XO. "It was about to be a good Friday."

The room deflates. There's a feeling that they've been outfoxed today, that they're being watched.

"Look, there could be a panga five miles away, just watching us now and we wouldn't see it if it sat low," says XO, looking out over the horizon.

OTHER MISSIONS GO OUT INTO the night. But they keep returning empty-handed. People take to the back of the ship and look out into the void. One day on the horizon we see the one piece of land we will pass in two and a half weeks. The first recorded people who saw this rock in the middle of the Pacific were Spanish conquistadores five hundred years ago, in 1530.

The strange rock juts into the air like an act of violence, a stab at the sky. It's a mile long and half a mile wide. And three hundred miles off the Colombian coast. Frightened by this rock, the Spanish named it the ominous Malpelo, literally "bad hair." The Americas spooked the Spanish conquistadores, who saw hell and the devil everywhere they stepped in the New World.

There is nothing on Malpelo—a rock face covered in crabs and booby birds who swarm the island. In order to maintain its claim to the island, Colombia keeps a group of four sailors on there at all times. They live in a tiny hut, spending four weeks cut off from the world. They bring their own food, stacks of DVDs, and music and that's what they do for thirty days. A warship will pass by, pick them up, and drop off the next four poor bastards.

Malpelo doesn't have beaches. Small, agile boats must pull up as close as possible to the sheer rock faces as waves slam into the boat, pushing it closer and closer to the wall. Move to the front of the boat that is rocking up and down, look down at the smashing sea. The captain shouts: "Move quicker! The boat is being pushed forward. Jump! Jump!" And you jump into the air—grasping for the rope ladder than hangs from the rock face.

Before all this happens, the sailors have warned you not to fall in—with a story. Sailors were delivering a huge bag of meat, enough to feed four men for the next thirty days. It slipped through the sailors' hands, landing in the water. It floated for a few seconds as the sailors looked for a hook to rescue it. Suddenly the water bubbled, thrashed in a frothing red as a horde of sharks tore into the bloody beef.

Riding around the island's waist is a solid ring of hundreds of sharks. Malpelo sits in the middle of the shark highway of the eastern Pacific. Years ago, I slid into the water.

Through the scuba mask, there was a gloom. My eyes, my brain struggled to adapt to this wonderous world. It was dark and at about thirty feet below the surface the sea turned gray. My eyes adjusted and this underworld came into focus: that gray was a solid mass of hammerhead sharks. Hundreds of hammerheads glided through the waters with the confidence that the food chain comes to an abrupt end in their mouths.

These hammerheads can grow to fourteen feet. It's a rare sight of natural beauty. I worried that all it would take is one hammerhead to nip me, an exploratory bite to get the blood in the water and for the rest to follow. Yet it felt strangely fragile, as if one shout and the sharks would vanish in a blue blur.

THE LACK OF COCAINE HAS the ship in a mood.

"You want to get in the fight. People are like wondering why are we not in the right spot because you know they're out there. Who's putting us in the wrong spot?" says Ty. "Training, training, training and people finally get tired of training and wanna see the action. People are antsy. And they're curious about why we're not getting stuff. But there's always a bigger picture that people don't see."

THERE IS A LOT OF downtime. The crew practices, they clean the ship, they work out. I read Bernard Moitessier, the French sailor who dropped out of the first nonstop solo race around the world in 1969. As he sailed alone in the Pacific, approaching the end and with a good chance to win the contest, he decided to abandon the race, in order to sail another lap of the globe. Using a slingshot, he fired a message on to the deck of a passing ship, explaining his decision:

". . . because I am happy at sea and perhaps to save my soul."

I sleep well on the *James.* Gently rocking, the boat soothes. The dreams are strange and new. Dark, swirling waters and I sink deeper, darker, further into oblivion. It ends with me swallowed by the black. And I wake.

AT 8:52 P.M., A CALL goes out: man overboard.

At the boat's stern, the *James*'s floodlights scour the black ocean surface for any sign. The moon hides behind clouds.

"There will be a small boat recovery, small boat recovery," says the PA.

Sailors shouts orders to each other as they prepare the rescue.

"Six hundred and fifty yards. Man been in the water two minutes," says the PA.

I strain my eyes in the darkness for any sign of man or woman.

"Eight hundred and forty yards. Man been in the water two and a half minutes."

The floodlights swing across the ocean's surface. I see nothing but the waves.

I imagine trying to stay afloat, the ice-cold water slapping your face, surrounded by darkness above, blackness below. And the lights of the *James* gently, so gently moving away. The terror you must feel if your foot touches anything, if something brushes against your leg. Some fear will snap a mind clean in half.

"Thirteen hundred yards. Man's been in the water four minutes."

Sailors on the deck above me are pointing out to the black ocean.

"Sixteen hundred yards. Man been in the water for five minutes."

I see the small boat race behind the *James* in search of the missing sailor.

Only then does a sailor tell me it's all a drill, and no one is overboard. Still, I think on what that must be like: any sailor who fell overboard and watched their boat sail off . . . I do believe that as they floated there in the eastern Pacific at night, they would be the loneliest person in the universe.

ANOTHER SHIP'S MEETING.

"Ahoy, *James*," the XO begins. It's noticeably quieter than before.

"Ahoy, XO," the boat responds.

The meeting begins with admin. An officer addresses the boat.

"So, I've got a list of letters and packets that have been sitting at my door for about a month. Pick 'em up, sign 'em by the end of today or I'm going to throw them out. . . . It's your deal. . . ."

The audience goes wild, whooping and cheering. This is the most I'll hear them cheer, even when it's announced later that they're getting an extra day of holiday. These are the politics of the day: everyone is convinced that everyone else is getting away with it and they're angry about it. Left, right, that's where we're at.

The captain picks up the mic.

"Lots of stuff going over here in this neck of the woods. I don't think anyone doubts otherwise, or wonders otherwise. So, we've had a couple of what I would call swings and misses."

No busts.

THERE'S A SUSPICIOUS-LOOKING FISHING SHIP, with three pangas attached. Two teams are sent to investigate. It's been seven days without a bust.

The fishing vessel looks like a floating white bathtub. The seven-man crew have run a clothesline across the deck where T-shirts and trousers dry. The teams report back to the *James* that they want to investigate. This request is transmitted to

Ecuador, under whose flag the boat is sailing. Much of the co-caine in southern Colombia is pushed across the border into Ecuador because of the blockade put around the Colombian port of Tumaco. Cocaine finds a way.

The wait turns into hours. The Coast Guard sit on their boats and the Ecuadorians sit on theirs. The hours drag on under the sun. Finally, after seven and a half hours waiting, they are given permission to board. Armed sailors perform a security sweep to make sure there are no threats. And then they begin the search. One team takes the fishing vessel. KC takes the pangas.

On hour eight, I write myself the note: "It's kind of boring."

After an hour of searching all over, they've found nothing. The Ecuadorians are pissed. Who can blame them? Ten hours being held up for nothing.

There's another meeting of the boat.

"Captain, the deck is yours, sir."

The captain takes the mic and stands before his entire crew.

"All right . . . fits and starts is the name of the day. Fits and starts," the captain says. "Right, so we had this [semi-sub] we were looking for. The [semi-sub] went underwater on us somewhere and now we don't know where he is. It happens. We tried."

The fluorescent white light is harsh.

"We thought we were going to do something and we ended up doing nothing. Some of that's on us, and some of that is just the way the game goes. But we'll be a little bit smarter for next time, I suppose. We had a very successful week last week. I know it's been a little slower now. It's not for lack of trying. Then we're going to try to make some of our own bulk in the process. That's what I'm here to do—find more bulk cocaine out here and I know it's around."

The crew take it in.

XO looks to the captain.

"I was going to sacrifice a chicken for good luck."

FUEL FOR THE *JAMES* IS running low. Fuel for the helicopter is running low. The eastern Pacific has never felt emptier. The day before Halloween, Ty spots a go-fast boat dead in the water, leaning into the ocean, taking on water. Three men are standing, manically waving their arms over their heads to attract the helicopter's attention.

That's how the Coast Guard hears the strange tale of three Ecuadorian fishermen, stranded and drifting across the Pacific for eleven days.

The three set out for some fishing on a Friday morning. They plan on a weekend at sea. They lay down hooks Friday and sleep overnight. Early Saturday morning, they check to see what they've caught.

Suddenly a speedboat is almost on top of them. It's a go-fast boat, leaning heavily to one side, and is clearly taking on water. It has huge cargo in the middle.

"It was new, but badly built. It was off balance. All the gasoline and merchandise meant it sank too low into the ocean. You know out there, the waves are huge," says Juan Carlos.

All the men are armed, two aiming their handguns at the fishermen and the other two brandishing knives. Pirates!

The go-fast pulls up next to the fisherman's boat. The pirates bark orders. The fishermen guess by the accent they're from Tumaco. The pirates board. They punch and kick Juan Carlos twice. They explain that they're here to take their boat, leaving the fishermen their leaky go-fast boat. The Colombians start unloading bales and bales of cocaine from their boat on to the Ecuadorians'. The Ecuadorians are pushed onto the leaky go-fast. The Colombians leave them bags of crackers, drinking water, and just three canisters of gasoline. And the Colombians jet off. The hijacking took thirty minutes.

The fishermen guess they're 350 miles off the coast of Ecuador. They have no compass, no radio, and a tiny amount of gasoline. The boat drifts, and slowly takes on water. It's dire. They decide not to turn on the engines. They're too far out in the ocean for the three canisters of gasoline to get them home. And they're not sure which way home is. If God is merciful, the boat will drift closer to the coast of Ecuador, where they'll see the outline of land and fire up the engine to close the gap. So they drift and scoop out the encroaching sea.

They keep lookout for passing boats for help. And as the night sets that first day, there is a new fear.

"It was scary. You lie down with your eyes open, terrified that a boat would come at night and run us over and destroy us," says Jose.

They hang two torches from two fishing rods, one on each side of the boat. By the end of the first day, they've done everything they can.

The true horror sets in. There is nothing to do and nowhere to go. Nothing changes. The true horror of the void. They see nothing.

"The water was coming on board. So we would wake each other up and say: 'Hey, you need to scoop out the water.' The other would say: 'Hey, wake up, you have to scoop out the water,'" says Jose.

They can feel it. Madness is setting in. On the fifth day— hope! They spot a massive freight ship. They crank the engine up and navigate toward it. They shout and wave, but they're too far away. The ship doesn't see them and the boat falls behind.

They return to waiting.

"It was horrific. You woke up in the morning and saw the sea. You sat down and saw the sea. In the night, you saw the sea. The next day, it was the sea. Every day," says Jose.

The water keeps coming on, and they keep scooping.

"We thought we were going to die," says Juan Carlos. "I've had friends who have gone out fishing on the Pacific Ocean and never come back."

The waves toss their tilting boat from side to side, ever worrying them that they will flip the boat. Hope runs low. On the night of day ten, the three men kneel, hold hands, and pray to God.

The next day, they see the Coast Guard helicopter.

"God sent us that helicopter."

The three are taken on the *James*. They're overwhelmingly grateful. Their first conversation with the Coast Guard, they realize that the sailors are skeptical, but they repeat their story. Eventually their interrogation comes to an uneasy end. The fishermen are put in the hangar with the prisoners, but without handcuffs. They will be returned to Ecuador.

Still no cocaine.

"GET YOUR COCAINE. COME GET your free cocaine. Get your cocaine," jokes Ensign Nikki Nottingham, walking through the metal corridors. There's a buzz on the boat—they're back in business. The *James* is doing what it is meant to do—seizing cocaine on the high seas.

The sailors are hauling the loads, and it's tiring work, but they're grinning. The bricks have the Gucci logo on them.

An aircraft flying above the ocean spotted bales bobbing up and down in the middle of the ocean with not a soul in sight. There's a beacon on the bales.

"Obviously somebody was moving it and got spooked. I don't know if it was because the aircraft came down out of the clouds or what. But they jettisoned their load and you know what, it floats. So it's entirely possible it was sitting out here for someone else to pick up," says XO.

He beams.

"We're looking at approximately eighteen million dollars. The mood is good. We've had a couple of cases where we were not able to get drugs on deck. And that takes a toll. Those are long days. We put everything we have into it. You know the desired endgame to get drugs on deck. And we came up short a couple of times, so now we have drugs on deck, we're feeling good about it. And we'll go right back out there tomorrow."

IT'S A GRAY SKY IN Fort Lauderdale, Florida, a week before Thanksgiving. The *James* is docked and a press conference is taking place on the deck. The captain is there and the acting deputy secretary of homeland security Claire Grady; Admiral Karl Schultz, the commander of the Coast Guard; and the US attorney for the Southern District of Florida, Ariana Fajardo Orshan.

Behind them is the entire crew of the *James,* standing in lines, their hands formally clasped behind their backs. And there on the deck is 18.5 fat tons of cocaine. The piles and piles of the drug was the result of the Coast Guard's three-month missions in the eastern Pacific. The cocaine is the result of eight ships' work, like the cutters *Venturous* and

Dauntless. The *James* is the star, having nabbed half of it all. The war trophies are blasted-out engine covers, bullet holes on display under a gray sky.

The Coast Guard says we're looking at half a billion dollars' worth of cocaine.

"Every bale or kilogram of cocaine on this flight deck that doesn't make it to our shores, represents a life saved and a significant blow to these criminal organizations and the instability they foster through their illegal networks," says the captain.

The Coast Guard commander takes the mic. He's brusque and speaks quickly.

"Coast guards interdicted more than 1.3 million pounds; that's 1.3 million pounds of illicit cocaine in the last three years. And that rolls up to be about eighteen billion dollars in wholesale value on American streets."

He repeats a request for more funding for the Coast Guard: "We have visibility of eighty-five percent of that activity; we action because of the capacity of the number of ships, the number of aircraft about twenty-five to thirty percent of that. So, it's a conversation; with more capacity we could remove more drugs in the water."

Men and women have tried their best out there on the Pacific Ocean to stop cocaine. But they're trapped fighting a war that can't be won, so the war on drugs rolls on. The answer to every setback in the war on drugs is always more war on drugs.

All that cocaine on the decks of the *James,* the trophies of war. What's missing? All the cocaine that got through.

EPILOGUE
THE END
(IT NEVER
ENDS)

I DON'T SEE ALEX FOR SIX MONTHS. No war among narcos breaks out. The plan for a mass handover fades from the newspapers' pages and seems out of time as the violence in the country-side spirals ever worse.

Alex plans to set up a business to launder money from other people's cocaine deals, to step back from trafficking. There will be jobs for all his crew. Diana and Alex prepare to marry. Alex has enjoyed his time trafficking cocaine; now he looks to the next stage of life: starting a family with Diana.

ALEX AND DIANA LEAVE TOWN for a few days. It's dinnertime.

Out of the night, the gun emerges, the muzzle pointed at Alex. Alex jumps up, pushing himself away from the table, grabbing for his gun. Diana throws herself on the ground—

just as Alex had taught her when the guns come out. Hands over her head, she thinks: "It's going to be a shoot-out."

Three shots, so gentle in the night. Like a finger flicking a sheet of paper. Pup. Pup. Pup. And nothing. No screams. Diana feels a calm descend. She gets off the floor and looks around. Alex is lying on the floor fifteen feet away from her. She's frozen. She watches someone apply a shirt to Alex's chest. Why is she doing that, she wonders. The woman removes the shirt to glimpse Alex's wound, and blood spurts in the air. It slaps Diana awake.

"I ran over, I grabbed his hand. I told him I would take him to the clinic. He needed to hang on. 'No,' he replied. 'I love you.'

"He had that lost look, he was going. Then in an instant . . ." Here she imitates her lover, her head suddenly drooping down. "He died. He didn't suffer."

She won't give up—she insists they take Alex to the hospital. "I never lost faith that we could save him." They bundle Alex into a car and drive him at high speed to the hospital. There a doctor tells her what she already knew but couldn't face. Her love is dead. She collapses.

"I never thought that this life would take him away so quickly."

The doctor takes pity and sedates her.

A MONTH LATER SHE IS still brittle.

"I still haven't really accepted it." Her eyes are so sad, the smile so weak. "I'll need help when I finally accept that he's gone.

"I don't know why they killed him and I don't want to know. For debts? To take him out of the inner circle [of drug traffickers]? To avoid paying what he was owed? It could have been a lot of things, but I don't want to know."

Smart—too much information in this world makes you dangerous.

"I won't forgive them. Let God forgive them," she says. "Maybe the person who did this is living well right now, but I'm in pain. For them, that pleasure will be short-lived. Everything comes around. It's karma."

Her anger rises. She knows these words are too dangerous to voice. With killings like this, the killers wait to see if there's any reaction. Anyone swears bloody revenge, promises retribution—it's time to call the men on the motorbike again.

"The good and bad of life, you pay here. You don't pay for your acts in heaven or hell, you pay here. Here on earth, we're in the flames of hell."

Her jaw hardens, her eyes dark. And for that moment, I glimpse the mafia girlfriend as she thinks on those who killed the love of her life. And it's gone.

"You know what? I normally dream a lot. But since the killing, I haven't dreamed," she says, showing a small smile.

"He told me he wouldn't be around forever. He said he would never reach fifty. He was working so he could set me up, so if in five years he was gone, I would be taken care of.

"I love my city and my country. These things have always happened. Now it looks like it's more civilized, more sophisticated, but these things will always happen. There are a lot of people like me, their loved ones killed."

She is one more of the city's young widows.

"I'M OUT," SAYS CACHOTE. "I can leave now; the one person who tied me to this life was Alex."

Cachote is agitated. He doesn't want to be in this city. He's agreed to meet a last time in a café before he leaves. He studies every person who enters the café. Cachote and all Alex's crew have gone into hiding. No one knows what comes next. Was the attack meant to kill Alex alone or his whole crew?

"If I had to guess, I would say that it was because Alex wanted to get out and take us with him. And someone didn't like that, so had him killed," Cachote says.

Will Alex be replaced? "Yes, someone in the organization will take over. We don't know how. It's easier to say, 'I'm going to take those neighborhoods,' than go up and take them by force."

He thinks of becoming a waiter, in some other city in Colombia or perhaps abroad. Cachote doesn't have many skills outside of killing.

"I realize I've done bad things in this life. I can't change that. But I can try to make a good life for myself now."

There is no mention of making amends for the damage he's done, only a desire to make a good life for himself. This isn't a call for a second chance. It's a call to outrun justice.

"It's going to be a big change. I won't earn the money. But right now, I'm terrified. So, yes, I'll take the wage cut. What's better? Your money or your life?"

Your money or your life. It was the deal they all made before getting into this life. They swaggered, drunk on their own bravado, and told Death to go fuck herself. Now the bill has arrived, the raven has croaked, the devil wants his due. Far too late in the night, they scream "Stop!" And all they see is grinning cocaine mouth the words, I've no more use for you.

In the end, he's just one more killer. Cachote probably doesn't have long left. There are those out there who harbor vengeful fantasies for Cachote's killings. He was immune to retribution because he was part of an outfit. Now he's naked and alone in a world with long memories, where vengeance is a virtue.

I PIECE TOGETHER SOME PARTS of Alex's life after his death. I seek out different people who knew him to try to understand him better. Someone sends a message: "Why so many questions about a dead man?"

The answer is in the question. He's dead. It's over. So why keep asking?

One Monday morning, winter is near. The sky is one vast mural of gray. It will rain. I can't find Alex's grave.

Colombian cemeteries are wild places. Muggers, prostitutes, and other entrepreneurs of the street rub peso-bills on the tomb of the country's most famous scientist in the belief the notes will multiply. At other tombs, people pray for the health of children. Thieves and crazies haunt the lonelier corners, attacking mourners and weeping grandmothers. Cemeteries can be dangerous.

This graveyard is nice, flat and dotted with trees. The tombstones are discreet acts of memory. A security guard helps me find Alex's grave and as we walk, we speak. He urges me to be careful here. Where do the thieves come from? The surrounding neighborhoods are all wealthy.

"It's not just the poor. Some do it for the adrenaline. There was a young man who drove in his bulletproof SUV, robbing people. He'd jump out of the truck and stick a knife at people's throats and take all their things. He robbed a bunch of people before we finally caught him as he was robbing a man. And when the police came and checked his documents? He's the son of one of our top generals. A general who's still active. Wild. That family paid a lot of money for the man not to press charges. That kid . . . some people just want the adrenaline."

Deranged little rich kids terrorizing and robbing hardworking Colombians sticking a knife to their throats. The powerful always get away with it. The kid will go far in Colombia.

As we walk, I'm curious: Will Alex's tomb be full narco, a monstrosity of dollops of gold? Now dead and beyond discretion, was Alex going to give the finger to the country he preyed on? Some gaudy mausoleum dripping with jewels, a fifty-inch plasma screen of a smiling Alex, ten grandmothers hired to weep and pray for his soul, and round-the-clock strippers strutting and rutting while a speaker blares out night and day "The Cross of Marijuana" by the Grupo Aquilus del Norte?

Over my tomb raise a cross of marijuana. . . .
In my luxury coffin,
Are my treasured machine guns.
I enjoyed everything in life:
Jewels, women, and gold.
I am a drug trafficker,
I know the gamble of cocaine. . . .

And all the time, the prim upper class wandering by and looking the other way, examining the flowers, the grass, the sky, any damn thing except the narcos now among them, lying next to their loved ones.

But no, we're saved a narco embarrassment. His is a discreet tomb, no different from those that surround us. There is a single gray plaque and a glass vase filled with bird of paradise flowers and lilies. Invisible in life, invisible in death.

Fresh red roses lie at the bottom of the tomb.

The inscription salutes Alex's bravery, his ambition, and his determination.

If life in cocaine is like a weekend on the drug itself, here we are on the Monday morning wondering if it was all worth it. And I'm tired. God, I'm so tired. The corruption, the cruelty is catching up with me.

Alex thrived in an ecosystem of cocaine built upon greed and murder. If words like "evil," "immoral," or "wicked" don't apply to a man like this, then burn them from the dictionaries. And if he is not in hell, hell does not exist.

Is the afterlife some hideous Dantesque hallucination of rivers of boiling blood and fire? God knows which circle of hell he'd be allocated—he reveled in every single deadly sin.

He was one more cog in the mass delirium that is cocaine. Cocaine sucked everything out of him and when she had no more use for him, she tossed his arid corpse aside. Her blessings now fall on the next capo. Here, under a graying sky that promises rain, another trafficker is dead and it won't make a spit of difference. The world is better off with Alex dead. Still, the world that created him keeps turning. The cocaine will flow; the mound of corpses will grow taller.

The drug trade leaves an international trail of murder and mayhem, to end in a consumer's nose on a Friday night. A failed war on drugs makes monsters billionaires and misery for those caught in the daily crossfire.

Every year, the war on drugs offers up its losses and yet on it rolls, never-ending. The cavalry is not coming to win this war. They've come, fought, and lie dead on the battlefield, ugly corpses. The war is unwinnable because at its center sits an unsolvable equation: the more cocaine is destroyed, the more the traffic is interrupted, the more the drug's value will rise. So, making it more attractive to produce and smuggle. Supply and demand, iron laws of economics.

What other public policy has failed so spectacularly as the war on drugs, yet keeps chugging along? And when we ask when this war on drugs might end, we're told that all that's missing is a little more war on drugs.

Prohibition failed once before when teetotaling politicians blamed beer drinkers for the rise of gangsters like Al Capone. Prohibition fails again and drug users are blamed again for fueling the trade. It's the prohibition itself that makes a brick of drugs worth tens of thousands of dollars.

The cocaine trade has killed more than any soul could count. And many more will die in the war on drugs, men and women cut down by a conflict we know we lost.

May we hope for a sane drug policy for the future? A Colombia where the farmers can grow legal crops and live in dignity?

We can hope.

In the meantime, Latin America bleeds. There is enough blame to go around for us all. Producers, consumers, politicians too cowardly to admit the truth of the problem, reporters who know the war is unwinnable but dutifully jot down the latest good news from the police. So, the war on drugs grinds on. Colombia keeps producing it, the world keeps buying it. And we keep doing the same and hoping for a different outcome.

So, let us build more cemeteries as glorious monuments to the forever war on drugs and all the beautiful dead still yet to come.

ACKNOWLEDGMENTS

MY MOTHER, CHARLOTTE MUSE, PUSHED ME TO write this book, before I knew I needed to write this book. The book would not exist without my agent, Ethan Bassoff, who has been there from before the beginning. Matt Harper and the team at William Morrow got this book across the finish line, getting it into shape along the way. Monica Villamizar always knew what worked and what didn't. Rafael Rios always knew the deal. Nicoló Filippo Rosso produced amazing photos out there every day in the jungles. Danny Gold started this. Brother Ed Poole helped the original drafts. Anastasia Moloney gave great feedback. Carmen opened locked doors. Simone Bruno helped record some of the interviews and provided great images. Alirio Castillo has been a friend for years. Brother Bhairav Patel gave amazing notes. Diana Castrillón put things in order. The Colombian police took me on missions that helped me see their work. The Coast Guard welcomed me abroad, taking me on an unforgettable journey of the high seas. The people of Antioquia, Norte de Santander, and Nariño always fed me, put a roof over my head, and a smile on my face as I researched this book. Thank you to Colombia for being my home for more than fifteen years.

ABOUT THE AUTHOR

TOBY MUSE is a British-American writer, television reporter, documentary filmmaker and foreign correspondent, working for such outlets as the *New York Times,* the *Guardian,* CNN, and others. Having reported from the front lines of the conflicts in Colombia, Iraq, and Syria, he lived in Bogota for more than fifteen years, reporting across South America and the endless drug war.